## Welcome . . . and congratulations!

Congratulations? For what? Well, studies show that the single most important factor in a divorce is starting off with the right information. The fact that you are reading my book shows you have a desire to know and participate that will lead you to successful solutions. You are definitely on the right path.

My life's work has been to develop ways to help people take some control when going through a divorce. Divorce is hard enough without having to struggle against a legal system that tends to make things worse instead of better. If you follow my advice, you won't have to go through that.

**Divorce Helpline.** In 1989, after nearly 20 years of producing books and software to help people help themselves, the next step was to reinvent the practice of law. My goal was to develop a way for lawyers to help people in a way that would be effective and affordable; a practice that would solve problems, not cause them. That was the beginning of Divorce Helpline.

Divorce Helpline attorneys do not take cases to court, but rather they serve as your coach and guide, helping you solve problems, develop options, talk to your Ex, and negotiate or mediate a fair settlement.

I left Divorce Helpline in 2007, but I still know their attorneys and trust them completely. They have vast experience and are very effective, honest and sincere. You can call to ask just one question, or they will stand by you all the way to your Judgment. You get to choose how much or little they do for you.

Many people can get through a divorce without any help outside the covers of my books—and well over a million people have done so. But, as good as they are, books can't replace years of experience and personal attention. People with some assets to protect or problems to solve will find that doing their own divorce with the help of an experienced Divorce Helpline attorney can save money and bring peace of mind.

**This is a book you can talk to.** If you have questions to ask or problems to solve, or if you want a friendly, reliable attorney to act as your coach or "just do it" for you, call Divorce Helpline. Tell them Ed Sherman sent you.

Ed Sherman

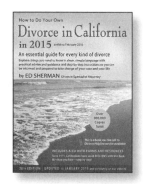

## Start any case and finish it if no opposition in court
### HOW TO DO YOUR OWN DIVORCE

This is the book you use to start any case. It is the only book you'll need if your spouse doesn't oppose you in court. Could be long gone, doesn't care, or you two can settle divorce issues peacefully. Explains the law, provides advice and step-by-step instructions with a sample agreement and all the forms you'll need to complete a peaceful divorce.

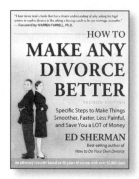

## For cases that aren't going smoothly (or might not)

This is the book you use to keep easy cases easy, or turn difficult cases into easier ones. Shows you specific steps you can take to reduce upset, insecurity and conflict, and to protect children. How to talk to your Ex, how to negotiate, how to organize your facts, documents and your thinking. This is the newer, better version of the famous, award-winning *Divorce Solutions*. CD with worksheets included.

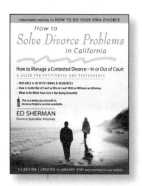

## For cases that seem headed for court
### HOW TO SOLVE DIVORCE PROBLEMS—*In or Out of Court*

This great book shows you how to get the information you need from your Ex, how to defend against legal action or take your own case to court if you need to go there. Or, if you *want* an attorney to take over your case, how to choose and supervise one and know if your case is being handled competently, and how to fire an attorney who is not giving good service. Includes free Bonus CD full of forms and resources to help make your job easier.

To use *Solve Divorce Problems,* you also need *How to Do Your Own Divorce.* For cases in court, they work together. So for convenience, in the text of both books we sometimes refer to *DYOD* as Book 1 and *SDP* as Book 2.

How to Do Your Own

# Divorce in California
## in 2015 and thru February 2016

## An essential guide for every kind of divorce

Explains things you need to know in **clear, simple language** with **practical advice** and **guidance** and step-by-step instructions so you can be informed and prepared to **take charge of your case and your life**

## by ED SHERMAN Divorce Specialist Attorney

**Nolo Press**
o c c i d e n t a l
Carlsbad, CA 92008
(831) 466-9922

# DATED MATERIAL
## THIS BOOK WAS PRINTED IN
# JANUARY 2015

## Do not use an old edition of this book!
## Out-of-date information can cause trouble

Laws and forms change often, usually in January and sometimes July. This book is printed at least once each year, sometimes twice, to give you the latest information. Using an old edition can be dangerous if the information or forms in it are wrong. **Make sure you are using the most current edition.** If the date above is over one year old, you are taking chances.

## FREE UPDATE NOTICES
## Check for new laws and forms
## at www.nolodivorce.com/alerts

## 30% OFF ON UPDATES

If you have an old copy of this book and want to update, tear off the cover and send it to us with $27.69, which includes tax and shipping. You can also get our great companion book, *How to Solve Divorce Problems,* for 30% off, too—only $54.19 including tax and shipping for *both* books! If you bought your book from our site, just call up and say so, no cover needed.

© 1971–2015 by Charles E. Sherman
ISBN13/EAN: 978-0-944508-97-8
ISSN: 2324-9102

| | |
|---|---|
| Interior design and graphics: | Ed Sherman |
| Cover design: | Dotti Albertini |
| Photo credits: | Page 1 and 3: Todd Tsukushi |
| | Page 2: David Weintraub |

Nolo Press Occidental
2604 El Camino Real, Suite 353B
Carlsbad, CA 92008-1297
(831) 466-9922

# TABLE OF CONTENTS

## Part One—All About Divorce

# Part Two—How to do your own Regular Dissolution

# Part Three—Summary Procedures

# Index

# Forms

**CD** with forms, worksheets, links, more . . . . **Inside back cover**

Part
One:

All About Divorce

This book is dedicated
to all of my clients
and to my ex-wife,
from whom I learned so much
about the subjects in these pages.

•

Special thanks to Sandra Borland
for contirbutions to this book
and to this company.

•

Thanks to former partners Anne Lober and
Peggy Williams who helped so much, and
to Hamid Naraghi, Charma Pipersky
& Allison Hardin of Divorce Helpline
for their valuable contributions.

# 1

# DOING YOUR OWN DIVORCE

You might not know it, but you are going through two divorces at the same time—your Real Divorce and your Legal Divorce. This book is about getting yourself through the legal divorce with little or no involvement with courts and lawyers. It explains California divorce laws with practical advice to help you make decisions, and shows you exactly how to do the paperwork to get your divorce or find someone to do it for you inexpensively.

**The real divorce** is your life, your relationships with your Ex, family, friends, and yourself. It's what you go through in practical, emotional and spiritual terms. The real divorce is about breaking old patterns, finding a new center for your life and doing your best with the hand you've been dealt. These matters are not assisted or addressed in any way by the legal divorce.

**The legal divorce** cares only about how you will divide marital property and debts, whether there will be spousal support, and how you will arrange parenting and child support if you have minor children. If you can settle these matters out of court, there's nothing left but paperwork and red tape to get your Judgment.

If you have trouble agreeing on terms, the problem is almost never legal, but almost always about personalities and emotional upset, for which there is absolutely no help and no solutions—zip, zero, nothing—in court or in a lawyer's office. In fact, getting involved with lawyers and courts almost always makes things worse—much worse. If you follow my advice, you'll avoid the traps and pitfalls of the legal system, and things will get much better much sooner.

## 1.1  Can you do your own divorce?  Should you?

**Yes! You can!** Since this book was first published in 1971, *millions* of Californians just like you have used it to do their divorces without retaining lawyers, so you can almost certainly do it, too. Over 60% of California's divorces are now done without either side being represented by an attorney, saving California families between 500 *million* and a *billion* dollars *every year* in unnecessary legal fees. This book can save you thousands of dollars!

**Yes! You should do your own divorce!** Taking charge of your own case leads to a smoother, faster, less painful, and less expensive experience. Most people would be better off if they reduced or eliminated their use of attorneys, because the legal process and the way attorneys work in it tends to cause trouble, raise the level of conflict, and greatly increase your expense. While you might decide to get advice from a family law attorney who primarily practices mediation or collaborative law, you should not *retain* an attorney to "take your case" unless you have an unavoidable need for doing so. In section 1.8 below, I explain when you should get help and how to get the right kind of help from an attorney without *retaining* the attorney to take over your case.

**What if things don't go smoothly—easy and difficult cases.** If your spouse will not oppose you in court because he/she is gone, doesn't care, or you expect no trouble agreeing on terms, then you only need some paperwork to get your divorce done, and this is the only book you'll need. However, if you have trouble agreeing on divorce terms (or think you will), or if you prefer to have a professional stand with you and take an active role in negotiating for you, or if your case seems headed for court, you can still do your own divorce, and this book is an important place to start, but you will need more help. Solving divorce problems is discussed below in section 1.7 and getting the right help is discussed in section 1.9.

## 1.2 What "do your own divorce" means

Doing your own paperwork is not the important part—the essence of it is thinking things through and making informed decisions. It means that you take responsibility for your case, your decisions, your life. You find out what the rules are and how they apply to your case. You explore all options, then decide what you want and how you want to go about it. If you use an attorney, *you* make all the decisions and control how your case is run. If your spouse is in the picture and cares what happens, doing your own divorce means having detailed discussions—perhaps with help—to reach a thoroughly negotiated agreement.

Above all, doing your own divorce means that you do not *retain* an attorney (section 1.3). No one should *retain* an attorney unless they have an emergency situation like those discussed in section 1.8, but that doesn't mean you can't get advice and help from an attorney if you feel the need (section 1.9).

Many people find it difficult to think things through carefully and make decisions about their divorce, and they are *extremely* nervous about discussing divorce details with their Ex. This is completely understandable, but it is something you need to do if you don't want to become a victim of divorce. If you want it, you can get help from an attorney-mediator or a collaborative law attorney (section 1.9) to help you think things through, talk to your spouse, and work out an agreement.

## 1.3 What it means to "retain" an attorney—and a better idea

It's okay to use an attorney, but most people should not *retain* one in their divorce unless there is a clear reason for doing so. Here's why.

When you *retain* an attorney, you sign a "retainer agreement" where the attorney takes professional responsibility to act in your behalf—to represent you. You are *literally* handing over your power and authority to act. Standards of professional conduct require any attorney who represents you—even one with good intentions—to act in ways that will complicate your case and make it worse instead of better. Attorneys typically start cases in court quickly, even when that is likely to cause upset and make settlement more difficult.

An attorney who represents you must go to great lengths to protect himself against later malpractice claims by his own client—you. This means doing things for the attorney's benefit instead of yours. California's leading family law authority advises attorneys to either get clients to waive the attorney's responsibility or else "do the absolute maximum" in every case. Doing the maximum may or may not help you, but it will certainly raise the level of conflict, and it will cost plenty.

Never forget that when you *retain* an attorney, the more trouble you have, the more money the attorney makes. That's hardly an incentive to keep things simple.

Our system of justice is known as "the adversary system." It began in the Middle Ages, when trial by combat meant a battle and whoever survived was right, and that approach to justice forms the basis of our legal system today. The attorney works in our system as a combatant, but that is not what you want for solving family and personal problems.

It would be nice if you could get help from an experienced attorney with a good attitude who does not want to be retained, but few attorneys will take an interest in your case unless you retain them. That's why Divorce Helpline was created. This is the only law firm I know of that works exclusively on divorce settlement. Instead of "taking" your case, Divorce Helpline attorneys serve as your guide and assistant. When you use Divorce Helpline, you are still doing your own divorce because the control of the case stays in your hands. They guide you, help resolve problems, and handle the red tape and paperwork, but your case doesn't get out of control because *you* are in charge.

## 1.4 Advantages to doing your own divorce

### Getting a good divorce

Studies show that active participation in your divorce is the single most important factor in getting a good divorce. "Good divorce" means such things as better compliance with agreements and orders after the divorce, less post-divorce conflict, less post-divorce litigation, more good will, and better co-parenting.

People who take an active role generally do much better emotionally and legally than those who try to avoid the responsibility for solving their divorce problems. This doesn't mean you shouldn't get help from an attorney or mediator—it means you should be actively involved, become informed about the rules, and make your own decisions. Be in charge of your case and your life.

### It's much cheaper

A huge advantage to doing your own divorce, even with the help of Divorce Helpline, is the savings in cost. When an attorney takes your case, the initial retainer could be anywhere from $750 to $5,000, but the retainer is only the beginning. The average cost of a divorce is about $20,000 *for each party*, but that's only because the average couple has no more than that to spend. If you have more, it will cost more—much more. Depending on the size of your estate, a contested case can cost many tens or hundreds of thousands of dollars *on each side!*

### Keeping it simple

Most people start off with a case that is either fairly simple or one that could probably become simple if handled right. Such cases don't usually stay simple after an attorney is retained. Divorces tend to be fairly sensitive, so it doesn't take much to stir them up, but lawyers and the legal system tend to make things more complicated, more stirred up, worse instead of better. This is because of the way the system works and the way lawyers work in it.

When one spouse or partner gets an attorney, the other is likely to get one too, and then the fun really begins. Two attorneys start off costing just double, but pretty soon they are writing unpleasant letters, filing motions, and doing attorney-type things as a matter of routine that may not be helpful. Now we have a contested case, more fees and charges, and a couple of very upset and broke spouses.

In the end, you will still have to negotiate a settlement with your Ex. Over 90% of all cases settle without trial, but when attorneys are retained, settlement usually comes after the parties are emotionally depleted and their bank accounts exhausted. Why go through all that?

The moral of this story is this: don't *retain* an attorney unless you absolutely must (section 1.8). If you do it entirely yourself, or with the help of Divorce Helpline, you have a much better chance of keeping a simple case simple and of reaching a settlement much earlier.

## 1.5   How to start a divorce—Petitioners and Respondents

**The Petitioner and the Respondent.** Every divorce starts with a Petition. The Petitioner is the person who first files papers and gets the case started. The Respondent is the other party. A Response need not be filed, but it is a good idea, otherwise the inactive person has little say about when or how the divorce is completed, unless there is already a written agreement. In general, the more both parties participate, the better. After a Response is filed, the divorce can be completed only by written agreement or court trial. Agreement is better.

**Equality.** Once a Response is filed, Respondent has equal standing and there is no legal difference between the parties or their rights, and either party can take any available legal step. Where instructions in this book indicate "Petitioner," Respondent can substitute "Respondent" and take the same action.

**The Petition.** To get your case started, you file a Petition and serve it on your spouse or partner. The only thing you need to know before you do this is that you want to start a divorce. The issues can all be sorted out and resolved later. On the other hand, it wouldn't hurt to read through Part One before you start.

**Advantages to serving the Petition:**
- Starts the clock ticking on waiting periods.
- Causes automatic restraining orders to take effect.
- Helps establish the date of separation.
- Has psychological value for Petitioner and tells Respondent a divorce is really going to happen.

**Possible downside.** Serving papers can upset the Respondent and stir up conflict if you don't properly prepare the Respondent ahead of time.

**Getting a smooth start.** Unless your Ex is an abuser/controller, you will probably want to start things off as nicely as possible. An abrupt start will probably increase conflict as an upset spouse is more likely to run to an attorney who will probably make your case more complicated. So take some time to prepare your Ex and let him/her get used to the idea that a divorce is about to start. If you aren't comfortable discussing things in person, write a nice letter. Let your spouse know you are committed to working out a settlement that you can both agree to and live with. Unless you are under time pressure, don't serve your Summons and Petition until your partner seems ready to receive the papers calmly.

**The Response.** A Response *should* be filed within 30 days of receiving the Summons and Petition, but *can* be filed any time before Petitioner declares the Respondent's default (chapter 17). Filing a Response is not an aggressive act. In fact, it is usually a good idea for Respondent to take part in the action, especially if you have kids or property or debts to be divided. It is easy to do. The only disadvantages are Respondent's filing fee of about $435 (chapter 7.3), and the possibility that you might have to file a questionnaire about your case in order to avoid a case conference hearing (last page of chapter 11).

There are numerous advantages to filing a Response. If there's no Response, Respondent has little control over when and how the divorce is completed, so the Respondent feels insecure. By filing, Respondent joins the case on an equal standing with Petitioner, so Respondent feels more a part of the process, more in the loop, more confident. Experience and studies show that the more Respondent participates, the better the divorce outcome is likely to be.

## 1.6  Three ways to get it done

After you file your Petition, there are only three ways you can get your Judgment of Dissolution: (1) by default, (2) by contest, or (3) by written agreement.

### The default divorce

In a default case, Respondent is served with the Petition but does nothing. No Response is filed, so the case is completed by default, without participation by Respondent. Default should be used only if you have little property or debts, no children, and no need for spousal or partner support, or in cases where Respondent is long gone or doesn't care to participate. If Respondent is around and cares what happens, it is better if a Response is filed.

## The contested divorce

If a Response is filed, you can complete your divorce only by written agreement or by taking the case to court and having a judge decide issues that you can't settle. Until there is an agreement, your case is *technically* considered to be contested. Whether or not there is a battle and a lot of legal activity depends on how you go about solving problems and reaching agreement. If you have problems reaching agreement, read *Make Any Divorce Better*. If you find yourself headed into a court battle, get Book 2, *How to Solve Divorce Problems*.

## Divorce by settlement agreement

When the problems are all solved and you finally reach an agreement, one of the parties files a stipulation (chapter 12.7) and steps out. The case is now uncontested and sails through. If your spouse is in the picture and you have children, significant property or debts, or you need to arrange spousal support, then you should make *every* effort to reach a written agreement on all issues. Look what you gain:

- You can be certain exactly what the orders in the Judgment will be.

- You can complete your case by mail and almost certainly won't have to go to court;

- Both parties participate, so the Respondent can feel confident about letting the divorce go through without contest or representation because the terms of the Judgment are all settled;

- It invariably leads to better relations with your ex-spouse or partner. Where there are children, this is extremely important; and

- You are far more likely to get compliance with terms of the divorce after the Judgment.

These advantages are so important that you should struggle long and hard to work out an agreement, with or without the help of a mediator or collaborative law attorney (section 1.9). Chapter 6 discusses written agreements in detail.

# MAP – How to get there from here

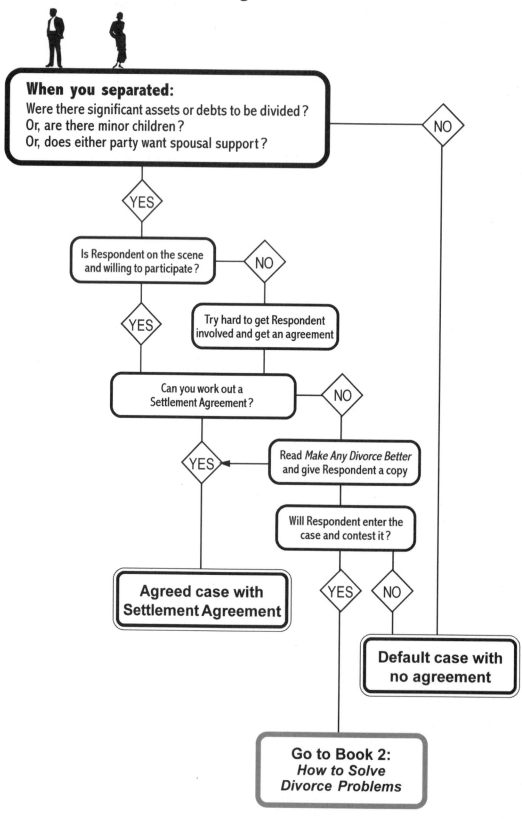

**When you separated:**
Were there significant assets or debts to be divided?
Or, are there minor children?
Or, does either party want spousal support?

NO

YES

Is Respondent on the scene and willing to participate?

NO

YES

Try hard to get Respondent involved and get an agreement

Can you work out a Settlement Agreement?

NO

YES

Read *Make Any Divorce Better* and give Respondent a copy

Will Respondent enter the case and contest it?

YES

NO

**Agreed case with Settlement Agreement**

**Default case with no agreement**

**Go to Book 2:**
*How to Solve Divorce Problems*

## 1.7  Solving divorce problems

The steps you take to make your case go more smoothly depend on what your situation is right at this moment. Five divorce profiles are described below with steps you should take in each situation. See which profile best fits you.

### Early cases

You haven't broken up yet, or broke up only recently. This is good, because the earlier you start, the easier it is to heal wounds and lay a foundation for a smoother trip. The way you go about doing things now will have a powerful influence on how things work out in your future—for better or worse.

**Your goal** is to solve problems and settle issues without taking problems to court or spending much (if any) time in a lawyer's office. Your goal is to end up with an Easy Case (below).

Here are steps you can take to achieve these goals.

- Go to **www.nolodivorce.com** and look in the Reading Room for articles mentioned below and elsewhere in this book.

- Read my article, *The Good Divorce*, so you will have a model to keep in mind and an idea of things you can try to accomplish to keep your divorce peaceful.

- Read the *Pre-divorce Checklist* and start working on those items.

- Read Part One of this book to learn about divorce laws, and skim Part Two, especially chapter 6, to get a sense of how divorce paperwork is done.

- Get *Make Any Divorce Better* and learn specific things you can do to smooth things out. Get a copy for your Ex, too, so you can discuss ideas in it.

- **Do not talk to your spouse about divorce** until you learn how to reduce conflict, create a foundation for negotiation, and negotiate effectively.

- **Do not go to an attorney** until you are better informed and prepared—unless, that is, you face an emergency as described in section 1.8.

Before you visit an attorney, you want to have already organized all the facts and documents in your case (see below) and learned what you can and cannot expect from an attorney. To learn about various types of attorneys and other professional services, see section 1.9 below.

## Easy cases

If your spouse won't come to court to oppose you, you've got an easy case. It could be because he/she is gone, doesn't care, or because you are able to sit down and agree on terms. All that's left is to file papers and go through some red tape to get a Judgment. You can do the paperwork yourself with this book or get it done inexpensively (see listings in the back of this book).

**Spouse on board?** It's very difficult to divide major assets or arrange parenting without your spouse's participation, so your goal is to settle things in a written settlement agreement. Here are tools to help you complete an easy case and make sure it stays easy.

• Go to the Reading Room at my site, **www.nolodivorce.com** and read my article, *The Good Divorce*, so you will have a model to keep in mind and an idea of things you can try to accomplish to keep your divorce peaceful.

• Read the *Pre-divorce Checklist* and start working on those items.

• Read Part One of this book to learn about divorce laws and skim Part Two to get a sense of how divorce paperwork is done. If you have major assets (real estate, retirement funds), it would make sense to have expert advice and an agreement drafted by an attorney, so I recommend that you call Divorce Helpline (800) 359-7004 and find out how they can help you. For other options, read section 1.9 below and see the listings in the back of this book for a professional near you. If you're thinking of using online divorce forms, go to the Reading Room at **www.nolodivorce.com** and read my article that explains why online forms are *not* a good idea.

• **Keeping easy cases easy.** Most divorces are delicate and easily stirred up. To learn how to keep an easy case from blowing up into a difficult one, I recommend that each spouse have a copy of *Make Any Divorce Better* and follow specific steps to calm conflict and negotiate effectively. Discuss ideas in it.

• **Get organized.** As soon as you can, organize your facts, gather documents and start thinking about how to divide community property, how much spousal support will be paid (if any), and how children will be supported and parented. You'll find a set of Divorce Worksheets on the CD that comes with this book. These will help you organize, think about, and discuss the facts and finances in your case. They will definitely save you time and money.

• **A written settlement agreement** is very important in most cases. The sample agreement that comes with this book is not ideal for dealing with major assets, but **DealMaker** software is. It clarifies the many possible options for real estate or retirement funds and also guides you in the creation of a parenting plan if you have minor children. **DealMaker** guides you to enter information and make some decisions, then it writes a sophisticated draft or your settlement agreement ready for your signature or review by an attorney-mediator.

## Difficult Cases—when things don't go smoothly (or might not)

This profile fits most divorces. Your spouse is in the picture and cares about how things will end up, but you're having some trouble (or you expect to) with discussing and settling terms.

The reason divorce agreements are difficult is almost always personal—bad communication, bad history, bad habits, etc.—and almost never about the law. Neither the law nor lawyers have any tools to help you settle problems that originate in your personal relationship. In fact, the things you can do yourself are far superior to anything a lawyer can do for you.

**Your goal** is to take specific steps that will make your case smoother and easier, to turn it into an Easy Divorce (above), so you can make a written agreement and do the paperwork yourself or get it done inexpensively. There are a lot of things you can do for yourself to make things better, steps that have helped tens of thousands of couples, so they can help you, too.

Here are the steps you should take.

- Go to the Reading Room at my site, **www.nolodivorce.com** and read my article, *The Good Divorce*, so you will have a model to keep in mind and an idea of things you can try to accomplish to keep your divorce peaceful.

- Start working on early steps, noted in my *Pre-divorce Checklist*.

- Get *Make Any Divorce Better* and learn about the specific things you can do to smooth things out. Get a copy for your Ex, too, so you can discuss ideas in it. This book also contains a section on strategies for difficult cases.

- **Do not talk to your spouse** about divorce until you learn how to reduce conflict, create a foundation for negotiation, and negotiate effectively.

- **Do not talk to an attorney** until you are informed and prepared—unless, that is, you face an emergency like those described in section 1.8 below.

- **Organize your facts.** Start now to organize your documents and facts. I created a set of Divorce Worksheets to help you organize, think about, and discuss the facts and finances in your case. They will definitely save you time and money. These worksheets can be found on the CD that comes with this book.

- **DealMaker.** Your highest goal is to get a written settlement agreement of all issues in your case. The sample agreement in this book is not ideal for dealing with major or complex assets, but **DealMaker** software is. It is especially useful for dealing with the many possible options for real estate and retirement funds, and it helps you create a custom parenting plan.

- **Mediation.** If you have trouble working out terms, you don't need an attorney, you need a mediator. Call Divorce Helpline at (800) 359-7004.

- **Collaborative law.** If you want to be represented by an attorney, try to get a collaborative lawyer on both sides. Read more about this in section 1.9 below. Divorce Helpline does collaborative law as well as arbitration.

- **Arbitration.** If you can't resolve issues after mediation, you should consider taking your case to arbitration rather than court. It is similar, in that the arbitrator imposes a decision, but the setting is less formal and an arbitrator is paid by the hour, so will take all the time you need to understand the facts about your family and situation. A judge has to move cases along quickly, so will tend to hurry through divorce motions or trials.

## Domestic abuse and violence (DV)

DV includes physical attacks, threats, intimidation, personal verbal attacks (put-downs, insults, undermining your self-confidence) and other efforts to control you. It can be difficult to distinguish between high levels of divorce conflict and forms of domestic abuse and violence. The DV profile is about cases where your spouse is an habitual controller/abuser, someone who has abused repeatedly. These people are not responsive to reason because their need to control or abuse is too strong, so when dealing with an habitual controller/abuser, your only choice is to go somewhere safe and get specialized help.

**Safety first.** If you fear for the safety of yourself or a child, go somewhere safe where you can't be found. Ask the local police for domestic abuse support groups near you. What you need most now is personal advice and counseling from someone who specializes in domestic abuse.

### Legal battle

If you follow my advice, you probably won't end up in a legal battle, but sometimes you simply can't avoid one or you might be in one already. If you're already in a legal battle, or if you can't avoid a battle even after following the steps in *Make Any Divorce Better*, then you have to do what you have to do—get an attorney and fight. If you must fight, you might as well learn how to do it effectively, so welcome to the Battle Group. Keep in mind that this is a legal battle, which is all about business. You do not want to battle on a personal or emotional level. In fact, you will be more effective and healthier if you don't. But you do need to learn:

- How to deal with extreme conflict
- Damage control
- How to protect children
- Winning strategies—hardball or softball?
- How to fight effectively at less expense
- How to choose and use your attorney
- How to fire your attorney (if you want to)

*Make Any Divorce Better* discusses this information in detail. Also get *How to Solve Divorce Problems*, which discusses all stages of legal battle, so you can either handle them yourself or monitor and supervise your attorney's conduct of your case. This allows you to call the shots and maintain a degree of control over your own case.

If you're in a legal battle, you should make persistent efforts to move your case toward negotiated or mediated agreement, using all the steps discussed in *Make Any Divorce Better*. Discourage legal action or activity that you think is not necessary and instruct your attorney that you want to mediate as soon as possible and be kept informed of every effort to make that happen. Also talk about this directly with your spouse, if possible, either in person or by mail.

## 1.8  When you should get some help

### Emergencies—when retaining an attorney makes sense

If your situation is described below, read the recommended articles to decide if you need to retain an attorney. If your situation is not described below, you should read Part One of this book and also look through *Make Any Divorce Better*, then take some time to think things over and take the steps I recommend for your type of case.

### A. Personal Emergencies

• **Fear for the safety of yourself or your child.** If your spouse is an habitual controller/abuser and you fear it will happen again, you need advice from a domestic violence counselor. Ask your local police or Superior Court Clerk's Office for a list of local DV support groups and call them to ask for names of people who can advise you and, if necessary, help you find a safe place to stay.

• **Fear of sneak attack.** If you think your spouse might do a sneak attack by filing for court orders for custody and support without discussion or warning, or maybe just take the kids and the money and run, or both, read about strategies in chapter 5D of *Make Any Divorce Better* and decide if you are going to be defensive or take the offense first.

• **Desperately broke.** If your financial situation is truly desperate—or if your spouse feels this way—go to the Reading Room at **www.nolodivorce.com** and read my article, *Funding Your Separation*.

• **Parenting children.** Many people run to an attorney because they are afraid they won't get to see their children often enough. If this describes you, go to the Reading Room at **www.nolodivorce.com** and read *Parenting in the Early Stages*.

### B. Legal Emergencies

• **Divorce papers served on you.** This may not be an emergency. If you've only been served with the Summons and Petition that start a divorce action in court and you want to have some say in the outcome, you need to file a Response (chapter 11) before the deadline stated on your papers. If the deadline has passed, call the Superior Court Clerk and ask if you are still able to file a Response even though the deadline has passed. If so, quickly file a Response. If not, you'll need an attorney to help you make a motion to allow you to enter the case late. In either situation, read section 1.9 below about how to find the right kind of help.

However, if a motion has been filed and a hearing scheduled in the near future to determine support or child custody issues, you need to get an attorney right away to either represent you at the hearing or seek a continuance so you can prepare. Read section 1.9 about what kind of attorney you want. If you don't have time to get an attorney, show up in court at the time and place indicated on your papers and ask the judge for a continuance so you can get an attorney. Even if you are in litigation, you should read *Make Any Divorce Better* and look for ways to move the action out of court and into mediation. Also get *How to Solve Divorce Problems*.

- **You are already in litigation.** If you are already in a legal struggle with attorneys on both sides, read *Make Any Divorce Better* to learn how the law works and how to guide your case toward negotiation, mediation, or collaborative divorce. If all else fails, arbitration is better than going to court. Get *How to Solve Divorce Problems* so you can see how a contested divorce works and use it to monitor your own attorney's performance. What you do not want is to end up stuck in a court battle where everyone loses but the attorneys.

## Legal advice—when to get it and from whom

In some situations, you can get a lot of good from a little advice. In *any* case, you can get peace of mind from knowing you are doing things right. A few hundred dollars for advice may not seem unreasonable when weighed against the value of your property, debts, possible tax savings, all future support payments, and the importance of a good parenting plan. You can often save more than you spend.

If you have any of the situations listed below in your case, you have good reason to get some legal advice. Section 1.9 suggests who to go to.

### Property
- The division of assets and debts is not equal.
- A major asset is being divided or sold—avoiding capital gains problems.
- You aren't sure how to value some assets, such as a business or a professional practice, etc.
- You have stock options—valuation, division, relationship to child and spousal (partner) support.
- Separate and community money was mixed together in a major asset.
- Pension or retirement funds accumulated at least in part during marriage—how to value and how to divide without penalty.

### Debts
- You have lots of debts and/or you want to protect yourself from your spouse's debts.
- Either party might declare bankruptcy.
- Joint credit card or other accounts have not been not closed.

### Your spouse (solutions are discussed at length in *Make Any Divorce Better*)
- You can't agree about important issues.
- You can't get information from your spouse about income, assets, debts.
- You suspect your spouse might be hiding assets.

### Children

- There is disagreement over parenting arrangements.
- One parent doesn't want the other to move.
- One parent earns much more than the other—consider saving on taxes by arranging for family support instead of child support.
- There are special needs or health problems.

### Spousal or partner support

- You have been married five years or more.
- There is more than 20% difference in incomes.
- One spouse is not self-supporting.
- One spouse put the other through school or training.
- You have preschool children.
- There are special needs or health problems.

### Personal

- With a good income and busy schedule, you would be better off if someone else did the paperwork.
- You want to be sure you're doing the right thing and know things are being done correctly.
- You don't understand your situation or what to do about it.
- You want help and suggestions for how to negotiate with your spouse.

## 1.9   Who can help?

Friends and relatives are the least reliable sources of advice. Accept all the moral support you can get, but when they give you advice, just smile and say, "Thank you," but do not take it to heart. Also be wary of "common knowledge." If you didn't get it from this book or a family law attorney in California, *don't trust it!* Just because you like or trust someone doesn't make them right.

### Legal Document Assistants (paralegals)

Non-attorneys who offer legal forms services directly to the public are called Legal Document Assistants (LDAs) and must register unless working under the supervision of an attorney or non-profit organization. In theory, you tell an LDA what you want to say on which forms, then they type them up and handle the secretarial work. In practice, they provide more guidance. We introduced this innovation in legal service in 1972, and it has since changed the face of the legal map. See the listings in the back of the book for someone near you.

No particular education or training is required to be an LDA, but the California Association of Legal Document Assistants (CALDA) offers its members training and promotes high standards in education, ethics, and business practices. We are a Sustaining Member of CALDA. There are many CALDA members in our Directory of Professional Services Near You at the back of this book, or you can find one near you at their web site: **www.calda.org**.

LDAs can't give you reliable legal advice, nor should you have one prepare your settlement agreement unless they are using Nolo's DealMaker software or following the example in this book. Just as when hiring a lawyer or mechanic, be careful who you hire. Ask how long he/she has been in business and check references. If you know exactly what you want and have no legal questions or problems, an experienced and reliable LDA is a good way to get your paperwork done.

### For a list of divorce services near you, look in the back of this book or go to www.nolodivorce.com/dir

### Court Facilitators

Every county has a Family Law Facilitator's office where you can get free assistance, at least with support issues: determining the correct amount, understanding rules and forms, establishing a child support order and enforcing it. In many counties, that's all they do, while in other counties they will help you with other aspects of your case. Most offer self-help seminars. We hear that the quality of service ranges from poor to excellent, mostly depending on the availability of additional funding. Demand far exceeds supply, so it takes a fair amount of time and persistence to actually get in and get help. If you have time to spare—or no better option—you should go see what help you can get. The more prepared you are, the more effective their help will be. Don't forget to take all your notes and paperwork with you when you go in. For contact information, call your Superior Court Clerk's office or go to **www.nolodivorce.com/links**.

### Mediators

If you can't work out an agreement on your own, you should try mediation. A mediator can help you communicate, balance the negotiating power, develop options you haven't thought of, solve problems, break through impasse and help you reach a fair agreement. If your problems are primarily personal or about parenting, a non-attorney mediator can be used, but if property or legal issues are involved, it might be best to select a family law attorney-mediator.

Mediation is not just for friendly divorces. Angry, conflicted couples are especially in need of mediation and stand to gain the most, particularly if they have children. Mediation can be very effective, even in cases with high conflict, when conducted by a good family law attorney-mediator like those at Divorce Helpline. If the parties can't even agree to try mediation, they are willing to contact the other side and try to arrange a meeting. Divorce Helpline works by phone throughout California or at their offices in San Jose, San Francisco, San Rafael, Oakland, Walnut Creek, Santa Cruz, Sacramento, Roseville, Folsom, Nevada City, Los Angeles, Encino, Irvine and San Diego. They can even do telephone mediation, which can be surprisingly effective and a lifesaver if parties can't meet at one location in person.

## Lawyers

**Advice.** Unless you expect (or want) a legal battle, the best place to get advice is from a family law attorney who mostly does mediation rather than litigation. This way you are more likely to get practical advice designed to solve problems rather than contentious advice that can lead you to court.

**Traditional lawyers** who *specialize* in divorce and work in the court system know a lot that could help you, but, because of the way the system works and the way lawyers work, they will almost certainly create unnecessary conflict and expense if you retain one. Unfortunately, getting information and advice from traditional attorneys without retaining them can be tricky, because they don't really want to help you help yourself; they want to be retained to do it all.

Attorneys will frequently do the first interview for a fairly small fee, but too often they spend that time convincing you that you need them to handle your case. Hourly rates can run from $150 to $450, but $175–$350 per hour is normal. Most attorneys require a retainer—$1,200 to $5,000 is typical—but the amount doesn't matter because the final bill will be *much* higher. Few attorneys will give you a definite maximum figure for the whole job. You are doing *very* well if you end up spending less than $5,000 *per spouse* on the *simplest* case. The average in urban areas when both spouses are represented is *well* over $18,000 *per spouse*, but couples with larger estates can expect costs to run into tens or hundreds of thousands of dollars—*per spouse!*

**Limited representation.** A small but growing number of lawyers are offering representation limited to specific tasks or portions of your case while you keep overall responsibility. For example, they will represent you only to draft your agreement, or only to appear in court if you are asked to show up there for some reason, or only to file and appear on one motion. If you need a bit of service from a family law attorney, call around and ask if they offer "limited representation" or "unbundling," the two names by which this service is known. Better yet, call Divorce Helpline, as they've been doing this sort of thing since 1990.

**Attorney-mediators.** See "Mediators" above. When you're looking for advice, it would be best to get it from an attorney who does mostly mediation, as the advice you get is more likely to be practical and about solving problems rather than going to court.

**Collaborative divorce.** Increasingly popular, spouses and their attorneys pledge in writing not go to court or threaten to go to court as a way to solve problems. Instead, they will use advice, negotiation, and mediation to reach a settlement. If there's no settlement, the spouses will have to get different attorneys to take the case into litigation. In some cases, the collaborative team might include other professionals, such as a divorce coach, family counselor, child specialist, accountant, or financial planner. Collaborative divorce has a good track record and, even with all the professional services you get, it will still cost less than a court battle.

## Divorce Helpline

Divorce Helpline was created to change the way attorneys practice in divorce cases and to provide expert support for people who are doing their own. Divorce Helpline attorneys will not litigate (go to court) because they don't believe in it. Instead, their expert family law attorneys work exclusively as your guide and assistant, helping you plan, solve problems, develop your options, talk to your Ex and reach a fair settlement. They offer advice, mediation, arbitration, and collaborative law, working by telephone throughout California, or at their offices in San Jose, San Francisco, San Rafael, Oakland, Walnut Creek, Santa Cruz, Sacramento, Roseville, Folsom, Nevada City, Los Angeles, Encino, Irvine and San Diego. Divorce Helpline attorneys are trained in mediation and are excellent at solving problems. They'll answer your questions, but they can do a better job for you when they do the *whole* case—the paperwork and the settlement agreement—as well as giving you advice. That way they have *all* the information, not just the small bit you are asking about. When they do the whole case they often find problems to solve and ways to save money that people don't know to ask about. Their methods have proved to be highly successful and very affordable. Learn more about Divorce Helpline, including their rates and services, at **www.divorcehelp.com**, or call (800) 359-7004 for a free explanation of how they work and how they can help you.

## 1.10 Looking ahead

As mentioned in section 1.5 above, you can file your Petition and serve it at any time, assuming you have arranged for a smooth start by preparing your spouse or partner to receive it. You can then take some time to make decisions and work out the details about your property, support, and children. We discuss the basic rules of these subjects in chapters 3 through 5, then in chapter 6 we show you how everything can be wrapped up in a settlement agreement once you get things worked out. If you have a more complex estate, real estate, or retirement funds, you should get **DealMaker** software (inside front cover), which uses the power of software to make it easier for you to deal with the many options available for major assets. You just enter requested information, make requested decisions, and **DealMaker** prints a draft settlement agreement ready to sign or have reviewed by an attorney-mediator.

**Preparation.** Eventually, to complete your divorce you will have to create a complete list of all of your assets and debts, and it will be extremely useful if you start doing that now. Start filling out the worksheets that come on the CD with this book and gather all documents and records related to your assets, debts and family. If you don't want to do the worksheets on a computer, you can instead fill out the disclosure documents described in chapter 14. Getting prepared in this manner will help organize your facts, your documents, and your thinking. It will suggest other information or questions you might have.

If you have trouble getting information you need, read *Getting the Information You Need*, which is the Appendix in *Make Any Divorce Better*, or chapters 8, 17, and 18 in *How to Solve Divorce Problems*.

Go to my web site, **www.nolodivorce.com**, look in the Reading Room, get the free article, *Pre-divorce Checklist*, and start working on those items right away.

**Study the Judgment.** While you are reading through the next few chapters, at some point you should jump ahead to chapter 18 and take a look at the Judgment form and the various attachments to the Judgment that are relevant to your case. Read the language in the various orders that are used in Judgments so you can understand where all this information you are reading about will end up. Then you'll have a better idea of where you are going while reading about how to get there.

# 2

# BASIC INFORMATION ABOUT DIVORCE

**Divorce = Dissolution.** In California courts, marriages are dissolved, so what you get is technically referred to as a *dissolution*. Still, we've never heard anyone say, "I'm going to dissolve you!" so we use both "divorce" and "dissolution" and you can call it anything you like outside of court.

**Domestic partners and same-sex marriages.** California marriage and divorce laws now apply equally to officially registered domestic partners. Same-sex marriages were very briefly authorized but currently are not permitted, although such marriages validly entered into in other states will be recognized, at least for now. This book can be used to end any valid form of same-sex relationship, but some allowances must be made for our terminology. Domestic partnership and same-sex marriages acquire their rules almost entirely by reference to existing marriage laws that use terms like *spouse, marriage, husband, wife,* and so on, mostly without adaptation to suit same-sex couples. Therefore, we ask same-sex couples to understand that all marital terms apply to them, too, unless clearly stated otherwise.

## 2.1 Dissolution, nullity, and legal separation

There are three ways a court can end a marriage or registered domestic partnership: dissolution, nullity, and legal separation. In any of these procedures, the court can make orders on property, debts, child custody, child support, and spousal or partner support.

**A nullity** (formerly called annulment) declares that the marriage or partnership never existed, while a dissolution says that the relationship will cease to exist at the end of the dissolution. Both have the effect of restoring the parties to single status, but the nullity permits you to remarry immediately after the hearing, while with a dissolution you sometimes have to wait a bit. Since the grounds for nullity are more complicated than for a dissolution, and since courts tend to be more strict in nullity cases, we recommend that you do not try to do your own nullity. This book does not show you how to get one. If you want a nullity, see an attorney or call Divorce Helpline.

**A legal separation** makes orders about children, support and property, but the parties remain legally joined while living apart. This is useful to couples who can't divorce for religious or moral reasons, but also can't continue to live together. There are a few situations where legal separation is a better choice—where sizeable Social Security benefits, Veterans' benefits, retirement, or other benefits may be lost if there is a dissolution, or where a long-term spouse with an illness or disability *might* be able to stay on the employed spouse's health insurance—call the plan to see if they allow this. The companion CD that comes with this book has an article about legal separation in the Reading Room section, and the Kit section has instructions for how to get one using the forms in this book.

**A dissolution (divorce)** will usually serve your purposes as well or better than either of the other methods. That's what the rest of this book is about.

## 2.2  Regular vs.  Summary Dissolution

In this book, we call the traditional way to get a divorce a *Regular* Dissolution. There are simpler procedures called *Summary* Dissolution for married couples and *Termination* for domestic partners. Not everyone is eligible, and of those who are eligible, not everyone will want to do it that way. The regular method has advantages even for those who are qualified to use the simpler methods.

**Summary Dissolution for married couples** can be filed if there were no more than five years between date of marriage and date of separation (date of separation is defined on page 44). The couple *must* prepare and sign a property agreement dividing marital assets and allocating responsibility for debts, and both must give up all rights to spousal support. When you sign the Petition, you and your spouse will be swearing that:

1. Both spouses have read and understood the Summary Dissolution Booklet (this is FL-810, found in the Summary Dissolution folder that is in the Forms folder on the CD that comes with this book;

2. One spouse has lived in California for at least six months and in the county in which you file for at least three months immediately before you file your Petition;

3. There are no minor children and the wife is not pregnant;

4. Neither spouse has *any* interest in real estate *anywhere*, not including a lease of a residence occupied by either party if it terminates within one year after the petition is filed and there's no option to purchase;

5. There is less than $6,000 in community debts, not counting car loans;

6. There is less than $40,000 in community property, not counting cars;

7. Neither spouse owns over $40,000 separately, not counting cars.

Still interested? If you meet these requirements, you can use the Summary procedure. But, there is a waiting period of six months after you file the Petition, during which time either spouse can revoke the Summary proceeding just by filing a simple form. If that happens, either spouse can start a Regular Dissolution, but some time will have been lost. If neither party files a revocation, then after the six-month waiting period, either party can ask the court to enter the Judgment, or the court *might* enter the Judgment without being asked. Until the Judgment has been entered, there is no divorce.

How to get a Summary Dissolution is discussed further in chapter 22 and Termination a Domestic Partnership is discussed in chapter 23.

**Notice of Termination of Domestic Partnership** is almost exactly parallel to the Summary Dissolution procedure above, so read those requirements to see if you qualify. The only differences are that the mandatory booklet and Notice of Termination form are obtained from the Secretary of State and the Notice of Termination is filed with that office, and there is no residency requirement *if* your partnership was created in California—in that case, you can file even if both partners no longer live here. How to do the Termination of Domestic Partnership is discussed further in chapter 23.

## Comments

A simple procedure is a good idea, but there is some risk. This is because either spouse (or partner) can revoke the proceeding at any time before the relationship is dissolved. For *at least* six months, maybe more, your dissolution is at risk. Divorce often involves personal drama and emotional turmoil—a time when otherwise reasonable people can play bad games. Are you absolutely certain your spouse won't spoil the process for the next six months or so?

## Advice

Even if you *are* eligible for the simpler procedure, don't do it unless you can start in plenty of time to make important decisions, get the property agreement worked out and the papers filed without feeling under pressure to meet the deadline. Divorce is too important to rush, and mistakes may come back to haunt you later. And you should not do the simpler procedure unless you can be certain your agreements with your spouse are firm and mutual. If there is even a small chance that during the next six or more months one spouse might become temperamental, uncertain, or unstable enough to revoke the procedure, then you would both be better off filing a Regular Dissolution to begin with. It's a bit more trouble but it is a lot more stable and certain. It costs the same for filing fees.

## 2.3  Grounds for dissolution

The primary ground for dissolution in California is "irreconcilable differences." In a Regular Dissolution you are also allowed to use "incurable insanity," which refers to people who are medically, scientifically crazy. Your spouse may seem weird to you, or even dangerous, but that may not be enough to be found legally insane. The insanity case is too complicated for you to present without an attorney, but if you are disturbed because your spouse is "different," then you can definitely go ahead and use the grounds of irreconcilable differences. In practice, anyone who wants a divorce has irreconcilable differences. You have irreconcilable differences when there is any reason at all for not continuing the marriage *and* if you are sure there can be no reconciliation. You don't need to actually state a reason—just the fact that one of the spouses wants a divorce is enough. Almost all divorces are granted on these grounds.

## 2.4  Residency requirements

**For married couples,** California has jurisdiction over their marriage and the power to dissolve it only if at least one spouse has lived in California long enough: either you or your spouse must have lived in California for at least six months, and in the county where you file your papers for at least three months, just prior to filing the Petition. Being away temporarily, as on a business trip or vacation, does not count against your residency time.

**Domestic partners** who registered in California have no residency requirement because they consented to the court's jurisdiction when they signed the registration form. Partnerships created elsewhere can be dissolved only if the same residency requirements as for married couples are met.

**After you file your Petition** there is no more requirement for residency, so you can move anywhere you wish. However, if you have children, you can't take them out of the state without the written consent of your spouse (section 2.7), and while most cases can be completed by mail, there is a small chance that you *might* have to return for a hearing (chapter 20.1).

## 2.5 Serving papers—giving notice to your spouse

In our system, any lawsuit is a struggle between two contestants conducted before an impartial authority, the judge. It seems obvious (doesn't it?) that you can't have a fair contest if the other side doesn't know one is going on. The essence of notice is that your spouse or partner is given or sent a Summons and a copy of your Petition and can therefore be presumed to know what the suit is about, what you want, and when and where the contest is to be held. The court cannot act in your case unless you properly notify your spouse or partner of the lawsuit. Chapter 12 shows how this is done. The notice requirement is especially important in cases that go by default, which is what happens when your spouse or partner gets notice and doesn't file a Response. Your spouse or partner has seen the Petition, so not showing up is like saying that you can have your way. Subject to the judge's approval, that is what you will get.

## 2.6 Jurisdiction and the power of the court to act

Your marriage or partnership might come under the court's power (jurisdiction) for reasons discussed in section 2.4 above, but that does not mean it has *personal* authority over your spouse or partner. To make an *enforceable* order against a *person*, the court must have power (personal jurisdiction) over that person. This can get complicated, but what it comes down to is this: if you want the Respondent to pay money (support, debts), transfer property, or do or not do any other act, the court's power to make that kind of order will be most clear if your spouse is either served in person *inside* the State of California (chapter 12.4), or your spouse signs the Appearance and Waiver form (chapter 12.7). If neither of those methods of giving notice is possible, the enforcement of personal orders depends on whether or not your spouse had sufficient "minimum contacts" with California. If you can't serve your spouse as described, get advice. Possibly your local Facilitator's office will help you, or you can call Divorce Helpline for advice.

## 2.7 Automatic restraining orders

Some basic restraining orders are built into the Summons and become automatically effective in every case when the Summons is served. Both parties are ordered by the court not to: (1) remove a minor child of the parties from the state apply for a new or replacement passport for a child without prior written permission of the other parent or order of the court; (2) cash, borrow against, cancel or change beneficiaries of any insurance or other coverage (including life, health, auto, and disability) held for the benefit of the parties or their minor children; (3) transfer, encumber (borrow against), conceal or in any way dispose of *any* property except with written consent of the other party or order of court, except in the usual course of business or for necessities of life; (4) create a will or trust that affects the disposition of property without written consent of the other party or order of court; and (5) each must notify the other party at least five days in advance of any extraordinary expenses, not including attorney fees or court costs for this case.

Read the orders on the Summons carefully and follow them. They remain in effect until the date you get your Judgment. If you have use for even one of these orders in your case, get the Summons served on your spouse as quickly as possible. The restraining orders may not be enforceable if you can't serve your spouse personally inside the state (section 2.6). If you want any order to last beyond the date of the Judgment, you have to ask for it at the time of the hearing, give a good reason why the order you want is necessary, and write the order into your Judgment.

**Nonautomatic restraining orders** are also available, but they must be requested by special motion. Most significant of these are orders prohibiting your spouse from abusing, harassing, or otherwise disturbing you or the children, and orders that your spouse must move out and stay away from the family residence. It is also possible to get quick, temporary orders for support, custody, or visitation. If you need any of these orders, see Book 2, *How to Solve Divorce Problems,* or call Divorce Helpline.

**Enforcement of orders.** Whoever violates a court order is guilty of contempt of court, a civil offense punishable by a threatening lecture from the judge and maybe (just maybe) time in jail or a fine, depending on the seriousness of the offense. You will need Book 2 to take your spouse or partner to court for contempt.

**Police.** It is a crime if either parent violates the order against taking a child from the state without written permission from the other parent. Violation of the other orders is a misdemeanor. If your spouse violates a restraining order, call the police first, then the District Attorney's office. Make sure you have a copy of the restraining order to show them, otherwise not much will happen.

If your spouse or partner abuses you physically or harasses you, call the police immediately—but *don't* call them unless you are willing to follow through and have your spouse prosecuted criminally. If you have good reason to believe that your spouse may abuse or harass you in the future, don't wait for something bad to happen—go to court immediately for a restraining order. Restraining orders are 85–90% effective, but practical things you can do to help yourself are very important. Get in touch with a domestic abuse support group in your community. The law requires police agencies to keep a list of domestic abuse services in your area. Call the police with jurisdiction over your residence, work, or school for a referral.

## 2.8   Mandatory disclosure of all marital information

Spouses and partners in a dissolution or legal separation are *required* to exchange court forms that disclose complete information about all their property and debts, as well as details of their income and expenses. Until the divorce is completely settled, you are required to keep each other updated immediately, in writing, of any new information. Disclosure forms are required to be exchanged by both parties before a written agreement is made for support or division of property and before the court can enter a Judgment of Dissolution. The disclosure law is an extension of the duties spouses and partners owe each other, described in chapters 3.2 and 3.3. It is intended to ensure a full exchange of information between spouses and partners. How to do disclosure is discussed in chapter 14.

A side effect of disclosure law is that lawyers get to do lots of extra work in every divorce. If you want to keep your case simple and inexpensive, it is more important than ever that you do not *retain* an attorney and that you try very hard to settle differences on your own or with a mediator. You can probably do better by managing your own case. Read this book and use Divorce Helpline if you want help.

## 2.9   When is it over? How final is your Judgment?

If you enter into a complete settlement agreement, the minute you sign it you have settled everything by contract. Your agreement will actually become your Judgment and all you have left is the red tape it takes to get it. You are, for most practical purposes, done. When your Judgment is entered, your divorce is legally complete and you can remarry. *However . . . .*

**How final is your Judgment?** To be final, your Judgment must have been obtained fairly and be based on complete and accurate disclosure. Traditionally, laws favor the finality of Judgments in the belief that society is best served by having things over and done with for good and forever. Exceptions were few and limited until 1993, when lawmakers decided to make sure no spouse enters into a divorce agreement or suffers a Judgment taken under unfair conditions. A divorce Judgment can now be attacked and some or all of its orders can be set aside under the following circumstances:

- Within two years of Entry of Judgment in case of duress (unfair pressure or force).

- Within one year of Entry of Judgment in uncontested or agreed cases where there was some mistake of law or fact by one or both parties.

- Within one year of the time a party discovers, or should have discovered, an actual fraud, where the party was kept in ignorance or otherwise fraudulently prevented from full participation.

- Any time within one year of the time a party discovers, or should have discovered, perjury in the Declarations of Disclosure or Income and Expense Statements.

- Any time within one year of the time a party discovers, or should have discovered, the failure to comply with disclosure requirements.

In all cases, the facts alleged must have materially affected the outcome and the party seeking relief must be benefited if relief is granted.

In summary, any divorce agreement or Judgment is potentially subject to attack for an indefinite period of time due to high standards of care between spouses and partners, disclosure requirements, and the new rules extending the time for setting aside all or part of a divorce Judgment. The greater risk is borne by a spouse or partner who managed community affairs because that person is presumably in possession of more information that can be hidden, overlooked, or forgotten.

These rules are meant to ensure disclosure of all information between spouses, but they also increase the opportunities for litigation and provide new weapons for revenge. These laws concern property and, to a lesser degree, support, but upset over any matters—child custody, for example—could easily find an outlet in property issues. What to do? How to make a Judgment or an agreement stick?

**How to make your Judgment final.** Attacks against the Judgment are limited more by practical considerations than legal ones. It costs a lot of money and more in emotional determination to conduct a legal battle. This means your risk increases with the value of your estate *and* the amount of upset between the parties.

If you want to get on with your life and not have your divorce become a career, it is more important than ever to work for a fair resolution of all issues, emotional and financial, that satisfies both sides. Be open, fair and temperate in all dealings with your spouse; listen more than you speak; don't argue. If necessary, use mediation and even counseling or therapy. Be *very* careful and thorough with your disclosure declarations. Make sure you have a high-quality settlement agreement. If you have enough income or property to make a legal attack worthwhile, it is *not* a good idea to write your own or have a paralegal do it. A good agreement is one that has been thoroughly discussed, worked out in great detail, and is very carefully drafted, and all facts have been disclosed and the parties have given each other open access to every document and record. If you do these things, you can go a long way toward making sure the divorce is really over when it's over.

## 2.10 Taxes

Almost every aspect of divorce can *possibly* have important tax consequences. Depending on your property and income, you might be able to save a lot of money by looking carefully into your tax situation and maybe getting expert tax advice, especially before making a settlement agreement, arranging support, or dividing or selling a major asset.

**Domestic partners and same-sex married couples** have significant differences from married couples when it comes to tax rules. Federal law does not recognize domestic partnership or same-sex marriages, so you can file only as single or head of household, depending on whether you have dependents that will be recognized under federal tax law, and earned income may not be treated as community property for income tax purposes. California law is in flux, so go to the Franchise Tax Board site at www.ftb.ca.gov/forms and do a search for "domestic partner" or "same-sex" and get the latest information. Better yet, see a tax accountant.

**Married couples.** If you don't want to file a joint return, you should know that Married Filing Separately may cost you more. To file as a single person for any year, your Judgment must be entered no later than December 31 of that year, and that means your Petition must be filed *and* served on your spouse before June 30. If you are desperate, you can get a Legal Separation first (no waiting period) and get your divorce later. As all issues are settled in the Legal Separation, the divorce case will be relatively simple, but you do have to pay a new filing fee and do another round of paperwork.

Some common tax issues will be raised elsewhere, more to call your attention to basic tax issues than to give detailed tax advice. Tax rules are too complicated and they change too frequently to be covered here in detail. Fortunately, there are some excellent pamphlets that tell you much of what you should know, and they are absolutely free at your local IRS office. After that, if you want tax advice, see a tax accountant.

- IRS publication 504, Divorced or Separated Individuals. If you only get one, get this one.
- IRS publication 523, Selling Your Home.
- IRS publication 596, Earned Income Credit.
- IRS publication 503, Child and Dependent Care Expenses.
- IRS publication 594, The IRS Collection Process.

## 2.11  Attorney fees

In the past, people representing themselves couldn't get attorney fees because they had no attorney. However, the appellate court in Los Angeles decided in October 2002 that while you can't be reimbursed for your own time, you *can* be awarded the cost for attorneys who help you represent yourself. Asking a judge to award attorney fees is part of a *contested* case, so unless you make it part of your settlement agreement (chapter 6), we won't be dealing with it in this book. However, if your case fails to settle and you end up in court, you will be working in Book 2, *How to Solve Divorce Problems,* where it will then be appropriate to ask for an award to cover the cost of any attorney assistance.

## 2.12  Common questions and answers

◆ **How much will it cost to do my own dissolution?** It now costs about $435 to file your papers in most counties. If Respondent files papers, there will also be a Response fee of a similar amount (chapter 7.3). Add a few dollars for photocopies and postage, and that's it for costs. If you hire a lawyer, all of these charges will be added to the legal fee, so you will be paying them either way. People who are very, very poor can file an application to have the fees waived (chapter 7.3).

◆ **How long will it take?** Several months, at least, probably longer. You can turn in the final papers for getting your Judgment 31 days after notice was served on your spouse (if no hurry, you can take up to five years to request the Judgment and finish your divorce). *But,* the earliest your marriage or partnership can be dissolved is six months after notice was served on your spouse or, for a Summary Dissolution, six months after the Petition was filed.

**Backlogs.** For many years, courts have been hit hard with budget restraints and cuts. This means staff are undermanned, overworked and overwhelmed, so service is slow. Papers can take a long time to process, from many weeks at best to several months, even up to a year in some counties. Things go even slower as year-end holidays approach. Call or visit your Superior Court Clerk's office and ask for an estimate of how long it takes to process an uncontested divorce once your final papers are filed.

**Need for speed?** If you need things done quickly for any reason—say, you want to remarry, or get your Judgment by December 31 so you can file as a single person, you have the option of hiring a private judge.

**Private Judges.** If you think it's worth a few hundred dollars to hurry things through, you can hire a private judge to process your paperwork very quickly. A private judge is an attorney who has been trained and certified to hear cases and process paperwork. Divorce Helpline has two on staff, so if you are interested in speed, privacy and special attention, give Divorce Helpline a call. Get our free report on how to get a faster divorce at **www.nolodivorce.com/PJ**.

◆ **What if we've already divided our community property?** It is still community property and it stays that way until it is formally divided by a court. Even if it has already been divided by agreement of the parties and already transferred, both parties own it as tenants-in-common until changed by court order. Same for debts.

◆ **What if we reconcile?** Reconciliation is a state of mind that goes beyond dating or occasionally sleeping together. But what do you do about the dissolution if you are certain you no longer want a divorce? If no Response has been filed and no Judgment has been obtained, the case can be dismissed if Petitioner alone can file a Dismissal form. If there's been a Response, both parties have to sign. You can get a Dismissal form with instructions in the Kit section of the companion CD that comes with this book. However, if an order for support has been entered, you will need help to get the case dismissed.

◆ **When can I remarry?** You can't remarry (or repartner) until after the Judgment has been entered and the date specified on it for termination of your marriage has passed—at least six months after the date the Summons was served. It is quite all right to wait longer.

◆ **What about those quick, cheap divorces from the Dominican Republic?** Divorces from a foreign country are generally valid in the U.S. if they are valid in the country that granted the divorce. However, in cases where neither of the parties actually goes there to establish residency, such divorces will almost certainly be invalid in any U.S. court, and any orders regarding your property, children, and support will not be enforceable. Unless acting on the advice of a reliable attorney, don't waste your money on a phony piece of paper from a mail-order Dominican divorce scam.

◆ **Resident aliens** who become divorced after less than two years of marriage are in danger of losing their resident status, and they and their dependent children may be in danger of deportation. There will, however, be no prejudice to status if the divorce was caused by child or spouse abuse. If there's a recent green card in your case, you should definitely consult an immigration attorney.

◆ **Divorce after legal separation.** If you get a legal separation Judgment and later want to be divorced, you have to start from scratch and file a new case. However, it should be smooth and easy, just paperwork, as all issues will already have been decided in the legal separation.

# 3

# DIVIDING PROPERTY AND DEBTS

In every divorce, you have to divide your community estate—the property and debts of the marriage or partnership, if there are any. Debts are a form of property (the negative form), so when you see the word "property" below, always remember to think of your debts in the same terms.

- If you have *very* little or no property, just read sections 3.1–3.4 and 3.8.

- If you have *some* property, read it all!

## 3.1 Income, debts and your date of separation

Income, accumulations, and debts of either party that are acquired *after* the date of separation are their own separate property, whether or not a divorce action has been filed. An exception would be retirement benefits or any other forms of delayed compensation that are community property to the extent earned during marriage or partnership, even if paid out after separation or divorce.

Debts are a negative form of property, so along with any other property you may have, all unpaid debts must be characterized as either separate or community property; then, by agreement or court order, they must be either confirmed as the separate property of one party or assigned for payment by one party.

You are responsible for all *community* debts incurred by either party between the dates of marriage or partnership and separation. Debts from before marriage are the separate property and responsibility of whoever incurred them. Loans for the education and training of a spouse or partner are treated as the separate property of that person. In general, neither you nor your share of the community estate is liable for your spouse's debts after separation, *except* that you can be liable for debts incurred for "common necessaries of life" for your spouse or the children—food, clothing, shelter, medicine—*unless* you have a written waiver of support or have settled the matter in court. So move right along; file your Petition and establish your claimed date of separation, even if nothing else is understood or settled yet.

*Anne can be liable for spouse's debt after separation for common necessaries of life unless you have a written waiver.*

You are responsible after separation for accounts that are in both of your names, or in the name of one party with anyone who extended credit knowing you were married or partnered and who has no reason to know of your separation. It is very important to actually *close* all credit card accounts and accounts that were in use during your marriage—it is not enough to simply have your name removed. Open new accounts and get new credit cards in your separate names. Give written notice to all creditors that either party might have dealt with during the marriage—tell them that you are separated and will no longer be responsible for your partner's debts. Be sure to tell your spouse well in advance when you close accounts or take other steps that could have an effect on his/her life.

You will *always* be liable for any debt for which you were originally liable when it was incurred. This means that orders of the court and agreements between parties about who must pay which debts are *only* effective between the parties and do *not* affect the people you owe. If a debt incurred during marriage is assigned by court order to your partner and he/she fails to pay it, *you* still owe the money. The creditor can come after you or repossess the property or both. Your spouse may be in contempt of court or breach of contract, for all the good that does you.

If one spouse is worried that the other will not actually pay off debts as agreed—a reasonable concern—try to get all debts paid out of community funds *before* community assets are divided. Or have each spouse get a new loan *after* separation to pay off their share of community debts. If nothing else works, make paying debts a matter of spousal or partner support, so that all or part of the support will be paid directly to creditors, but get help if you want to do this—it's tricky.

**Burdened by debts?** Divorce is often accompanied by severe debt problems. Both are incredibly stressful, either can overwhelm and undermine your confidence and your health. Together, they can be truly devastating. The good news is that both debt and divorce problems can be relieved by careful exploration of your total situation and all available options, together with sound advice leading to your best course of action. The highly experienced attorneys at Naraghi & Woodcock—the firm that operates Divorce Helpline—are ready to help you find your best solutions. Call them at (800) 359-7004. Expert advice at an early stage can be very important. For divorce and debt issues, it is often important to take some steps as soon as possible in order to preserve your best options. Delay can often cause things to become worse. The sooner you set out on a sound course, the sooner you will regain control of your life and peace of mind.

**Date of separation** affects the character of both income and liability for debts, yet this is an ambiguous date, both emotionally and legally. In most cases, it won't particularly matter whether separation occurred one time or another. But if the date of separation has significant financial consequences and there is a contest over the date, the date of separation is whenever you can prove that one spouse intended to make a complete, final break (not just a temporary separation), with simultaneous conduct furthering that intent. Living physically apart is indispensable, which generally requires a separate residence. It is possible to "live apart" in the same house, but this must be shown by clear, unambiguous conduct. Living physically apart does not by itself determine the matter, because one can live apart without intending a final break. Courts consider evidence of all conduct and circumstances.

Let's say Jane earned a big commission on April 1. And say that January 15 she had said, "I'm leaving you for good and this isn't like other times I said it, this time I really mean it," and they stopped sleeping together from that time on, but it took until April 15 for Jane to move out. John thinks the date of separation was April 15, so therefore the commission is community property and he should get half. Jane thinks the separation was on January 15, so her earnings thereafter are entirely her own. Here's another case. Does Sue have to pay half of a loan that Sam got two months before she moved out when six months before he had announced (again) the he intended to divorce her and she believed him so she started sleeping with another guy? It's often hard to say exactly when separation actually took place. In the examples, though John and Sue should win, any lawyer would be happy to fight on either side until the couples' funds run dry. Weigh carefully the cost of fighting against the amount at stake. If you have trouble, read about Difficult Cases in chapter 1.7 and about mediation in chapter 1.9.

## 3.2  Management of property and the duty spouses owe

**Management and control of property.** Spouses and partners have equal rights to manage and control their community property. When doing so, each party owes the highest duty of good faith and fair dealing to the other, including openness, honesty, and full access to whatever books and records happen to exist. Disclosure duties and penalties for breach are discussed in the next sections.

Either party can sell community *personal* property (other than furnishings or clothing of other family members) without having the written consent of the other, but any such transfer must be for fair and reasonable value. Neither spouse may mortgage or give away community property without the written consent of the other spouse, with the exception of a gift between spouses or by both spouses to a third party. A non-consenting spouse can void an improper transaction if action is taken within one year of transfer of personal property or three years in the case of real property.

**Businesses.** A person operating a community property business (or in which the community has an interest) has primary control and may act alone in all transactions, but must give prior written notice to the other spouse if all or substantially all of the personal property used in the operation of the business is being sold, leased, mortgaged, or otherwise disposed of.

**Duty spouses owe each other.** When dealing with community property, spouses owe each other a very high standard of care, the highest good faith and fair dealing. This duty continues beyond separation and lasts until all property has been legally divided. Even after the divorce, if any property was hidden or just simply overlooked, the spouse's high duty of care continues with respect to that undivided property.

## 3.3 Duty to disclose all information

The standard of care that one spouse owes the other also includes a high degree of openness and disclosure:

- To provide each other with full access to whatever books and records happen to exist on community transactions or transactions with third persons that involve community property,
- To account for and hold as trustee for the other spouse any benefit or profit derived from investment or use of community property, and
- To give, *on request*, full and true disclosure of *everything*, including all material facts and information regarding the existence, character, and value of all assets and debts that are or may be community property.

**Mandatory disclosure.** The duty to disclose *requires* that disclosure forms be exchanged in every dissolution or legal separation, as discussed in chapter 14. A spouse *must* also disclose any investment opportunity that results from any activities of either spouse during the marriage. This investment disclosure must be done in writing in time for the other spouse to decide whether to participate. Absent disclosure, any gain from such an investment would be held as tenants in common and subject to the continuing jurisdiction of the court to divide later. So be very careful about investments after separation; make sure they are either disclosed or obviously clear of involvement with activities of either spouse during the marriage.

**Remedies.** A spouse who fails in the fiduciary duties of care and disclosure may be liable for 100% of the value of any undisclosed or transferred asset or—what may amount to much more—50% of the value *plus* attorney fees and court costs for the legal action on the breach.

**Set aside.** If material information is withheld, misrepresented, or even simply overlooked, a disadvantaged spouse can set aside all or part of an agreement or Judgment. Thus the settlement of your divorce is potentially open to attack for a very long time. To make sure your case is really over when it's over, read and heed chapters 2.9 and 14 very carefully.

## 3.4  Cases where there is no community property

Do not conclude that you have no community property or debts without carefully going over the Schedule of Assets and Debts in chapter 14.3. Use it as a checklist to make sure you have thought of everything, especially pension plans, retirement benefits, intellectual properties (writing, painting, music, software, etc.), or other kinds of property that are easily overlooked. Read section 3.6(b) below about retirement benefits, and also read section 3.1 above about income and debts.

**Caution!** Do *not* assume there is no community property just because you have already divided it up, especially if the assets have significant value or if there is property with title (autos, real estate, pension or retirement accounts, etc.). Such assets, even though divided informally, will remain community property until divided and awarded in a Judgment.

If you truly have *very* little or no community property, you may not want the court to get involved with it at all. In your Petition, simply tell the court that there is no significant property to be divided, and the court will do nothing. There will be no inquiry into your property and no orders about it.

## 3.5  Cases where there is some property

If the community estate is valuable or contains titled property, pensions, or debts of significant value, then you need to have things divided properly before you can complete your dissolution.

Before you make an agreement or take your case to court, make sure you understand your estate and know *all* that it contains. Read sections 3.1 and 3.6 and work through the Schedule of Assets and Debts in chapter 14.3 to make sure you have thought of everything. You have to do a complete inventory in every case to satisfy disclosure requirements. Be careful and complete; a court can reopen old cases to divide overlooked community property assets or debts that were not previously divided by Judgment. Hidden or overlooked property is owned after the divorce as tenants in common until it gets divided, however long that takes. Coming back to court will cost both sides a lot of time, trouble and money, so get all your property listed and divided correctly now.

If you think your spouse may have hidden assets, either see an attorney or get Book 2, *How to Solve Divorce Problems* and read chapters 8 and 17 in that book to learn how to get information, including how to force your spouse to give information under penalty of perjury.

In a dissolution, all separate and community property must be itemized, characterized, valued, and divided.

- **Itemize.** Make a list of *all* of your property using the Schedule of Assets and Debts (chapter 14.3) or use the worksheets on the CD.

- **Characterize.** Define each item as either "community" or "separate." See section 3.6.

- **Value.** Determine the fair market value of each item or group of items of community property.

- **Divide.** Community property (CP) can be divided by a judge or the parties in a written agreement. A judge *must* divide CP equally, unless your CP has a net value (assets minus debts) of less than $5,000 *and* your spouse can't be located after a diligent search. Otherwise, the only way to get an *unequal* division of CP is with a written agreement (ch. 6). But be careful, because when spouses are not represented undue influence in the signing can be presumed if one spouse gets significant advantage over the other. This does not apply if the agreement is the result of mediation and more than six months have passed. So, if you want a significantly unequal division of a your CP estate, call Divorce Helpline for advice.

**Date of valuation.** The date property is valued can make a big difference in rising or falling markets. If the spouses can't agree, the law says the date of valuation is as close as practical to the time of trial. But you don't want a trial, therefore you need to agree to a date of valuation that seems fair to both, like the date of separation or the day you sign your settlement agreement (chapter 6).

**Basic principles.** When thinking about dividing your property, keep in mind that getting the last cent might not be your best or highest goal. On the other hand, you have a responsibility to your own future and a right to your fair share. Consider the children (if any), your relative earning abilities, your general situation, fairness, and other such things. Consider what will be best for everyone.

**How to proceed.** If you have community property but no written agreement when you file your Petition, you have two choices. First, and usually best, simply state in the Petition that property will divided by agreement. This shows your peaceful intentions. If you fail to get an agreement, simply file an amended Petition listing all property and serve it again. It doesn't cost more. If you have trouble agreeing, get my book *Make Any Divorce Better* and learn specific steps that will reduce conflict, solve problems and settle disagreements, including ten clever ways to divide property without going to court. Or call Divorce Helpline. The second way to do a Petition is to list all property and debts; then if there is still no agreement by the time of the hearing, your community property will be divided *equally* by a judge (unless the net value is less than $5,000 and your spouse can't be located). Neither spouse will be entirely in control of exactly how the property gets divided, although the judge will be strongly influenced by the suggestions of the Petitioner.

**Promises to pay.** If there will be a note or any other promise to pay in the future as part of your divorce settlement, make sure such promises are *correctly* secured by a lien on real property or some other form of security, if at all possible.

If the court awards you property that is in the possession of your spouse, you still have to figure out how to get it. If this might be a problem, be sure to read chapter 2.6 about the power of the court to make orders against your spouse and get advice if the court may not have jurisdiction.

Property law can get extremely intricate, but the section below will give you some basic rules. If you have a lot of property, think about getting professional advice or letting Divorce Helpline supervise your case. How much is "a lot" is up to you and depends in part on how concerned you are about whatever you happen to have. A professional can tell you how to locate, value, divide, and transfer property and, especially, how to protect your interests.

## 3.6 Understanding your estate

### a. Community and separate property

Only community property needs to be divided, since separate property already belongs to one spouse or the other. However, to prevent disagreement in the future, you should list any items you want to have clearly understood as separate. The list is made in a settlement agreement, on your Petition, or in a Property Declaration attached to your Petition. If listed with the Petition, by not filing a Response your spouse concedes that your list is accurate.

**Separate Property** (SP) belongs just to one spouse and not the community. Separate property is a) property that was acquired before the marriage; or b) property that at *any* time was given specifically to one spouse by gift or inheritance. After the separation, the earnings, accumulations, and debts of each spouse are generally separate. Community property that has been informally divided by the spouses does not become separate—both spouses still own it equally until it is officially divided by the court.

**Community Property** (CP) is anything earned or acquired by either spouse during the marriage that is not separate property. This includes debts incurred by either spouse up to the time of separation. Don't forget accumulated vacation pay, pension funds, employee stock options, tax refunds, and equity in insurance policies that may have accumulated during marriage. Any part of intellectual property (writing, painting, music, software, etc.) that was created during the marriage will be CP. Personal injury awards are usually SP, but characterizing Workers Compensation awards is tricky. Rules in this area are complicated and evolving, so get legal advice if there are injury awards in your case.

Because spouses are like partners, community property belongs to both spouses equally, no matter who actually earned it. Each spouse is entitled to an equal share on dissolution. In a written settlement agreement, spouses can agree to divide their property any way that seems fair to them, but if divided by a judge, community property will be awarded so each spouse receives an equal share. But, if the CP has a net value of less than $5,000 *and* your spouse can't be located after diligent search, the judge can award all or any part of your CP to you.

The term **"quasi-community"** property appears in the Petition and property forms. It refers to property acquired before establishing residency in California, which would have been community property if it had been acquired in

California. It is treated the same as community property, but must be identified separately on your forms.

**Jointly owned property.** Title documents define ownership of cars, real estate, bank or investment accounts, and so on. Any property acquired by spouses during the marriage in any form of co-ownership—both names on the title document—is *presumed* to be community property. However, spouses can make valid agreements that change the character of property, or there might be a right of reimbursement (more on this below). One spouse acting alone can take all the money out of a joint bank account (unless the account is set up to require two signatures) or sever jointly owned titles to other kinds of personal property (unless there is a written agreement otherwise). This means that any property in jointly owned accounts is at risk until you serve the Summons with its automatic restraining orders.

There are four kinds of joint title for real estate. Each has its own advantages:

**1) Husband and Wife as Joint Tenants.** Each owns an undivided half of all the property, which will pass automatically on death to the survivor without tax or probate, a result you may not want any longer. Creditors of either spouse can reach it all. The right of survivorship is not affected by your separation or by a will, but can be terminated *only* by a new title, a Judgment, or a termination by just one co-owner, *if done correctly*. If you terminate and keep your half-share as a tenant-in-common, your share will pass according to your will. Should you do this? Maybe—but it means you will lose *your* right of survivorship, too, and will not take all if your spouse dies first.

**2) Husband and Wife as their Community Property.** This is like joint tenancy, except there is no right of survivorship. Each spouse's share passes on death according to his/her will, so it has to go through probate. This form of ownership has valuable tax advantages not available to joint tenants, and a spouse's share cannot be taken to pay a *separate* debt of the other spouse.

**3) Husband and Wife as their Community Property with right of survivorship.** If formed after July 1, 2001, this has the tax advantages of community ownership and the property passes automatically, without probate.

**4) Husband and Wife as Tenants-in-Common.** Each owns an undivided portion as his or her separate property. The shares need not be equal. No right of survivorship. Creditors of one spouse can't reach the share of the other spouse.

**Mixed-up property.** The general rules about property are fairly clear, but if you mixed separate and community property together, you may have a situation that is easy to argue about and difficult to unravel. Here are some guidelines.

**Changing the character of property (transmutation).** Sometimes spouses have an agreement or "understanding" to change separate into community property or the other way around. But if made after January 1, 1985, such agreements are not valid unless made in writing. However, even if the character of property was not effectively changed, there could be a right to reimbursement. Keep reading.

**Tracing.** In order to sort out community from separate property, you *must* be able to trace it—that is, show very clearly where certain money came from and how it was spent. This sometimes requires expert evaluation and assistance. If you have questions about whether or not assets in your case can be traced, you should consult a local attorney or call Divorce Helpline.

**Return of SP used to benefit a community asset**—*Reimbursement I.* After 1983, if a spouse used separate property to buy or improve a community asset, that spouse is entitled to reimbursement if it can be traced (see above). It will not be presumed to have been a gift, unless stated in writing. The reimbursement includes down payments and any payments that reduce the principal of a loan used for the purchase or improvement of community property, but does *not* include payments on interest, insurance, taxes, or maintenance. No interest will be paid nor adjustments made for changes in the value of money. The amount reimbursed is limited to the amount paid and also to the net value of the property at the time of the divorce hearing. Separate property spent on living expenses or vacations is not reimbursed, nor is separate property spent to benefit the other spouse's separate property.

Before 1984, separate property spent on a community asset was considered a gift to the community unless a written agreement or an "understanding" existed that it would be paid back some day. There is a large collection of cases about how to establish an oral "understanding." Very messy and expensive to litigate.

**Return of CP funds spent on education, support, debts**—*Reimbursement II.*

1) The community may be entitled to reimbursement, with interest, for community contributions to the education or training of a spouse that substantially increased that spouse's earning ability. This does not include ordinary living expenses. This rule is most likely to be applied when a divorce takes place shortly after completion of training, before the community has had a chance to benefit from the increased earnings.

2) The community is entitled to be reimbursed for payments for support obligations from a prior marriage, but only to the extent the person who owed the support had separate resources available that were not used.

3) Reimbursement is possible where, after separation, separate funds are used to pay community debts or improve or preserve a community asset. But if one spouse acting alone decides to make the improvement, reimbursement is limited to the actual increase in market value.

4) **Big gifts.** Uh-oh! SP that was used to buy a "substantial" gift for a spouse is entitled to reimbursement unless there was a written statement of intent to "transmute" SP to CP. Do you know anyone who sends statements with gifts? "Substantial" is subjective and related to the size of the estate.

**Apportionment**—*Community funds used to benefit a separate asset.* If community funds were used to help pay for or improve a separate asset, the community has an interest in it. For example, if wife had her own home before marriage, and during the marriage the couple used community income to make payments or improvements, then the community has an interest in wife's separate house. If you have this situation, you will need expert help to figure the exact amount of the community interest.

If your estate is tangled, complicated, or in any way difficult for you to understand or deal with, call Divorce Helpline and they will help you untangle it.

## b. Pensions and retirement funds

This category includes company or government pension plans, Keoghs, 401(k) and 403(b) plans, Individual Retirement Accounts (IRAs), SEP IRAs, Tax Sheltered Annuities (TSAs), and Employee Stock Option plans (ESOPs). On dissolution, each spouse is entitled to half of that portion of any retirement plan or fund that was earned during the marriage. **Joinder:** it is very important that you file papers to join retirement funds or plans as parties to your divorce action (see below).

**Could be worth more than you think.** If your marriage was very short, or employment meager and irregular, there may not be enough community interest in a pension fund to worry about. But if regular contributions to a pension plan were made during marriage, you may have a valuable right that is worth protecting.

**Must be valued correctly.** To decide what to do with a pension plan, you need to know what the community interest is worth. You also need the correct value to fill out your Disclosure Declaration (chapter 14). If a spouse fails in his/her disclosure obligation by reporting "unknown" or an incorrect pension value, a judge *must* set aside the settlement agreement or Judgment if the other spouse discovers later that the pension was worth more than he or she thought. You *must* disclose the correct value.

Periodic summary statements that report plan value might be misleading and might not reflect the true value of the community interest:

- If your plan is a tax-deferred savings account like a 401(k), the value is probably the figure shown on the summary statement.
- For plans where you have to wait for a certain age or number of years of employment to begin receiving payments, then the correct value is probably *not* the same as the figure on the summary statement. It is often *much* more, but it takes an expert to say how much. You *must* have your plan appraised by a professional pension actuary. This costs from $150 to $300, but it is money well spent! If you need an appraisal of a pension plan, call Divorce Helpline.

**Military and federal pensions.** Military retired pay and federal civil service annuities are community property, but military disability pay cannot be reached, nor can you reach military retirement that was waived in order to receive disability benefits. Spouses of marriages that last through ten years or more of military service gain big advantages in the enforcement of pension awards. Former spouses of marriages that saw at least twenty years of active military service are entitled to commissary and PX benefits. Don't rush the date of divorce if you are approaching a 10- or 20-year deadline. Note: a spouse retiring from the military can be bound to a written agreement to designate a former spouse as beneficiary under a Survivor Benefit Plan (SBP) *if* the agreement is incorporated, ratified, or approved in a dissolution Judgment, and if the Secretary concerned receives a request from the former spouse along with the agreement and court order. If you have this issue in your case, call Divorce Helpline.

**Social Security** is not community property and not subject to division by a court. It is a federal program with its own rules, so contact the Social Security Administration to get information about your rights after divorce. Note: benefits accrue to spouses of a marriage that lasted at least 10 years, so if you are near that deadline, don't rush into a Judgment that could conveniently be postponed.

## Joinder

If the community has an interest in one or more pension plans or retirement funds that have not already been awarded to the employee-spouse in a written agreement, then you need to join each such plan or fund to your case to make sure that no money is withdrawn before the fund is divided in a Judgment. Joinder only requires filing a few forms and is *extremely* important for the non-employee spouse. So, with the exception of federal government plans and individual IRA accounts (not including SEP IRAs), when you file your Petition, or as soon after as possible, you should join each plan or fund. For funds that are *not* joined, send them a Notice of Adverse Interest. Joinder forms, instructions and letters are in the Kits folder on the CD that comes with this book.

## How to divide a pension plan or retirement fund

Because of complexities involved with retirement and pension funds, if you are going to have a settlement agreement, we recommend that you use DealMaker instead of the sample agreement in chapter 6, and it would be a *very* good idea to get some advice before you start framing your agreement. Call **Divorce Helpline** (800) 359-7004 and ask about their special deals for DealMaker users.

Call the employer's personnel department right away, now, and get the name and address of the plan administrator and, if there is one, get a copy of the company's pension plan booklet, which will be full of information you'll need. Call the plan administrator and ask what they require when a plan is either divided or awarded entirely to the employee in a divorce Judgment.

Finally, choose one of the following three methods to divide it:

**1) The waiver** can be used if the community interest is truly worth very little. The non-employee-spouse simply gives up, in a settlement agreement, all interest in the employee's pension fund.

**2) The trade-off** (present day buy-out) is a clean and easy way to divide a pension fund; courts like it, and it has no immediate tax consequences. By this method, one spouse trades his or her interest in the employee-spouse's pension plan for something else of equal value, such as a larger share of the family home or a promissory note. Be careful—insist that any note be secured, preferably with a Trust Deed on real property.

Note that the employee-spouse trades hard dollars in the present for something that *might* be collected if he or she stays employed long enough and lives long enough to collect. The employee-spouse will pay taxes on that future income while the other spouse pays no taxes on the trade. However, the employee-spouse may need the entire pension to live on after retirement, so it may be better to pay now rather than have less to live on later. Or maybe the community interest is relatively low and easy to pay for now, just to get things wrapped up cleanly.

**3) The payoff** (division into two accounts) awards present ownership of a share of *future* pension rights (when they come due) to the non-employee-spouse. Transfers following a payoff *must* be done in strict accordance with IRS rules, or you might suffer an *immediate* tax liability.

This method costs several hundred dollars for a special order called a QDRO (see below). The non-employee-spouse may have to wait for his/her share, and the employee-spouse will have a smaller pension check to live on. It is most appropriate in long marriages where the pension is the only or largest asset. Sometimes the employee-spouse will use it to reduce or eliminate spousal support payments.

**QDROs.** To divide a pension plan or retirement fund, you need a Qualified Domestic Relations Order (QDRO), which is like an official title or "pink slip" to a share of the pension fund, 401(k), or annuity. This *must* be done at the same time or before the Judgment is signed or the non-employee-spouse could lose out. Besides, plan or fund administrators will probably not release funds without a proper order that meets their highly specific requirements.

Two different plans require two joinders (see above) and two QDROs. One pension plan with multiple parts may require more than one QDRO. QDRO orders are difficult to draft and any mistake could be very expensive, so we *strongly* recommend that you call Divorce Helpline or an attorney with a lot of pension fund experience to see if there is some way to get what you want *safely* without having to prepare a QDRO, or to prepare a QDRO for you. Don't take a chance with such an important matter—get expert assistance. It will be worth it.

**Death benefits.** Divorce automatically removes a spouse as beneficiary under some plans but not others, so the employee-spouse should notify the plan of the divorce and name a new beneficiary. The non-employee-spouse may want to be continued under the plan, but it is usually better to value this part of the plan separately and replace it with an annuity or life insurance of equal value and cover the cost in the settlement agreement, perhaps with a small increase in spousal support.

**Be careful** with pension plans and retirement funds as there are often tax consequences and penalties if pensions or 401(k)s are not correctly divided or if withdrawals are made before retirement age. Don't touch a fund without making sure your changes won't end up costing you. If you want advice about how to deal with pensions or retirement funds, or help deciding what's best for you, call Divorce Helpline. Their attorneys will help you achieve a fair division of your pension funds in the best and safest way. They can arrange a valuation for you and do the paperwork necessary to make your plans work correctly.

### c. The family home and other real estate

If you and your spouse own a home or other real property in any form of joint title, or if any real property was paid for or improved with funds earned during the marriage, then the community has an interest in it. You must now value the community interest and decide how to divide it.

**What is the community interest worth?** The amount one actually owns in property, the "equity," is the difference between what you can get for it on the current market less any amounts due on it. Deduct the cost of sale *only* if it is going to be sold immediately. The best way to find out the current market value of your property is to consult a professional real estate appraiser—call around for prices. You can get free estimates from local real estate agents, but this may not be as reliable. Once you know the market value, deduct amounts owed to get your equity. If, and only if, the house is to be sold right away, you also deduct an agent's commission and costs of sale, typically 7–8%. Next, deduct any traceable separate property contributions that need to be reimbursed (section 3.6(a) above). The amount left over is what the community interest is worth.

**To keep or not to keep.** In thinking about who, if anyone, will keep the family home, you will naturally consider the children, your emotional ties to the home and neighborhood, and the ghosts of the past. But you also have to carefully consider it as a business deal—even if you get it, does it make economic sense to keep it? Can you afford all the payments, taxes, insurance, and regular maintenance costs? Be sure to get advice about tax consequences of any decision you might make before you decide.

**Dividing the family home.** Some of the more common ways you can divide the community interest in a family home are:

- Sell it and divide the community property interest; or

- Transfer it entirely to one spouse in exchange for something worth half the community interest—other property; interest in a pension fund; a *secured* note for an amount to be paid monthly or on a specific future date, or upon some specified event, such as when the youngest child reaches a certain age, or when the house is sold, or the spouse remarries or moves; or any specific time or event that you can agree to; or
- Change title to tenants-in-common (separate ownership), with each spouse holding a stated percentage, and agree to let the custodial parent and kids live in the home until some time or event (as above); or
- The spouse that keeps it refinances the property to buy out the share of the other spouse (the preparation of documents and transfer of funds will be handled by the title company).

**Child on board?** Where there is a child (especially a disabled child) living in a long-established family home, a judge might not force a sale *if* a sale would cause economic, emotional, or social detriment to the child. But first, the judge must find that the spouse in the residence can afford to pay for mortgages, insurance, maintenance, taxes, and so on. If so, the judge will consider all circumstances and then *may* defer the sale, *unless* the economic detriment to the nonresident spouse would outweigh the other considerations. This kind of order, regarded as additional child support, *might* last until the youngest child reaches majority, but rather than defer the sale for a long time (if at all), most judges would look for some logical earlier date—for example, when the affected child would normally change from one school to another. Unless otherwise agreed by the parties, such an order can be modified or terminated any time on a showing of changed circumstances. Remarriage of the resident spouse strongly suggests that continued deferral is no longer fair. Once popular, these orders are uncommon now, because high property values have made them economically unfeasible in most cases. To get such an order over the objection of the out-spouse, there would have to be evidence of a special reason why a child should not be moved, something strong enough to outweigh the financial burden to the nonresident spouse.

**Transferring real property.** The best way to transfer title is by drawing up a deed and possibly a note (promise to pay money). Any note should *definitely* be secured by a Deed of Trust (a mortgage on the property) to simplify matters in case of nonpayment. To transfer real property from joint ownership by both spouses into sole ownership of one spouse is simple. Method 1: get a blank "interspousal transfer deed," complete it and take the notarized original to the County Recorder where the property is located and have it recorded. Method 2: if your Judgment orders a change in title for property in California, the Judgment itself can transfer title if you take a certified copy of it to the County Recorder. California note and deed forms can be found at **www.nolodivorce.com/CA/deeds.html.**

Deeds must be signed before a Notary and recorded at the Recorder's office in the county where the property is located. There will be a small fee for recordation and maybe a small transfer tax. Any transfer of real property requires a Preliminary Change of Ownership (PCO) statement, which is available at your County Recorder's office. This form will let the County Assessor know not to reassess your property to a higher rate. Notes must be properly drawn and should be secured by a Deed of Trust. If you need help making up your deeds and notes, you may be able to get assistance from a title company (escrow), a bank, or a local attorney. Call around to see what they charge.

**Caution.** Transfers of property do not remove a spouse's name from any mortgages that were originally on the property—both are still liable. This *could* create a credit problem, so you might want to see if you can get the property refinanced in the sole name of the spouse who is keeping it.

**Real property must be disposed of** in any settlement agreement or listed with your other property, as shown in chapter 15. If it is still not transferred by the time of the hearing or settled by written agreement of the spouses, the judge will divide it along with all the other listed property.

## 3.7 Taxes

Remember, federal tax laws do not recognize domestic partnership, but state laws do. Domestic partners should probably see a tax accountant to clarify the many issues created by this conflict in federal vs. state law.

Transfers of property between spouses as part of a divorce settlement are not taxable, but sales to third parties are. Always get expert tax advice before dividing or selling a major asset, as there could be significant tax consequences. Read the tax pamphlets described in chapter 2.10. Be very careful how you divide retirement funds or you might face a tax or a penalty.

**Family home and other major assets.** A spouse who keeps the home or any other major asset also keeps the *potential* liability for capital gains taxes and

*I do not understand the for consequences of the judgment*

sales commissions whenever the property is sold. Tax consequences should be understood by both spouses and negotiated as part of any agreement.

**Capital gains and exclusions.** You can't avoid tax on gains from the sale of a residence by rolling the funds into the purchase of another home, but *anyone* can exclude capital gains from the sale of their primary residence ($250,000 for single people and $500,000 for joint filers), but only if the house was your principal residence for two of the five years before sale. When one spouse takes possession of the house *as part of a court order,* the non-resident-spouse can claim the house as principal residence during the period of exclusion, so hurry up with that order! If the home was acquired as part of a divorce, the new owner can claim the period that the other spouse owned the home. There is also an exclusion amount for sales forced by health reasons or change of place of employment.

## 3.8   Wills, insurance beneficiaries, and nonprobate transfers

**Wills.** A dissolution *automatically* revokes bequests to a former spouse and children or relatives of the former spouse who are not related by blood to the testator, and it removes such persons as executor under any will made before the dissolution. If you want your former spouse or his or her relatives to be included in your will or one of them to be executor of your estate, you need to make a new will after the dissolution.

**Insurance beneficiaries.** A dissolution does *not* remove a spouse as beneficiary of life insurance policies. This should be covered in your settlement agreement. Contact your insurance carrier if you want to change your beneficiary.

**Nonprobate transfers invalidated.** A nonprobate transfer is any instrument other than a will that transfers property on death of the transferor, a living trust being one common example. Any nonprobate transfer of property made before or during the marriage will fail if the recipient is no longer the transferor's spouse due to dissolution or annulment, so all such documents should be reviewed at this time.

**After a divorce,** you should make a new will—or better yet, a living trust—and review persons you previously named as beneficiaries on insurance or bank/investment accounts, or named in a pre-divorce Health Care Directive. Call Divorce Helpline and let their attorneys answer questions, advise and help you with a new will, living trust or Health Care Directive.

# 4

# CHILDREN: CUSTODY and VISITATION

The parenting plan may be the most important matter you deal with in your divorce and it can sometimes be the most difficult. "Parenting plan" refers to all your arrangements for the children and how the parents will share responsibility for their care and upbringing.

**What is in the child's best interest?** This is the question asked by judges and by concerned parents. It is the question you and the other parent should ask. One thing that is clearly best for children, a huge gift that can be difficult to give, is for parents to resolve their personal issues so that bad feelings are reduced to a minimum and cooperative parenting becomes possible. This is *vitally* important.

Studies show that harm to children is more closely related to conflict *after* divorce. Everyone has conflict before and during a divorce, but if you want to protect your children, get finished with conflict and resolve it, at least within yourself, as quickly as possible. Remember that children need *both* parents, and parents need all the help and cooperation they can get from each other.

**Which children?** Divorce courts are concerned with *minor* children born to *both* parents or legally adopted. If the wife (or a partner) is pregnant, that child *must* be listed in the Petition as "one unborn."

**Whose child is it?** Any child born to a married woman is presumed to be her husband's. If they were cohabiting on the date of conception, and the husband was not medically impotent or sterile, the presumption is just short of conclusive. If there is or might be a dispute as to paternity, you had better contact an attorney or call Divorce Helpline for advice.

**Which court?** If a child has not lived in California for six consecutive months before the Petition was filed, it is *possible* for a parent to claim that some other state or country has superior jurisdiction over the children. Temporary absences (vacations) do not affect the six-month period. If you can't satisfy this time requirement, and if your Petition is in fact attacked, consult an attorney immediately.

**Parenting programs.** At least seven counties (Humboldt, Marin, Placer, San Luis Obispo, Santa Barbara, Santa Cruz, Tuolumne) require parents to attend a short but useful program about children before they can get a Judgment. When you file your Petition, the clerk will give you details about the program and local requirements. There's also the informational form FL-314 with information the state wants you to know about custody. It's in the CD. Take a look and consider sending a copy to the other parent.

**Child custody information forms:** FL-313 and FL-314. Both are on the CD. Each county can choose, or not, to require you to serve one or the other form with the Petition. They contain basic info about custody and parenting plans and, if you can't agree on parenting terms, they recommend mediation (FL-314) or counseling (FL-313). You can choose to send one or the other to the other parent even if your county court doesn't require it. Take a look.

**Modification.** All orders concerning minor children—custody, visitation, and support—are subject to modification at any time. This means either parent can go back to court and seek a change by showing that there has been some important change in circumstances since the last order and that a change in the order is necessary to protect the best interests of the child.

**Parental agreement.** If you have trouble working out a parenting plan, both parents should read *Make Any Divorce Better* for specific steps that will help you reduce upset, solve problems, negotiate, and reach agreement. Consider seeing a counselor or mediator, or call Divorce Helpline for advice. If your case seems headed to court, get Book 2, *How to Solve Divorce Problems,* to learn how to handle a case in court or supervise an attorney. On the other hand, if your spouse is gone or not interested in the children, you can probably get any reasonable orders you want. Make up something that will work and that will encourage stable parental contact if and when your spouse becomes interested in the children again.

If parents can't agree about their parenting plan, it must be decided in court. But before going to court on any custody matter, parents are *required* to meet with a court-appointed mediator. If you have already worked with a private mediator, the court mediator will decide if you satisfied the requirement. Mediation is confidential, but counties vary as to whether the court mediator will make a recommendation to the court if parents can't reach an agreement.

**Severe conflict.** In extreme cases, the court can appoint an attorney to represent children and/or order parents into counseling or substance abuse treatment for up to six months in an effort to reduce conflict and improve parenting. The spouses will bear the cost in a reasonable proportion determined by the court.

**Moving before Judgment.** Once the Summons is served and until the Judgment is entered, restraining orders are in effect (chapter 2.7) and, among other things, neither parent can take a child out of the state without the prior written consent of the other parent. When you get your Judgment, the court can be asked to extend the restraining order or to make a new order regarding moves. We recommend that your settlement agreement or Judgment require either parent to notify the other parent in writing at least 60 days ahead of any change in a child's residence that will last more than 30 days.

**Moving after Judgment.** If the custodial parent wants to move away, he/she should carefully consider how that will affect the children's relationship and visiting time with the other parent. In general, absent bad faith, a custodial parent is free to move anywhere, but the other parent can require a hearing to determine (a) if the move is made in bad faith, say, to impair visitation, and (b) if the move will cause such detriment to the child that a change in custody is required for the child's welfare. The result depends very heavily on the judge's discretion, so best to avoid the expense and trauma of a court hearing with uncertain outcome. If a parent wants to move, try to negotiate or mediate new co-parenting arrangements that meet the needs of both parents and the child.

**Child snatching.** It is a felony to take or keep a child with intent to defeat a custody or visitation right. If this happens to you, report it to the police and go see your District Attorney immediately. However, it is a defense if there is a reasonable belief that the child will suffer immediate physical or emotional harm. A pattern of domestic violence, not necessarily in the child's presence, is evidence of danger to the child. If you have reason to fear a child might be abducted (taken), see a family law attorney or call Divorce Helpline.

**Smoked children.** Secondhand smoke has an adverse effect on health, especially for children. The scientific evidence is nearly overwhelming and therefore difficult for judges to ignore, so if demanded by one parent, not smoking could likely be made a condition of custody or visitation. In fact, Health and Safety Code 118948 makes it unlawful for anyone to smoke in a motor vehicle if there is a minor on board.

## 4.1  Custody

The traditional terms, "custody and visitation," are losing favor because they encourage parents to think of the issue as something to win or lose rather than a child to be cared for. One parent ends up feeling that he or she has "lost" custody and somehow lost the child. This thinking needs to be changed. What you are trying to do is arrange the child care schedule when parents no longer live together. This is called your "parenting plan," and you should always call it that, too, even though the law still speaks of custody and visitation.

**Custody Terms Defined.**

- "Joint custody" means *both* joint physical and joint legal custody.
- "Joint legal custody" means that both parents share the right and responsibility of making decisions relating to the child's health, education, and welfare.
- "Joint physical custody" means each parent will have significant periods of physical custody arranged to assure the child has frequent and continuing contact with both parents. It need not be 50/50; even 70/30 would be okay.
- "Sole physical custody" means the child will live with and be under the supervision of one parent. A parent with sole custody *may* have an advantage when it comes to moving away over the objection of the other parent. "Primary physical custody" is often used instead—it has a similar legal meaning, but doesn't have the harsh implication that only one parent has the child. The other parent can think of himself or herself as having less time rather than no custody.
- "Sole legal custody" means that one parent has the right to make decisions relating to the child's health, education, and welfare.

Ideally, you will use these terms only in court, and outside of court you will continue to remember that the child still has and still needs two parents and you will think of each other that way. You both need all the help you can get raising the child. Remember, too, that parents who feel cut off and left out are less likely to make support payments in full and on time.

**Legal neutrality.** There is no *legal* preference for one form of custody over another, nor any *legal* preference for mothers over fathers, and physical handicap is not by itself a sufficient reason to deny custody. In court contests, the best interest of the child is the prime consideration, but the judge may have personal opinions as to what's best. In custody contests, the judge can require a family study before making a decision, but all other things being equal, for the sake of stability, the judge will often decide to keep the child in whichever home he or she has been living since separation. When the child is old enough to make intelligent choices, the judge will give some weight to the desires of the child. However, most children don't want to be put in the position of having to choose.

**Immigration status.** A parent, guardian or relative cannot be disqualified from having custody based on immigration status (Family Code 3040).

**Details, details.** In most cases, it is very useful for you to work out your parenting plan in as much detail as possible. Parents in agreement can arrange things any way they like from day to day, but if disagreements come up in the future, you will always have the specific terms of your agreement to fall back on as to who does what and when. Section 4.3 has two sample parenting plans you can use as a guide; one is very simple, the other is highly detailed.

**Joint custody.** There has been a growing trend for parents to request joint custody (both physical and legal) as a way to encourage the maximum involvement of both parents. Most judges now wisely require a plan for joint custody to be spelled out in some detail so that in the future each parent will know what is expected and when. Parents can freely arrange things any way they like by mutual agreement, but when you can't agree, the plan must be followed. For purposes of determining school district or welfare eligibility, your agreement or order can specify one parent as the primary caretaker who provides the primary home of the child. By law, an order for joint *physical* custody *must* specify the parenting time of each parent with enough detail that a judge can determine clearly if one parent is being deprived of custody by the other. If your request for joint custody is denied, the judge must state the reason in the decision *if* you request this in writing within 10 days of the order. It's best to do this at the hearing.

**Joint legal and primary physical custody.** This may have become the most popular parenting order today, and for good reason. It is used where one or both of the parents is not comfortable with full joint custody, yet it does not isolate the other parent as much as an order for sole custody and visitation. Under this plan, you award joint *legal* custody to both parents, with primary physical custody to one parent, along with a detailed parenting plan showing the times the child is with each parent. This arrangement is clean and clear, and judges are comfortable with it. The child has the stability of living primarily in one place most of the time, yet both parents are legally equal, thus minimizing the sense of loss to the parent with less child care time. An order for joint legal custody *must* specify any circumstances where consent of *both* parents is required. In all other situations, either parent alone can make decisions about the child's health, education and welfare.

**Primary custody with rights of visitation.** The old standard order grants sole custody, both physical and legal, to one parent, with detailed visitation rights to the other parent. The parent with sole custody has the major responsibility of caring for and raising the child, and that parent has the last word on all matters concerning the child's upbringing. The drawback is that it tends to make the non-custodial parent feel more or less cut off and at a real disadvantage in maintaining a relationship with the child.

**Domestic abuse and alcoholism.** When custody is an issue, a judge *must* consider abuse or threats of abuse by either parent to any family member, mate, or someone they dated, and continual or habitual use of alcohol or drugs. There is a presumption against awarding any form of custody—sole, joint physical, or joint legal—to a person the judge finds has committed domestic abuse in that family. The presumption can be overcome only by a preponderance of evidence. The judge can require independent proof of allegations made by one parent against the other, and a stiff penalty plus attorney fees can be awarded for a false accusation of child abuse.

If after reading this chapter and the possible custody orders in chapter 18.4, you still have questions about the parenting plan and its terms, or if you want help setting it up, you may want to discuss your case with a family law attorney. Call Divorce Helpline and make an appointment for a phone consultation. If you and your spouse are having difficulty communicating or working out terms for custody and visitation, then I strongly recommend that you both read *Make Any Divorce Better*. If that doesn't solve your problems, call Divorce Helpline or consider help from a counselor or mediator. Find out how to use your court mediation service; it is often a superb bargain. Custody fights are to be avoided at any cost, as they are hugely expensive and *always* destructive—especially to your children.

## 4.2  Visitation

A good parenting plan will keep the best interests of the child uppermost and help the parents to create as open and flexible an atmosphere as possible to permit a good relationship between the child and both parents. Both parents and the child will have a degree of certainty and stability.

In the past, the parent who did not get custody was often awarded "the right of reasonable visitation," meaning the right to visit at reasonable times and places, upon reasonable notice, and with the consent of the parent with custody. It is left to the parents to work out exactly what this means in terms of where and when visitation takes place. This can be very good if the parents are truly cooperative, but you can see how this vague order could create uncertainty and disagreement. Nowadays, most judges grant "reasonable visitation" only if given a good reason, and some won't accept "reasonable visitation" orders at all. If you enter into a settlement agreement, you can probably do as you wish. However, in almost all cases, it is much better to have very detailed parenting orders that set out specific days and hours for visiting, including overnights.

Day-by-day, parents can agree to any schedule they like, but whenever they can't agree, the specific terms of the visitation schedule will settle the issue and eliminate argument and further conflict. The next section has samples of parenting plans that you can use as a guide for thinking about your own. When you compose your plan, use simple words, be very clear, and be specific. Avoid terms that are subject to more than one interpretation. If you want help with your parenting plan, call Divorce Helpline.

**Virtual visitation** means staying in touch with your children via video calls, email, instant messaging, and cell phones. Relatively inexpensive, video calls allow you to hear and see each other, share documents, help with homework, play games, bring friends or grandparents into the visit, and so on. It is not a substitute for quality time spent together, but rather an extremely valuable supplement. Virtual visitation benefits all parties, as it allows the custodial parent to stay in touch with the child during extended summer or holiday visits with the non-custodial parent, and the child never has to feel cut off from either parent at any time. For more information, a tale of personal experience, tips on how to do it, and suggestions for how to word virtual visitation in your settlement agreement, look in the Reading Room folder on our companion CD. Other resources can be found at www.internetvisitation.org.

**Visiting for non-parents.** You can include in your agreement periods of visitation for a stepparent, grandparent, or any other person with an interest in the welfare of the child. Absent agreement, a judge has discretion to award visiting rights to grandparents whenever it would serve the best interests of the child. Grandparents can join in any action between the parents or bring their own action for visitation. Grandparent visitation time can be allocated between the parents for the purpose of calculating support. It is also possible to order support to a grandparent to cover the expenses of care and visitation.

**Problem cases.** The relationship between parent and child is so protected that courts rarely order no visitation at all. If you show good cause, you can get an order to conduct visitation only under supervision, but to get an order preventing any visiting at all you, must have a very strong case showing that even supervised visits will most likely be very dangerous or detrimental to the child. If you need a court order that prevents all visiting, see an attorney.

If your spouse has a history of harassing you, word your agreement or orders so you exchange the child in a public place, or even so that you never have to see your ex-spouse at all, possibly by arranging exchanges through a third person or agency.

Any parent who keeps or conceals a child to frustrate custody or visitation orders is guilty of a crime. The parent with custody is not entitled to forbid an arranged visitation for any reason other than the well-being of the child. If the visiting spouse arrives in a drugged or drunken state, for example, it would be reasonable to prevent the visit on that occasion. However, visiting cannot be refused because of a disagreement, ill will between the parents, or even because of a complete failure to provide support. Likewise, support cannot be suspended because visitation has been frustrated. In extreme cases, however, deliberate and persistent interference with visitation and the parental relationship has led to reduction or termination of support or a switch of custody to the other parent. Concealment of the child has been upheld in some cases as a defense to collecting unpaid support.

The law provides for additional support as compensation to help cover costs for periods when the visiting parent fails to assume caretaker responsibility. Conversely, a parent prevented from exercising visitation rights is entitled to compensation for expenses incurred.

Once you have your custody and visitation order, it is hoped that all will go smoothly. If not, and if you can't work things out peacefully and finally, you should try counseling or mediation.

## 4.3 Two parenting plans and some other ideas

Use these parenting plans and forms as a guide in making your own agreements and orders. You can (should) change them to fit your own ideas and circumstances or you can combine ideas from all of them. Other plans and good ideas can be found in some of the books listed at the end of this section.

**How much detail?** In general, more detail is better. Parents can vary from a detailed plan at any time by agreement, but if there's a problem, you just drag out the agreed plan and you know who is supposed to be where and when; end of argument. On the other hand, a very detailed plan might be harder to negotiate——especially if emotions are raw—and parents under detailed plans can sometimes become inflexible. The need for flexibility is always important, as parents must be prepared to accommodate the child's changing needs over time as well as the changing circumstances of the parents.

Carefully study the terms for visitation found in Judgment attachments listed below so you can see the kinds of terms attorneys have thought up for parenting plans to cover every kind of situation. Next, study the sample plans below to see a range of possibilities for customizing your own plan. Almost anything parents agree to, within reason, will be acceptable to a judge.

**Future moves.** What will happen if ever the custodial parent wants to move away usually shouldn't be addressed until it is actually about to happen. It is best negotiated at the time, based on circumstances existing at that time. Moves that tend to reduce the other parent's contact with the children are generally disfavored by judges, but may be allowed if in the child's best interest.

### JUDGMENT ATTACHMENTS

You can draft your own parenting plan, following the samples below, or you can attach forms to your Judgment to spell out custody and visitation. These forms are on the companion CD in the Forms folder. Take a close look at FL-341, FL-341(C), FL-341(D), and FL-341(E) to see the kinds of parenting terms devised by attorneys to cover almost anything that might come up in any kind of case. Better yet, get DealMaker™ and be guided to a refined, customized plan.

## SAMPLE PARENTING PLAN A

This plan represents the bare minimum for very cooperative parents. It's just a sketch of intentions, with lots of details left to be worked out day-by-day. It may be easier to write down now, but it won't help settle disagreements that may come up later about who is to do what and when. It's good for joint custody, but don't use this one unless you are secure with the relationship you have with your co-parent.

A. The parties agree to joint legal custody of their minor child. Primary physical custody of the child shall be with Wife. Husband shall have the child as follows:

1) for long weekend school holidays;

2) for half of the summer school vacations;

3) for the Easter school vacation in odd-numbered years;

4) for Thanksgiving school vacations in even-numbered years;

5) for half of the Winter Break school vacation;

6) for such other time as the parties shall agree.

B. At all other times, the child shall be with Wife.

C. Each party shall give the other two weeks' advance notice if the party is planning to take the child from the State of California for a period exceeding (one week/10 days/one month).

(Alternately, you could specify "the county of residence" rather than the state).

D. Both parties shall participate in making medical decisions concerning the child, and each party shall promptly inform the other of any medical emergencies that may arise.

## SAMPLE PARENTING PLAN B

This plan is relatively detailed so don't just copy it—think about it carefully and tailor the terms to fit your family and your particular circumstances.

1. (Mother/Father) shall be designated as the "Primary Custodial Parent." The Primary Custodial Parent shall have the primary physical responsibility for the children except for (Mother's/Father's) parenting time set forth below.

2. Basic Parenting Plan:

   a.  Weekends: Alternate weekends, commencing _____, from Friday at 6 p.m. until Sunday at 7 p.m. The weekend shall be extended to 7 p.m. on Monday if the Monday is a holiday when the children are scheduled to be with (Mother/Father).

   b.  Weekdays: Every (other) Wednesday, commencing _____, from 4 p.m. to 9 p.m.

   c.  Spring School Vacation: During the children's spring vacation from school, (Father's/Mother's) parenting time shall be from 6 p.m. Friday to 6 p.m. Wednesday if his/her regular weekend is before the vacation, or shall be from 6 p.m. on Wednesday to 7 p.m. Sunday if his/her regular weekend is after the vacation.

   d.  Summer School Vacation: Six weeks during the children's school vacation time during the summer, with starting and ending times to be agreed upon by the parties. During these six weeks, the children will spend alternate weekends with (Mother/Father) from Friday at 6 p.m. until Sunday at 7 p.m. The weekend shall be extended to 7 p.m. on Monday if the Monday is a holiday when the children are scheduled to be with (him/her).

   e.  Holiday Schedule:

Thanksgiving: In odd-numbered years, from 6 p.m. on the Wednesday before Thanksgiving until 6 p.m. on the following Sunday.

Winter:

In odd-numbered years, from noon on December 26 until 6 p.m. on the day before school resumes in January.

In even-numbered years, from 6 p.m. on the last school day before the Christmas school vacation until noon on December 26.

or

Seven consecutive days, including any regularly scheduled weekend time, during the children's Christmas holiday from school. The starting and ending times shall be agreed upon by the parties.

Other Holidays: As agreed by the parties.

3. Each parent shall be responsible for picking up the children at the beginning of his or her parenting time.

4. Either parent may designate any competent adult to pick up the children and to be with the children when they are picked up.

5. Each parent shall give at least 24 hours' advance notice to the other parent if he or she must change the schedule. The parent requesting the change shall be responsible for any additional child care costs that result from the change.

6. Both parents will cooperate in finding alternate child care for those periods when regular child care is not available, and the cost of said child care shall be included when the parties establish how the cost of child care is to be shared.

7. Neither parent may remove, or cause to be removed, the minor children from the state of California without 30 days' prior written notice to the other parent. This provision applies to vacations and trips outside of the State of California.

8. Neither parent may change his or her residence or the residence of the minor children without 60 days' prior written notice to the other parent.

# 5
# CHILD AND SPOUSAL SUPPORT

Child and spousal or partner support are discussed separately because they have different rules and priorities. But first, here are some points that apply to both.

**Support priorities.** Child support has priority over spousal/partner support. Spousal support will be considered only after children have been adequately provided for and will be based on the finances of the parties after child support has been accommodated.

**Earning ability.** Support is normally based on actual current income, but if a court finds that a spouse has voluntarily reduced income when employment at a higher level is available, then support can be based on that spouse's *ability* to earn. Occasional overtime and bonuses can be included in earnings if likely to continue in the future, but excessive overtime beyond a reasonable work schedule should not be included.

**New mate income.** For *spousal* support, you can't consider income or expenses of a *payor's* new mate to figure the amount of support, but if the *recipient* has a live-in mate, it can be presumed there is decreased need for support, at least to the extent expenses are reduced. For *child* support, new-mate income can be considered *only* if the parent intentionally quit work or remains unemployed or underemployed and relies on the new mate's income to do so, and if including it will not cause a hardship to any other child that the payor *or* the new mate supports. *For tax purposes only:* support is based on *actual* taxes paid, so if a party files taxes jointly with a new mate, the new mate's income and deductions have to be included in order to figure the correct amount of taxes attributable to the payor.

**Mandatory wage assignment.** Whenever there is an order for child or spousal support, there *must* also be an order assigning wages of the paying spouse. More about this in section 5.4 below.

**Jurisdiction.** Don't forget! To make an enforceable order for the payment of money, the court needs "personal jurisdiction" over the person ordered. Do you have this in your case? See chapter 2.6.

**Insurance.** The automatic restraining orders (chapter 2.7) forbid either spouse from canceling or transferring life or health insurance policies if the other spouse or a child are beneficiaries. Violation is a misdemeanor. On filing of a dissolution, a notice can be sent to insurance providers requiring them to continue named beneficiaries until the Judgment, and requiring notice of any lapse of payment or change of beneficiaries. Later, a copy of the Judgment can be sent to put the insurance provider on notice of orders that affect or protect beneficiaries.

**Life insurance** on the life of the payor should be considered to protect the recipients. This is especially important where the supported spouse keeps the home and the home mortgage as, if the payor dies, the supported spouse will get stuck with the mortgage and no support.

**Family support and tax savings.** Where the spouses' incomes differ significantly and child support will be paid, the family can save on taxes by ordering the payment of "family support," which is entirely deductible, whereas child support is not. Tax savings must be shared with the children, but your whole family profits when you pay less to the IRS. If you want a family support order, get help, because it takes expert advice and drafting to make it work, but it will probably be worth it. Call Divorce Helpline for more information.

## Modification of support orders

**Child support orders and agreements** can be modified at any time to accommodate changes, such as incomes, cost of living, needs, or other changes. A sudden increase or *unavoidable* decrease in income would be a reason to request modification of child support, as would the end of a major obligation. The parties can agree (stipulate) to a changed amount, or it can be done by motion in court. The court order is what determines how much is owed—informal agreements don't count. Don't fail to do it right!

**Spousal support** can also be modified, unless the Judgment or agreement has explicitly made it non-modifiable. If not fixed by Judgment or agreement, spousal support can be modified in either direction on showing of changed circumstances of income or need. The end of a companion child support obligation would be a valid basis for requesting a modification of spousal support, but the motion to modify must be brought within six months of the end of child support.

Once a year, either party to a support order can serve FL-396, a request for a completed Income and Expense Declaration, on the other party without going through the court. This will help you decide if a motion for modification is in order. The form is available in Book 2 or at the Superior Court Clerk's office.

## 5.1 Child support

**California's mandatory guideline.** California has a statewide guideline for *child* support based on the actual after-tax income of the parents and the amount of time each has physical custody of the child(ren). The guideline is mandatory, meaning a judge *must* order the guideline amount unless the parties have a written agreement or unless certain exceptions can be proved (see below). Knowing the guideline figures for your case will help you decide what's fair and make your negotiation much easier. You will know that there is little to gain by dragging the matter of child support into court because the judge has to follow the guideline, so you might as well follow it, too. In fact, you need to know the guideline, because even if you agree to an amount, you have to show the court that you knew the correct guideline amount before you made the agreement.

**Bottom line.** What people want to know first is the bottom line: "How much?" The court wants to see how you got there. In section 5.3 below, we explain the various ways you can get the correct guideline amount for your case.

### Details

**Duration.** A child is entitled to support until the child reaches 19 or reaches 18 and is not a full-time high school student, or dies, or marries, or becomes self-supporting, whichever occurs first. If parents agree in writing, support can be ordered to age 21 or through college or training. Support for a disabled minor or adult child who is unable to work can be extended so long as the disability lasts. Child support usually starts when ordered, but it is *possible* to have it made retroactive to the date the Petition was filed. Child support does not end automatically when the recipient dies, but a written agreement or Judgment can state that child support ends on death of the recipient if the payor takes custody of the child.

*add to judgement, that father will not take custody of child if Petitioner dies.*

**Additional support: insurance.** In addition to basic guideline support, health insurance for children *must* be made a part of a support order *if* it is available at a reasonable cost to either parent. "Reasonable" means that the difference between family and individual insurance is no more than 5% of the payer's gross income, but if the payer's net monthly income is less than $1,000, the court must first

*Reasonable: no more than 5% of payer's gross income*

find that it would be unjust not to order the health insurance. If not available, the order must require it to be obtained if ever it becomes available at reasonable cost in the future. A health insurer cannot refuse to cover a child because it doesn't live with the insured parent, lives outside the coverage area, is not claimed as a dependent on the insured's tax return, or was born out of wedlock. If your spouse won't cooperate, the court can order the employer directly to enroll the children in the health plan. The court can also award a sum of money to cover the cost of life insurance on the paying spouse to benefit the dependent spouse or children.

**Additional support: shared expenses.** In addition to guideline support, both parents are responsible for certain child care expenses which *must* be shared equally unless the parties agree or a court orders them shared in proportion to net incomes. The two *required* add-ons are (1) child-care expenses to enable either parent to work, and (2) uninsured health care expenses. The two *discretionary* add-ons are (1) educational or special needs of a child, and (2) travel expenses for a visiting parent.

**Uninsured health care expenses.** Every child support order must include an order that the parents will share reasonable uninsured health care costs for the child, either equally or in proportion to their net incomes. Amounts actually paid are presumed reasonable unless evidence is presented to show otherwise. A form stating the parents' rights and duties must be attached to any Judgment containing this order.

**Exceptions to the guideline.** The judge cannot depart from guideline amounts unless evidence is introduced in court to show one or more of the following special circumstances:

- Sale of the family home is being deferred to benefit children and the fair rental value of the home exceeds the mortgage, taxes and insurance;
- Extraordinarily high income would result in an excessively high award;
- Special circumstances that would cause the application of the guideline amount to be unjust or inappropriate;
- Necessary job-related expenses beyond normally allowed deductions;
- Financial hardship due to expenses from extraordinary health expenses or uninsured catastrophic loss or care of a live-in child by another relationship.

Evidence of any of these circumstances can be raised with the court, but because the judge has discretion to consider the total circumstances and the best interests of the children, you can't be certain of the result.

**Low income adjustment.** If the payor's net monthly disposable income is below $1,500, a judge can reduce child support, but by no more than the percentage by which payor's net monthly disposable income is less than $1,500. This amount will be adjusted annually on March 1 according to California's consumer price index.

**Taxes, exemptions and credits.** Be sure to read the tax information pamphlets (chapter 2.10). To be claimed, a child *must* have a Social Security number. The child dependent exemption is a valuable deduction that can be claimed by the *custodial* parent. However, the *non*-custodial parent can get it if the custodial parent signs IRS form 8332—each year—releasing the right to claim the exemption, and a copy of that form is filed with the tax return of the non-custodial parent. Because the high-earner saves more on taxes, it is usually best if the high-earner takes the exemption and pays part of the tax savings to the low-earner to cover any extra taxes. Don't forget, the person taking the exemption also gets the valuable child tax credit. Finally, parents may be eligible to take child-care expense deductions and a dependent-care tax credit. For more detailed advice, call Divorce Helpline.

**Agreed child support.** Parents can agree to any reasonable amount of support, but an amount different from the support guideline requires a written agreement (chapter 6) or the Stipulation to Establish Child Support (figure 18.3).

**Low or zero child support.** It is generally not easy to get an order for very low or zero child support, but it can usually be done when child care is substantially equal. Even then, it requires a carefully drafted settlement agreement and depends on continued good will between the parents, because a motion to modify can be made at any time when an order is below the guideline. If you want support ordered that is more than a little bit below your guideline amount, we suggest you have Divorce Helpline prepare your settlement agreement and see your paperwork through to Judgment.

Both parents are obligated to support their child. A parent cannot escape this obligation by voluntarily reducing income. Petitioners with children *must* include an order for child support in the Judgment in *every* case, even if the other parent is unemployed, unemployable, or long gone. Either parent can receive child support. It can even be ordered to a low-earning, noncustodial parent to help care for the child during visitation.

Child support is based on the *current* wealth of both parents, so a significant change in income can mean different support. If the payor enjoys a lifestyle that far exceeds that of the custodial parent, child support must reflect the richer lifestyle, even if this produces some unintended benefits for the custodial parent.

Child support can't be withheld even if visitation is being frustrated, and visitation can't be refused even if child support is not being paid. This is the law, but exceptions have been made in extreme cases. Where the child was hidden, a court reduced the amount of child support; several courts have discharged unpaid support arrearages for periods when a child has been concealed from the other parent; and in one case, deliberate and persistent interference with visitation and the parental relationship led to termination of the support obligation.

**Welfare cases.** If child support is ordered for a parent receiving welfare for the children, the support *must* be paid through the Department of Child Support Services (DCSS). Contact their office in your county.

## 5.2 Spousal or partner support

If you want spousal or partner support, it must be requested in the Petition or Response. Parties can agree to any amount, duration and terms, but if decided in court, the judge must follow the law.

Spousal support is not favored where the marriage is very short or where there are no children and both spouses can take care of themselves. For medium and longer marriages, the trend is to try to equalize the standards of living for the spouses after divorce. A wife can be ordered to support her husband if she earns more because the law is gender-neutral.

**How much?** Each county has guidelines for spousal support, but unlike child support guidelines, these are not mandatory and can *only* be used for a *temporary* spousal support order. The guideline amount can be useful in your negotiation but it does not tell you what a judge might order because the judge is not allowed to use a guideline for that purpose. If you can't settle by agreement and your case goes to court, the law insists that each case must be decided on its own merits based on the statutory factors in Family Code 4320.

### Family Code §4320

In ordering spousal support under this part, the court shall consider all of the following circumstances:

(a) The extent to which the earning capacity of each party is sufficient to maintain the standard of living established during the marriage, taking into account all of the following:

(1) The marketable skills of the supported party; the job market for those skills; the time and expenses required for the supported party to acquire the appropriate education or training to develop those skills; and the possible need for retraining or education to acquire other, more marketable skills or employment.

(2) The extent to which the supported party's present or future earning capacity is impaired by periods of unemployment . . . incurred during the marriage to permit the supported party to devote time to domestic duties.

(b) The extent to which the supported party contributed to the attainment of an education, training, a career position, or a license by the supporting party.

(c) The ability to pay of the supporting party, taking into account the supporting party's earning capacity, earned and unearned income, assets, and standard of living.

(d) The needs of each party based on the standard of living established during the marriage.

(e) The obligations and assets, including the separate property, of each party.

(f) The duration of the marriage.

(g) The ability of the supported party to engage in gainful employment without unduly interfering with the interests of dependent children in the custody of the party.

(h) The age and health of the parties.

(i) Documented evidence of any history of domestic violence, as defined in Section 6211, between the parties or perpetrated by either party against either party's child, including, but not limited to, consideration of emotional distress resulting from domestic violence perpetrated against the supported party by the supporting party, and consideration of any history of violence against the supporting party by the supported party.

(j) The immediate and specific tax consequences to each party.

(k) The balance of the hardships to each party.

(l) The goal that the supported party shall be self-supporting within a reasonable period of time. Except in the case of a marriage of long duration as described in Section 4336, a "reasonable period of time" for purposes of this section generally shall be one-half the length of the marriage. However, nothing in this section is intended to limit the court's discretion to order support for a greater or lesser length of time, based on any of the other factors listed in this section, Section 4336, and the circumstances of the parties.

(m) The criminal conviction of an abusive spouse shall be considered in making a reduction or elimination of a spousal support award in accordance with Section 4325.

(n) Any other factors the court determines are just and equitable.

**How long is a long marriage?** Section 4336, referred to above, presumes a marriage or partnership of 10 years or more to be of long duration, but under some circumstances a shorter marriage can also be considered to be of long duration, and a longer marriage with periods of separation could fail the test.

**How long does spousal support last?** The parties can set any term by agreement, but when decided by a judge, the duration will be related to the length of the marriage and the circumstances of the spouses. Cohabitation before marriage will *not* be considered. A rule of thumb is half the length of the marriage, as cited in the statute above, but note that this does not apply to long marriages. Unless agreed otherwise in writing, spousal support is not terminated by cohabitation with another party, but it automatically ends on remarriage of the recipient or the death of either spouse. To get support beyond the life of the payor, make life insurance part of the support agreement.

**Efforts to become self-supporting.** The supported spouse is expected to make *reasonable* efforts to become self-supporting. Failure to do so might be a factor considered as a reason for modifying or terminating spousal support.

**Impact of domestic violence.** Under clause (h) in the statute above, if domestic violence by the payor against the recipient is proven, it can affect the amount or duration of support. If the recipient was convicted of violence against the payor in the five years prior to the divorce or *at any time afterward*, there is a presumption that there should be no award for spousal support (Family Code §4325).

**Zero support vs. termination of support right.** Spousal support can stay steady, go down over time, or be set at zero. But there is a *big* difference between zero support and terminating all right to it. So long as the court keeps jurisdiction over spousal support, a spouse can come back later to ask for a modification of the original order. Even if support was ordered to end on a certain date, if a motion is made before that date, a judge can extend the term on a showing of need.

**Jurisdiction.** Courts should *not* retain jurisdiction over spousal support where the marriage was short and the spouses are in good health and self-supporting. For "long" marriages, the court *must* retain jurisdiction indefinitely unless the parties have agreed otherwise in a technically correct writing. What's long? A marriage of 10 years or more is long by legal definition, but shorter marriages can be considered long, depending on circumstances. In fact, a judge *might* be willing to retain jurisdiction—for a while—over spousal support in marriages of only four or six years.

In a written agreement, spouses can specify that the support amount cannot be modified, or that the time cannot be extended, or both. In fact, a written agreement is almost the only way you can be completely certain that spousal support will stay fixed at a certain amount or end on a certain date or condition.

**Termination.** To end forever all right to spousal support—that is, to terminate the jurisdiction of the court to make orders on the subject in the future—it must be waived in open court or in a written agreement. For long marriages (even some medium ones), a waiver or a written termination will not be approved if it isn't made clear that both spouses know that a judge *would* retain jurisdiction if asked to and that both spouses are capable of supporting themselves.

**Right to continue health insurance.** If one spouse is covered under the other's health insurance *at the time of the dissolution*, COBRA (a Federal act) gives that spouse the right under almost all plans to continue coverage for up to three years after the Judgment at similar rates, at his/her own expense. To exercise this right, within 60 days of Judgment you *must* deliver a written notice of the divorce to the Plan Administrator and tell them you want to continue under COBRA. The cost may seem to go way up after the employer's contribution is no longer applied, so here's what you do. Way ahead of the Judgment, call the plan or the employer's personnel department and find out what the coverage is and your cost under COBRA after the divorce. Then call other plans and shop around for a better deal. **Domestic partners** are not covered by this federal law unless their particular plan happens to have a COBRA look-alike written into it; but the law on this point is in flux, so check with the plan administrator.

**Creativity.** Spousal support has inspired a great deal of creativity; in fact, there are books much larger than this one devoted to nothing else. We cover the basics here, but if spousal support is a difficult issue in your case, call Divorce Helpline to explore options and get advice based on their long years of experience in dealing with this thorny subject.

## 5.3 Support software to calculate guidelines

The guidelines are so incredibly complicated that few lawyers or judges understand them completely, which is why they all use software to calculate the correct guideline amount. Meanwhile, if parents make a support agreement, they are expected to show that they know the correct guideline amount and state whether their agreed amount is higher or lower. All judges would like you to attach a computer calculation of guideline support to your paperwork, some counties require it, and having a printout is the best way to complete form FL-170 which is used to move an uncontested case toward Judgment. So what's a person to do?

Lawyers use expensive software to calculate guideline support. While guidelines are intended to assist the parents, legal software is designed for litigation, which is not the same thing at all, and their printouts are extremely difficult to understand, so when you *do* get your results, you will need a consultation to have it explained. Lawyers typically charge $150–$250 for a calculation, and it usually has to be done many times as you negotiate your way through various proposals.

Divorce Helpline attorneys will calculate the guidelines for $75, plus $25 for reruns. Many paralegals and mediators offer support calculation service, too.

Every county has a Family Court Facilitator's office (chapter 1.9) and a branch office of the Department of Child Support Services (DCSS). Either one of these can help you with child support issues, among other things. Call to see what help you can get and how long you'll have to wait to get it.

The DCSS web site offers a free guideline calculator, but at this writing the price is right because it is still difficult to understand and use even after you read the 34-page manual, and it does not calculate spousal support. To find it, go to **www. childsup.ca.gov**, click on "Calculate Child Support" in the left column, then click on "Go to Calculator" near the bottom of the next page.

**Your best option.** To make support guidelines accessible and useful, we developed CalSupport, a Windows program designed for ordinary people and sensible professionals who serve them. It is far easier to use and understand than other software, yet it is very affordable and, better yet, it is designed to help you communicate and settle. That's what guidelines are for, right?

It costs only $34.95 to register CalSupport, yet it gives you the same results you would get from a lawyer entering the same data in a $500 program. It is certified by the California Judicial Council for use in all courts, but if you use CalSupport™, you aren't as likely to end up in court because it produces reports that are easy to understand and designed to help parents settle.

When you use CalSupport™, instead of arguing about how much support should be paid, you go over documents to support the accuracy of data entered and let CalSupport™ tell you how much support any judge would order under California guidelines. That's the range you negotiate. You won't go to court because lawyer's bills could easily run from $10,000 to $25,000 for *each side,* and the outcome would be near the guideline amount anyway.

**How to get it.** A free trial version of CalSupport™ for Windows is on the CD that comes with this book. Even better, you can download the latest version at **www.nolodivorce.com/CA.** CalSupport™ PRO, a professional version with extended features, is also available for $149 at **www.nolodivorce.com/PRO.**

## Other ways to calculate support guidelines

You might wonder if there are alternatives to computer calculation of the child support guideline. In practical terms, not really, but here are two other possibilities.

• **Do without.** This is not recommended, and can't be done if your county requires a computer printout. Otherwise, you *could* try going to a court hearing (chapter 20.3) without a printout and ask the judge to award "the guideline amount" for child support. Some judges will calculate the figure at the hearing. If the judge asks *you* for the guideline amount, ask for a continuance and come back for your hearing after you get the figures.

• **Do it by hand.** If you have math ability and time, you can hand-calculate child support using the instructions at the end of this chapter. If you want to see the entire child-support statute, search Google for "CA Fam Code 4050" or ask at your county law library. When working by hand, figuring taxes will be a challenge, and if either parent has a live-in child by another relationship, the allowable deduction will be extremely difficult to figure. And, when all is done, the only thing you will have to show your spouse or the judge will be some pages of scribbled figures.

## 5.4  Enforcement of support orders

Support may be ordered, but it is not always paid. In fact, only 17% of all recipients are paid in full and on time. This is why you should make *every* effort to settle the amount of support by agreement because you get better compliance later.

**Mandatory wage assignment.** Every order for child or spousal support *must* include an order assigning the wages of the paying spouse to the recipient spouse or an agency appointed to collect support. If the order is served on the payor's employer, all or part of the support payments will automatically be deducted from wages by the employer. The wage assignment can be stayed by court order, but not easily. However, it is *entirely* up to the recipient *when* the wage assignment order is actually *served* (if ever) on the employer,  so, as described in chapter 19, the parties can agree in writing that the order will not be served on the payor's employer so long as payments are current (see chapter 19).

**Social Security benefits** can be attached for child or spousal support. If this is the payer's primary source of steady income, contact your local support collection agency or Social Security office and ask them how to proceed.

**Keep track!** Both parents should keep careful records of support paid or received because if ever the issue of overdue support comes up, the person with the best records wins. To make your job easier, we created **Tracker** software to help you keep track of support payments, amounts overdue, and interest that is automatically added to amounts overdue. For more information, see **www.nolodivorce.com/CA**.

**Teeth that really bite.** Cash-hungry governments are putting more teeth than ever in enforcement laws. Here are some of the sharper ones:

> **Security deposits** can be agreed to or required by a judge in the amount of up to one year's support. You can also ask the payor to provide life or disability insurance to replace support in case of accident or death. Requiring a security deposit is a very good idea where the payor is self-employed.

> **License and passport blocking.** Deadbeats face revocation of their drivers' licenses and business and professional licenses, and passports can be revoked or renewal refused.

> **Intercept** tax refunds, unemployment and State Disability payments, or lottery winnings.

**Credit rating affected** by nonpayment of child or spousal support can ruin the payor's credit rating. The Department of Child Support Services is *required* to report nonpayment of support to credit agencies and the agencies are required to include it in any report until cleared.

**It is a Federal crime** to willfully fail to pay a past-due support debt from another state.

**Contempt of court** if payor fails to make a good-faith effort to get a job.

**Penalties** of up to 72% can be added to amounts past due and interest can be added, but you have to take legal action to get it.

**Liens on real or personal property** belonging to the payor can be obtained.

**Seek a work order.** Deadbeats can be ordered to submit a report to the court, every two weeks or some other reasonable period, listing places where he/she applied for work.

**Help is available.** All child support services except for criminal prosecution are handled by the Department of Child Support Services (DCSS), with offices in each county. They get involved with spousal support *only* if it is part of an order for child support. The Family Law Facilitator will also help people with support orders. Unless a parent is receiving welfare, you should probably contact your county Family Law Facilitator first. Some offices are more effective than others and most are understaffed, so think about getting your own attorney. However, establishing and collecting child support is their primary function, so they should be experts on the subject. County attorneys do not actually represent you, but they can still be useful. Contact information for these offices can be found on our companion CD under "Links" or at **www.nolodivorce.com/links**. Give them a call or, better yet, go see them.

**Good record keeping** is extremely important for both parties in case of future claim or disagreement. Keep records safe and keep them until the obligation for support is long over.

**Register your Judgment** if you move to another state. This is essential if you might ever want the right to enforce the support orders in your new state.

**Don't put off collection too long.** If you don't bother to enforce your unpaid support for many years, this *could* be interpreted as evidence of a waiver of the right to support, especially in the case of spousal support. This is not a hard rule, but it has happened before.

# Calculating child support by hand

## Family Code Section 4055

$$CS = K [HN - (H\% \times TN)]$$

CS = Guideline child support for the first child. Calculate it in this order:

Figure TN = Total net monthly disposable income of both Mother and Father. See Note 1 in right column. Figuring the correct amount of state and federal income taxes and FICA deductions make this the trickiest part of the hand calculation and a strong argument for using CalSupport™ software to figure guideline child support.
- Add the results for both parents together to get TN.
- Whoever has the highest net monthly disposable income (HN) is High Earner.

Figure H% = Timeshare for High Earner (next page). If there are different arrangements for different children, use the average that the high earner spends with each child. If there's no evidence of timeshare, court will use 0% or 100% depending upon who has custody.

Figure HN = High Earner's net monthly disposable income.

Figure K = Percentage of parents' combined net incomes (TN) that is allocated for children. Figure the K factor like this:
- If H% is less than or equal to 50%
  K = ( 1 + H% ) times fraction below:
- If H% is greater than 50%
  K = ( 2 – H% ) times fraction below.

| Disposable income | | | Fraction | | |
|---|---|---|---|---|---|
| $0 | to | $800 | .20 | + | TN/16,000 |
| 801 | to | 6,666 | .25 | | |
| 6,667 | to | 10,000 | .10 | + | 1000/TN |
| Over 10,000 | | | .12 | + | 800/TN |

Figure CS: Multiply H% by TN, subtract result from HN and multiply by K. This is the Guideline figure for the first child.

Total Guideline Child Support:

If you have more than one child, multiply CS by:

| | |
|---|---|
| 2 children | 1.6 |
| 3 children | 2 |
| 4 children | 2.3 |
| 5 children | 2.5 |
| 6 children | 2.625 |
| 7 children | 2.75 |
| 8 children | 2.813 |
| 9 children | 2.844 |
| 10 children | 2.86 |

If the result is positive, the high earner pays the low earner that figure. If the number is negative, the low earner pays.

## NOTES & DEFINITIONS

1. "Net disposable income" is gross income reduced by actual amounts attributable to:
   - State and federal income tax actually payable (not necessarily the amount withheld from the paycheck). Unless the parties agree otherwise, this shall not include the tax effects of spousal support. Note: this step requires you to calculate the probable tax bill for both parties—one of the major reasons hand calculation is difficult and imprecise.
   - Federal Insurance Contributions Act. For people not subject to it, any amount actually used to secure retirement or disability benefits, not to exceed the equivalent FICA amount.
   - Deductions for mandatory union dues and retirement benefits that are required as a condition of employment.
   - Deductions for health insurance for the parent and any children the parent has an obligation to support and deductions for state disability insurance.
   - Any child or spousal support actually being paid pursuant to a court order to any person not a subject of the current calculation, or any child support actually being paid without a court order for a natural or adopted child not residing in the party's home and not a subject of the current calculation. No deduction under this section allowed unless it can be proved.
   - Hardship deductions: 1) minimum basic living expenses of minor children, natural or adopted, of other relationships who actually live with the parent; 2) extraordinary health expenses for which the party is obligated; 3) uninsured catastrophic losses. These deductions are discretionary with the court upon a showing of evidence.

2. Authorized add-ons. These are 1) child care costs related to employment or necessary education or training for employment skills; and 2) uninsured health care costs for the children. Discretionary add-ons: 1) costs related to educational or other special needs of the children; and 2) travel expenses for visitation. Sharing: Add-ons are generally shared equally, but a judge can order or parties agree that it be in proportion to their net incomes.

3. A hardship deduction for basic living expenses for a live-in child of another relationship can be taken from gross income by judge's order or agreement of parties. The amount may not be more than the prorated amount ordered for each child under the current order. If this is a factor in your case, you have yet another reason for getting a computer calculation that applies all formulas and takes all factors into account.

4. Low income adjustment. If payor's net monthly disposable income (HN) is less than $1,500, it is presumed that guideline child support (CS) will be reduced by an amount that may not exceed the percentage by which HN is less than $1,500. The maximum adjustment, therefore, is: CS x (1,500 - HN)/1,500. This presumption can be rebutted by evidence showing the adjustment would be unjust and inappropriate.

# Estimating Timeshare

Timeshare is the percentage of time the parent has primary physical control. There are no state rules for how to figure it, so you can calculate timeshare any way the parties can agree on.

Credit for time in school or day care. You should negotiate how to credit time the child spends in school or day care, but a judge would decide based on factors like who is on call for emergencies, who arranges and pays for it, who drops off and picks up the child, and participation in school and extracurricular activities. If you both do these things, share the time in proportion.

Some counties have voluntary guidelines in their Local Rules of Court (ask the Superior Court Clerk's Office or at the county law library).  As an example, here's the guide that Santa Clara County judges use when parties disagree about how to figure timeshare:

Definitions:

| | | |
|---|---|---|
| Weekend | = | 6 pm Friday to 6 pm Sunday |
| Extended weekend | = | Close of school Friday to opening of school Monday |
| Evening | = | After school to after dinner |
| Overnight | = | Close of school midweek to opening of school next day |
| Alternate holidays | = | New Year's, President's Day, Easter, Memorial Day, Mother's Day or Father's Day, July 4, Thanksgiving (two days), Christmas, child's birthday |
| Summer vacation | = | 12 weeks (84 days) mid-June to September 1 |
| School vacation | = | Summer, two weeks at Christmas, 1 week Spring, two days Thanksgiving, plus seven other days. (school holidays vary from one district to another). |

| Parenting arrangement | Days | % |
|---|---|---|
| 1 weekend per month | 24 | 7 |
| 1 extended weekend per month | 36 | 10 |
| 1 weekend per month plus one evening per week | 50 | 14 |
| Alternate weekends | 52 | 14 |
| Alternate weekends plus 2 weeks in summer | 67 | 18 |
| Alternate weekends and holidays plus 2 weeks of summer | 73 | 20 |
| Alternate weekends plus 1 evening per week | 78 | 21 |
| Alternate extended weekends | 78 | 21 |
| Alternate weekends plus 1 overnight per week | 78 | 21 |
| Alternate weekends and holidays plus 4 weeks of summer | 86 | 24 |
| Alternate weekends and holidays plus half of summer | 100 | 27 |
| Alternate extended weekends plus 1 evening per week | 104 | 29 |
| Alternate weekends and holidays plus 1 evening per week plus 4 weeks of summer | 112 | 31 |
| Alternate weekends and one evening per week, and half of school vacations | 135 | 37 |
| Three days per week | 156 | 43 |

# 6
# SETTLEMENT AGREEMENTS

This chapter explains why an agreement is the best thing you can do in most cases and how to make your own written settlement agreement (**SA**), either with the simple sample printed in this book or with the more sophisticated capabilities of Nolo's DealMaker software (see inside front cover).

**Here's why** you should work hard to get a well-drafted settlement agreement.

- With an agreement, you won't have to go to court. Without one, chances are you will.

- Your SA becomes your Judgment, and you will be ordered to comply with its terms, thus you get to decide everything ahead of time and have total control over the Judgment. Without a settlement agreement, you are more limited, and a stranger (the judge) who doesn't know you or your family decides everything after spending very little time getting to know the facts.

- With a settlement agreement, you can get far more depth, detail, flexibility, and protection.

- If your community property has a net value (assets less debts) of more than $5,000, a written settlement agreement is the only way you can arrange an unequal division.

- Once you sign, your divorce is mostly finished except for red tape and paperwork.

- Divorces settled by good agreements usually work out better afterward—spouses are more likely to comply with terms, have better post-divorce relationships, better co-parenting, faster healing, and it just feels better.

**Money and more.** Often, a lot of money can be gained or lost depending on how things are handled in your SA, especially if significant assets, debts or support are involved. Careful planning, problem-solving, and drafting can save thousands or tens of thousands of dollars.

A settlement agreement can be tailored to suit your specific situation: protection from a spouse's debts, dealing with the family home, avoiding taxes and penalties. For spousal support, you can be creative about fixing dates, amounts, and various conditions so that you never have to come back to court again. Your parenting plan can be designed to calm the concerns of both parents about their future relationship with the child and each other.

## Write your own?  Get help?

Writing your agreement yourself is not the main point. The true value of an agreement is the depth and detail with which you think things through, discuss issues, and work things out between you, so both of you end up with a complete understanding of what was agreed. So, should you write your own or get help?

**How much is good help worth?** The settlement agreement is virtually your entire divorce. Stop to think if it is worth it to get professional help. Add up the value of all your property and debts, then add all future support payments. Compare that figure to a couple of thousand for professional help and a settlement agreement that is done right. If expert help isn't worth it, or if you just prefer to do things yourself, use the sample agreement below as a guide for simple estates, or for larger or more complex estates, you should take advantage of the more sophisticated and powerful capabilities of Nolo's **DealMaker** software.

**Who can help?** To go beyond the simple sample agreement below, get the more sophisticated agreement produced by **DealMaker** software (see inside front cover), or have it done by a family law specialist like those at Divorce Helpline. Do *not* let a non-attorney draft your settlement agreement unless you have little property and they follow the agreement in this book or use **DealMaker** to produce your agreement. Do not use anyone else's agreement as a guide, as it may be from a different state or a different time, and it will certainly be for different people. Get one professionally tailored to your needs and today's laws.

**The three befores.** If you get help, be sure to get your information and advice *before* you state your position to your spouse, *before* you draft your settlement agreement, and *before* you sign anything.

## Getting your agreement

If you need help negotiating or otherwise working things out, read my book *Make Any Divorce Better* or call Divorce Helpline. They can help with suggestions, problem-solving, negotiating techniques, or they can mediate your disagreement if there's an impasse.

## Settlement agreement highlights

**Timing.** You need to file your Petition (chapter 10) before you finalize an agreement because you *must* complete disclosure (chapter 14) before signing an agreement, which is done *after* the Petition is filed. Also, agreements take time to work out, and you don't want to rush something so important. File your Petition, do the disclosure, then forget about it while you negotiate your agreement.

**Thorough discussion and complete agreement.** Because set-aside rules are relatively relaxed for divorce cases (chapter 2.9), you want above all to avoid a situation where either spouse has second thoughts in the months after the agreement is signed. This means you want and need a true meeting of the minds on all points, and that means a contract that has been thoroughly thought out, discussed, and negotiated in depth and detail by both spouses, personally.

**Never sign a settlement agreement without disclosure!** You can't make a sound agreement unless both parties have complete financial information. In fact, unless both parties fulfill disclosure requirements, you might not be allowed to complete your divorce, and your Judgment might be vulnerable to attack in the future. How to do disclosure is described in chapter 14. The law requires both spouses to serve each other with preliminary *and* final disclosures before or at the time of entering into any written agreement regarding property or support. Using form FL-144 (chapter 14), the spouses can agree to waive the Final Disclosure, but this is not recommended in cases with significant property because you *want* the other party's sworn disclosure on the record before you sign anything.

**Secure promises to pay.** A debt between spouses to settle their divorce case should be secured whenever possible, preferably by a trust deed (mortgage) on real property, if there is any.

**Death** of either spouse will terminate spousal support unless stated otherwise in your settlement agreement.

**Voluntary changes.** If you later agree to alter your arrangements for custody, visitation, or support, be sure to do it in writing and then get your Judgment modified. Informal understandings won't affect your written order, and obligations under that old Judgment are binding until changed.

**Modification.** If circumstances change, either party can make a motion to change the orders for child support or custody. Spousal support can be modified *unless* your agreement states in legally correct language that it can't be modified either as to amount or duration or both.

**Reconciliation.** A settlement agreement is not canceled if you reconcile later. To terminate a written agreement, you will have to change or revoke it in writing.

**Taxes.** Many aspects of a settlement agreement can have tax consequences, so be sure to read the tax information booklets (chapter 2.10) or get expert advice. You may be able to save quite a bit on taxes by customizing your agreement.

**Signing.** When the settlement agreement is being signed, you should also have prepared all other documents that need a signature: interspousal transfer deeds, notes, auto pink slips, and so on.

**Notarize.** It's a good idea to notarize both signatures to your settlement agreement in any case: some counties require it. In every county, you *must* have Respondent's signature notarized if you proceed by Default (chapter 17). Butte County wants the parties to have two different notaries.

**Welfare.** If a party is receiving welfare, the District Attorney's office will need to sign an approval on any SA or Judgment with provisions for child support. They will need proof of the payor's income.

## Warning!

Think carefully before signing an agreement for less than your fair share of property and support. Buying peace is not always a bad idea, but think carefully first, so you don't end up sorry later that you made that decision. Don't give away valuable rights because you feel guilty, or to make your soon-to-be ex-spouse like you better. It is very difficult and expensive to try to break an agreement.

### A sample settlement agreement
#### (also available on the companion CD for editing)

A *simple* settlement agreement (SA) is included here so you can see what one looks like and use as a guide. **Caution!** This agreement is suitable for simple cases—a few household goods, vehicles, a few debts—but nothing big or complicated. For a more sophisticated agreement, get Nolo's DealMaker software (**www.nolodivorce. com/CA**) or call Divorce Helpline (800) 359-7004 for assistance.

**Things not covered.** Here are some situations where we suggest professional advice or help with drafting:

- Zero child support in joint custody cases.
- Family support (instead of child support, to maximize tax savings).
- Child support beyond age 18 for college or technical training.
- Security for payment of debts or amounts to be paid later.
- Spousal support—stepping up or down; making the amount or duration depend on a condition; or terminating support in cases where there is a long marriage (chapter 5.2).
- Sale of a major asset to take place after SA signed—protection of respective interests until sale and allocation of expenses while you own it.
- Tax consequences of sale of a major item—maximizing tax savings, minimizing tax liability.
- Equalization payments to balance unequal division of property.
- Future interest in a pension plan, to be distributed upon reaching retirement age.
- Self-employment, solely owned business, sideline business—valuation and division.
- Intellectual property—ownership and future value of music, writings, art, software, inventions, etc.

**When.** Settlement agreements are filed with your Judgment. In most counties, it is attached to the Judgment, but in San Bernardino the SA is filed separately as Exhibit 1 (see "San Bernardino Rule" in chapter 18.2).

**Details.** You will need the original and three copies of the agreement, typed on one side only. When signing, both spouses should also initial each page at the bottom and initial any alterations or corrections.

**Doing your own.** If you write your own settlement agreement, use the parts below that apply to you. Change wording to suit your needs; disregard what doesn't fit, but *don't* leave out paragraphs X to XV. Use clear and specific wording because vague terms with more than one possible meaning cannot be enforced. Your settlement agreement will, in effect, become your Judgment, so it *must* be right. If you have trouble understanding the agreement, or wording it to fit your own case, get help.

## SETTLEMENT AGREEMENT

I, _____, Husband, and I, _____, Wife, agree as follows:

I. GENERALLY: We make this agreement with reference to the following facts:

A. MARRIAGE: We are now husband and wife. We were married on the ___ day of _____, 20___, and separated on the ___ day of _____, 20___.

B. CHILDREN: There are (no minor children/the following minor children of the parties):
**(list full name, age and birth date of each minor child of the marriage)**

C. IRRECONCILABLE DIFFERENCES: Unhappy and irreconcilable differences have arisen between us which have caused the irremediable breakdown of our marriage.

D. DISCLOSURE: We each acknowledge receipt of Final Declarations of Disclosure from the other.

E. We now intend, by this agreement, to make a final and complete settlement of all of our rights and obligations concerning child custody, child support, spousal support, and division of property.

II. SEPARATION: We agree to live separately and apart, and, except for the duties and obligations imposed and assumed under this agreement, each shall be free from interference and control of the other as fully as if he or she were single.

III. PARENTING PLAN: **(choose one):**

**Joint custody:** Husband and Wife shall jointly share the legal and physical custody and care of our minor children. Our parenting relationship shall be guided by the following terms and conditions: **(write your parenting plan in as much detail as possible; chapter 4.3)**

**Joint legal custody with primary physical custody:** Husband and Wife shall jointly share the legal custody of the minor children of the parties, and **(Husband/Wife)** shall have the primary physical custody of said children. Our parenting relationship shall be guided by the following plan: **(write your parenting plan in as much detail as possible; chapter 4.3)**

**Sole custody and visitation:** (Husband/Wife) shall have the sole legal and physical custody of the minor children of the parties, subject to the right of (Wife/Husband/other) to visit said children as follows: **(write your parenting plan in as much detail as possible; chapter 4.3)**

**Optional:** Each parent shall give the other parent at least 60 days' prior written notice before making any change in a child's residence that will last longer than 30 days.

**More options:** consider other provisions such as a) visits with grandparents; b) a successor to visitation rights in case of death of visiting parent; c) written notice to other spouse in case of changes in health, education, well-being, educational progress; d) provide documents to allow spouse to inquire directly with doctors, hospitals, school personnel. **Still more options:** That the children will keep the father's surname and not take on the mother's maiden name or name of any new spouse, at least until the child is old enough to make that decision. Some spouses want an agreement about the children's religious upbringing and education.

IV. BASIS OF AGREED SUPPORT: The support established by this agreement is based on the following facts:

A. Before separation, our gross combined family income was $_____ per month, and our average expenses were $_____ per month.

B. At the time of this agreement, Husband's gross monthly income is $_____ and average monthly expenses are $_____. Wife's gross monthly income is $_____ and average monthly expenses are $_____.

C. **(If there are children)**  Under our agreed parenting plan, the children will be in the physical care of the Wife __% of the time and in the physical care of the Husband __% of the time.

D. The mandatory Wage Assignment Order for support will be issued.

**(Optional):** E. AGREEMENT NOT TO SERVE WAGE ASSIGNMENT ORDER: We understand that a Wage Assignment Order (WAO) must be issued by the court whenever support is ordered, but so long as support payments are no more than ___ days in arrears, (Wife/Husband) agrees not to serve the WAO on (Husband's/Wife's) employer. Until the WAO is served, support payments will be made directly to (Husband/Wife) and both parties will keep a record of all payments made and received for the duration of the support obligation.

V. SUPPORT OF CHILDREN: Pursuant to California Family Code §4065, the parties make the following declarations: (1) We are fully informed of our rights concerning child support; (2) The child support award is agreed to without coercion or duress; (3) The agreement is in the best interests of the children involved; and (4) The needs of the children will be adequately met by the stipulated amount. **(Do not alter foregoing language.)** We are aware that the guideline amount for our case is $____ **(chapter 5.3)** and acknowledge that this agreement (does/does not) follow the guideline. **If not on welfare, add:** The right to support has not been assigned to the county under Section 11477 of the Welfare and Institutions Code and no public assistance application is pending.

As and for child support, _____ shall pay to _____ a total of $____ per month, payable in advance on the __ day of each month, beginning on the __ day of _____, 20__. Support shall be apportioned for each child as follows: **(Use guideline apportionment shown in the child support order, chapter 18.4, or substitute your own. This is not done if you have different time share with different kids).** Support shall continue for each child until said child dies, marries, becomes self-supporting, reaches 19, or reaches 18 and not a full-time high school student, whichever occurs first.

HEALTH INSURANCE: (Husband/Wife) shall obtain and maintain an insurance policy providing major medical, dental, and vision coverage for each child for the duration of the support obligation. The child's reasonable health costs that are not covered by any policy of health insurance shall be (paid by Husband/Wife) (shared equally) (paid __% by Husband and __% by Wife).

CHILD CARE: As additional child support, _____ shall pay to _____ for child care a total of $__ per month, payable in advance on the __ day of each month, commencing on _____, 20__, and continuing as long as child care is necessary and actually being paid.

**Life insurance option:** During the term of the support obligation for each child, (Husband/Wife/both equally/other) shall carry and maintain a policy of life insurance in the amount of $_____, and shall name as sole irrevocable beneficiaries (Wife/Husband/said minor children), and shall not borrow, assign or otherwise encumber said policy.

**Note on tax status:** To file as Head of Household, during the tax year you must have actually paid more than half the cost of maintaining a home for yourself and a party you are entitled to claim as a dependent. To cover time when a supported child is away at school, you can include this clause: When (child) is living at school, college, or other post-high school training, the principal abode of (child) shall be with (Husband/Wife) and said parent shall pay more than half the cost of (child's) support and maintaining a home for (child) during (child's) temporary absence at school.

**Termination option:** The child support obligation shall terminate upon the death of the recipient if the payor assumes full custody of the children.

**Optional payment for college or training:** Many parents prefer the flexibility of renegotiating this point when the child graduates high school, to examine the child's level of commitment or the parent's ability to pay, but if you think the payor may be stingy later and you can get the agreement now, you might want to pin it down. Get advice on the pros and cons of making this kind of agreement now and how to word it.

VI. SUPPORT PAYMENTS TO SPOUSE: The parties agree that the following amount of spousal support (does/does not) completely meet the current needs of the recipient for support. (Use A or B)

**A .** Waiver of Right to Support: In consideration of the other terms of this agreement, and whereas both spouses are fully self-supporting, **(choose one of the following)**

. . . there will be no order for spousal support at this time, but the court shall retain jurisdiction over spousal support.

. . . we each waive all right or claim which we may now have to receive support from the other. No court shall have jurisdiction to award spousal support at any time regardless of any circumstances that may arise. We understand that either of us could ask the court to retain jurisdiction over the subject of spousal support. For marriages over five years, add: We are informed and aware that, if requested by either party, the court is required by law to reserve spousal support for long-term marriages of over ten years, and may be disposed to do so for marriages shorter than ten years. Even so, we each waive the right to receive spousal support now or at any time in the future.

**B.** In consideration of the other terms of this settlement agreement, _____ agrees to pay to _____ the sum of $_____ per month, payable on the __ day of each month, beginning _____, 20__, and continuing until **(any or all of the following—some certain date, the death of the payer, death of the recipient, remarriage of the recipient, some specific condition. Note: unless specified here, no amount of cohabitation will equal remarriage, so be exceptionally clear if you intend otherwise)**, whichever occurs first.

**Optional:** Said (termination date/amount/date and amount) is absolute and no court shall have jurisdiction to modify the (termination date/amount) of spousal support at any time regardless of any circumstances that may arise. Spousal support may not be requested for any period after the termination date, nor will any court have jurisdiction to order spousal support to be paid for any period after the termination date, regardless of any circumstances that may arise and regardless of whether any motion to modify spousal support is filed before, on, or after said date.
**More options:** 1) amount decreases at set times; 2) amount adjusted automatically for increases in paying spouse's income; 3) court retains jurisdiction over spousal support, but no payments now; 4) a policy of life insurance required naming support recipient as sole irrevocable beneficiary (see life insurance option under child support, above), or specify that spouse and/or child to be named or retained as irrevocable beneficiary under some existing policies; 5) spouse to be dropped as beneficiary under a certain policy.

VII. CONFIRMATION OF SEPARATE PROPERTY:

A. The following property was and is the separate property of Husband, and Wife confirms it to him and waives any claim to or interest in it: **list—describe clearly.**

B. The following property was and is the separate property of Wife, and Husband confirms it to her and waives any claim to or interest in it: **list—describe clearly; for example, use vehicle license numbers and VIN, assessor's parcel numbers and legal description for real estate.**

VIII. DIVISION OF COMMUNITY PROPERTY AND DEBTS: The parties warrant and declare under penalty of perjury that the assets and liabilities divided in this agreement constitute all their community and quasi-community assets and liabilities. In the event that the division is unequal, the parties knowingly and intelligently waive an equal division of the community property.

A. Husband is awarded and assigned the following assets as his share of the community property: **(list each item or groups of items. Give legal description of real estate, including assessor's parcel number; license and VIN for vehicles).**

B. Wife is awarded and assigned the following assets as her share of the community property: **(list as instructed for Husband).**

**Option for cases with little or no significant property or bills, instead of A & B above:**
Husband and Wife agree that their community property and bills are minimal and that they have already divided them to their mutual satisfaction. Each hereby transfers and quitclaims to the other any and all interest in any property in the possession of the other, and agrees that whatever property the other may possess is now the sole and separate property of the other.

C. Husband shall pay the following debts promptly when due and indemnify and hold Wife harmless therefrom: **(list—identify clearly, give value of each item).**

D. Wife shall pay the following debts promptly when due, and indemnify and hold Husband harmless therefrom: **(list—identify clearly, give value of each item).**

E. Husband and Wife each warrants to the other that, after the date of this agreement, no debt or obligation will be incurred for which the other may be liable, or that could be enforced against an asset held by the other. We agree that if any claim be brought seeking to hold one liable for the subsequent debts of the other, or an undisclosed obligation of the other, or for any act or omission of the other, then each will hold the other harmless, defend such claim, and indemnify the other for any liability on the obligation, attorney fees, and related costs.

F. If either party has any knowledge of any community asset other than those disclosed and listed in this agreement, warrantor will transfer or pay to warrantee, at the warrantee's election, one of the following: (a) If the asset is reasonably susceptible to division, a portion of the asset equal to the warrantee's interest in it, plus 10% per annum compounded annually from the effective date to the date of payment; or (b) The fair market value of the warrantee's interest in the asset on the effective date of this agreement, plus 10% per annum compounded annually from the effective date of this agreement.

G. If either party decides to claim any rights under bankruptcy laws, that party must notify the other of this intention in writing at least 14 days before filing the petition, including the name, address, and phone number of the attorney, if any, who represents the party in that petition and the court in which the petition will be filed. The party receiving notice will have five business days to elect to participate jointly with the notifying party in a consolidation proceeding and may choose to be represented by the same attorney, if any.

H. These provisions will not impair the availability of any other remedy arising from nondisclosure of community assets or debts.

**Note about pension plans.** Read chapter 3.6(b). If there is a community interest in a pension plan, it must be dealt with in your settlement agreement. If it is to be given entirely to the employee-spouse, list it in item A or B above. If the pension will be divided by the payoff method (see 3.6(b)), you shouldn't try to do the SA or the Judgment orders yourself. Call Divorce Helpline and get help.
**Note about family home.** Spouses may agree to (a) sell and divide the home now; or (b) a buy-out by one spouse, maybe with a promissory note to the other (payments can be deferred to some future time or event); or (c) joint ownership. Get DealMaker software or call Divorce Helpline for help if you plan to use method (c).

IX. TAXES:
A. Any tax refunds for the current fiscal year shall be distributed as follows: **(specify).**
B. Any tax deficiencies for the current year shall be paid as follows: **(specify).**
C. For any year in which support payments for said child are not over ___ days in arrears, the parent paying support may claim the tax exemption for **(names of children)**, and the recipient will execute a waiver of the right to claim the exemption for that year. (Note: before you do this, be sure

to analyze the effect on the amount of support paid and the net income of both parties. **CalSupport™ can give you this analysis.**)

X. RESERVATION OF JURISDICTION: The parties agree that the court shall have jurisdiction to make whatever orders may be necessary or desirable to carry out this agreement and to divide equally between the parties any community assets or liabilities omitted from division under this agreement.

XI. ADVICE OF COUNSEL: The parties recognize that the termination of the marriage, issues of child custody, visitation, child and spousal support, and division of marital property will be determined by this instrument. We recognize that we each have a right to seek advice from independent counsel of our own choosing and that we knowingly and with due regard for the importance of same have elected to proceed with this agreement.

XII. EXECUTION OF INSTRUMENTS: Each agrees to execute and deliver any documents, make all endorsements, and do all acts which are necessary or convenient to carry out the terms of this agreement.

XIII. PRESENTATION TO COURT:
    **A) Los Angeles & San Bernardino:** This agreement shall be presented to the court in any divorce proceeding between the parties, the original of this agreement will be placed in the court's case file, and the court shall be requested to accept the agreement and order the parties to comply with its provisions. It is the intention of the parties that all warranties and remedies provided in this agreement shall be preserved.
    **B) All other counties:** This agreement shall be presented to the court in any divorce proceeding between the parties, it shall be incorporated into the Judgment therein, the parties shall be ordered to comply with all its provisions, and all warranties and remedies provided in this agreement shall be preserved.

XIV. DISCLOSURES: Each party has made a full and honest disclosure to the other of all current finances and assets, and each enters into this agreement in reliance thereon. Each warrants to the other and declares under penalty of perjury that the assets and liabilities divided in this agreement constitute all of their community assets and liabilities.

XV. RESOLUTION OF DISPUTES:
With the exception of emergencies involving an imminent threat to the physical safety of either of us or a minor child, or the custody of a minor child, or the collection of back support, all disputes arising between us on any matter whatever will be resolved as follows:
    (1) If we are unable to resolve any dispute ourselves or with counseling, then we each agree to make a reasonable good-faith effort to resolve the matter in mediation. On the written request of either party, we will within 30 days submit our dispute to mediation with a mediator agreed upon by both of us. If we are unable to agree on a mediator, we will each choose one person to make a choice on our behalf, and those two persons together will appoint our mediator. We will participate in mediation in good faith, and we will each be responsible for half the cost of mediation.
    **Optional.** Unless we agree otherwise, our mediator must be a California family law attorney who specializes in family law mediation.
    (2) We are each entitled to representation in mediation by an attorney of our choice. Each party will be responsible for his or her own attorney fees.

XVI. BINDING EFFECT: This agreement, and each provision thereof, is expressly made binding upon heirs, assigns, executors, administrators, representatives, and successors in interest of each party.

Dated: _____        _____, Husband

Dated: _____        _____, Wife

**If the Department of Child Support Services (or some other court office) is providing support enforcement in your case, add this:**
The Department of Child Support Services (or other office) for the County of _____, State of California, approves the child support as agreed herein. This office claims jurisdiction only to approve the matter of support.

Dated:

_____        _____
Type or print name                              for the Department of Child Support Services

**Note: Child support, some counties.** If your settlement agreement has child support in it, some counties (Alameda, Imperial, Santa Barbara, Santa Cruz, Solano, Stanislaus, and possibly some others) want the Stipulation to Establish Child Support (Figure 18.3). A computer calculation (chapter 5.3) of the guideline amount is also required in Alameda and Imperial counties.

**Note.** If your case involves any kind of support, you *must* file an Income and Expense Declaration (chapter 16) unless you have a settlement agreement. Even if you do have a settlement agreement, many counties (Alameda, Contra Costa, Monterey, San Francisco, Santa Clara, Solano, probably many others) want to see an I&E form from *both* parties—see local rules (chapter 7.4) or call the Superior Court Clerk to see if they are required in your county. File them along with the other paperwork when you are ready to get your Judgment (chapter 20).

## Mediation and arbitration

Sometimes it isn't completely over even when it's over, especially for parents. So if any disagreement should arise after your divorce is completed, clause XV will help you stay out of court, where no family should ever go. This clause says that any disputes between you in the future will be resolved by mediation, which has a high rate of success. A mediator is trained to help people talk reasonably and listen to each other, develop options, solve problems and reach a fair settlement that they can both agree to.

**Arbitration.** In case mediation does not resolve all issues after a reasonable number of sessions, I strongly recommend that you next give serious consideration to taking your disagreements to binding arbitration rather than to court.

Like court, arbitration is an adversarial proceeding where each side presents facts, documents, witnesses and arguments to the arbitrator and a decision is imposed. This is far better than court because it is more informal and conducted in a private conference room by a paid arbitrator instead of a judge in a public courtroom. Binding arbitration is final on all issues and will almost always be incorporated directly into a Judgment once you present the arbitrator's decision to the court. As with any Judgment, when it comes to minor children, if facts change over time, courts will always be willing to review child custody and child support decisions.

**Speed and privacy.** Mediation and arbitration are often referred to together as alternative dispute resolution (ADR). Court hearings and records are open to the public, while ADR is private and discreet. More important, courts are slow, complicated, expensive, and impersonal. If you were ever to end up there, the judge won't know you or your family and won't have much time or patience to learn about you or your problems. Unlike court, when you select your mediator, you can pick someone with a talent for conciliation who can take some time to explore options and solutions for your problems.

**Choosing a mediator.** In general, you are looking for a local family law attorney who primarily does mediation, very little or no litigation in courts. However, it might be reasonable to choose a mediator who is not a family law attorney if the primary issue is parenting or if your problems are primarily due to your rocky relationship. However, if your issues are more about money and property than personalities or parenting, a family law attorney-mediator is a good choice. All of Divorce Helpline's family law attorneys specialize in mediation.

**Choosing an arbitrator.** Your arbitrator should definitely be a family law attorney or a retired family court judge from your state. Legal knowledge and experience with the law is essential to conducting an arbitration correctly. Divorce Helpline attorneys are expert arbitrators.

**Private Judges—Maximum speed and privacy.** A private judge is an attorney who has been trained and certified to act as a temporary judge. A private judge has the same power as any judge and can decide disagreements, process your Judgment and all of your other paperwork, and get your case filed in court without the long delays involved in having the clerk's office process your paperwork. This will save you a lot of time and effort. A private judge can also manage your paperwork and settlement agreement so that the financial details of your divorce remain private. Get our free report on private judges at www.nolodivorce.com/PJ. Divorce Helpline has two private judges on staff, so if you are interested in speed, privacy and special attention, give Divorce Helpline a call.

## Looking ahead—Getting off to a smooth start

The most important thing you need to know about getting your case started is how to do it in a way that minimizes upset and smooths the path toward a peaceful outcome. Whether you do your own paperwork or have someone do it for you, be sure to read page 106, "Softening the Blow."

## DealMaker™ Settlement Agreement Software $64⁹⁵

DealMaker™ guides you through every step—entering information and making decisions—then it produces a comprehansive draft agreement for you ready for signatures or review by an attorney-mediator. The power of software takes you much further than the simple sample agreement in this book. DealMaker offers excellent guidance when dealing with real estate or retirement funds, and it is especially good with parenting plans. DealMaker is easy to use, with tips on each screen and in help files that guide you with information and advice. Requires Windows and monitor resolution of 1024 x 768 or higher.

**Get more information or DOWNLOAD a free trial version at www.nolodivorce.com/CA**

**DealMaker Divorce Helpline bundle**       **www.nolotech.com/DHL.html**
You get **DealMaker** software plus **two consultations** with a Divorce Helpline attorney—one pre-agreement consultation of up to 30 minutes and one re-view of your agreement—after it is completed but before you sign it—of up to 30 minutes. The two can't be combined. **You save 31%** . . . . $425 **$290**

**Divorce Helpline special rates for DealMaker users** . . . . . . . . . Call (800) 359-7004

# Part Two:
# How to do your own
# Regular Dissolution

# The Chapters in Part Two

## WE·CAN DO IT FOR YOU

You probably have important things to do with your time, so if your plate is already full, let us take this red-tape burden off your hands. You will feel better knowing that your paperwork will be done promptly and correctly by Divorce Helpline's staff of family law attorneys and documents experts.

 (800) 359-7004

# DOING YOUR OWN FORMS

This part of the book tells you exactly how to do your own Regular Dissolution. Chapter 2.2 describes Regular and Summary Dissolutions and tells you how to choose which one to use.

## How hard is it? Should you get help?

Doing your own divorce is not about filling out forms—it's about thinking things through and making decisions. Doing your own paperwork takes a bit of clerical skill, care and persistence. Even easy cases take some time and careful thought, so don't expect to do these forms in one day or even a few days. Just take it one step at a time and you'll be fine.

Millions of people have done divorces entirely by themselves using this book. The law and paperwork may seem complicated, and while the majority of clerks are lovely and will help you as much as they are allowed, dealing with the court bureaucracy can sometimes be trying (to put it nicely).

**Can you do your own paperwork?** Yes, almost certainly. Your real question is, "What do I have to lose if I don't do it right?" Not much? Do it. A lot? Get help. If you can afford a few hundred dollars, your time might be better spent on your job, your children, and getting on with your life.

Skim the next chapters to get an idea of how it might feel to do it yourself. Then review chapter 1.9 (Who can help?) to decide if you want to get help and from whom. Even if you do get help, if you use this book you will still be in charge, still "doing your own divorce," still far better off.

## When and how to start

**Respondent.** If you are the Respondent, your case has already been started, so go to chapter 11 and find out how to file your Response.

**Petitioner.** You need to plan carefully when and how you will deliver the papers, as how you do this will set the tone for the future. Typically, one spouse is ready to act long before the other has accepted the idea of a divorce—a primary cause of a lot of conflict. You don't want to frighten or anger your spouse into running to an attorney and taking the case into conflict. Take some time to prepare your spouse and let him/her get used to the idea that it's going to happen. However, if you are dealing with an abuser/controller, there's not much point to talking until you establish a position of power. There are a variety of ways to do that, from the beginning (see *How to Solve Divorce Problems*, chapters 3–4).

## Softening the blow

Unless you *want* your Petition to arrive as a shocking surprise—a sure way to start a war—you should tell your spouse ahead of time that papers are coming and there's lots of time to talk and work things out before a Response is necessary. Send a letter saying that you are filing papers to get the case on record, but you very much want an agreement and you promise not to take the case further without giving 30 days' written notice. If you prepared your Petition so that you *can't* go forward without either an agreement or filing an Amended Petition (page 125–126), be sure to point this out. These steps let your spouse know there's no need to respond in a hurry, that there's time to talk. Send Respondent a copy of this book. Good information really helps.

**If your spouse responds,** you have only two ways to proceed: by agreement or by trial. You *really* don't want a trial, so work hard on getting an agreement. Get *Make Any Divorce Better* to learn how to reduce conflict and negotiate an agreement, and send a copy to your Ex. Or call Divorce Helpline for expert problem-solving assistance. Ask your spouse to call, too, so they can explain things to both of you.

## 7.1  How to use the forms

All dissolutions in California must be filed on forms published by the Judicial Council. There is a complete set on the companion CD that you can fill out on a computer. Almost all forms have been "enabled," so you can save the data you enter by using the File > Save function in Adobe Reader 8 or later.

**No computer? No problem!** Use a friend's or go to an internet cafe. Many public libraries have computers for public use. As a last resort, just print the forms in blank and fill them out by hand or with a typewriter, as described below. For more information on how to use these forms, read the file "How to Use the Forms," found in the Forms folder on the companion CD.

You won't need all the forms on the CD. You won't even need all of the forms discussed in this book—just use the ones you need for your case, as explained in the instructions. In chapters below, you'll find a description of each form with detailed instructions on how to fill it out. But first, here are some general instructions that apply to all forms.

## Generally

**Get it together.** Keep your papers safe, neat, organized, and all together in one place.

**Type size.** If you prepare forms on a computer, the type is already specified in the official forms, so just accept whatever appears there when you enter data. For other documents (attachments, settlement agreement) use 12 point Times or Times New Roman.

**Typewriters.** Does anyone still have a typewriter? If so, you'll need to print the blank forms from files on the CD and then fill them out with your typewriter. You have to use the larger size type (Pica), as some clerks will occasionally refuse forms with smaller type (Elite).

**Hand printed?** If you have no other choice, you can fill out forms by hand. Black ink is okay, but dark blue is better, so you can tell which copies are original. Print very neatly, because forms that are difficult to read will irritate clerks and judges and you don't want that.

**Color your world.** Some counties used to require that certain documents be filed on colored paper, but in 2007, Rules of Court §§ 1.31(f), 1.35(f), and 2.103 superseded local rules and all court documents must now be filed on white paper, at least 20-pound weight. If a clerk returns a document and requests it on colored paper, you have two choices: either file it again with a note calling the clerk's attention to the above Rules of Court, or just do as the clerk asks. Sometimes that's easier.

**Printing and stapling your forms.** When you print a two-sided form, it is okay to print it on two one-sided sheets. Whenever you file a form that is longer than one page, the pages of each copy of the form should be stapled together at the top. If you want to make an extra effort, courts like two-sided forms tumbled—that is, printed with the second side upside down on the back. But doing it this way is more trouble and entirely optional.

**Sign in blue.** Not a legal requirement, but it's a *very* good idea to sign documents in blue ink so both you and the clerk can tell easily which copy is the original.

## Figure 7.1 HOW TO FILL OUT THE CAPTION

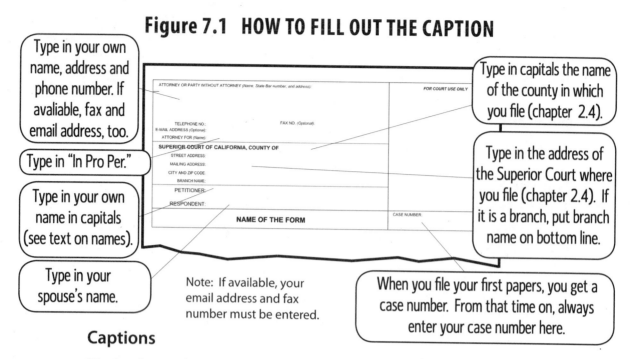

Type in your own name, address and phone number. If available, fax and email address, too.

Type in "In Pro Per."

Type in your own name in capitals (see text on names).

Type in your spouse's name.

Note: If available, your email address and fax number must be entered.

Type in capitals the name of the county in which you file (chapter 2.4).

Type in the address of the Superior Court where you file (chapter 2.4). If it is a branch, put branch name on bottom line.

When you file your first papers, you get a case number. From that time on, always enter your case number here.

## Captions

The heading at the top of each form is called a caption. Slight variations cropped up over the years, so you'll have to adapt, but basically, it goes as shown above.

## Petitioner/Respondent/In pro per

The Petitioner is the person who files papers to start the case; the Respondent is the other person. The words "in pro per" appear in various places. This is abbreviated Latin, meaning that you are appearing for yourself without an attorney.

## Dates

Best to spell them out, e.g.: August 12, 2012. If cramped, abbreviate: Aug. 12, 2012.

## Names

While not required, it is best to use full names, but be consistent: names should appear exactly the same each time, including your signatures. The court won't know that John Smith, J.W. Smith, John W. Smith and J. Wilson Smith are the same person. It is better to type names in capitals. Use names in normal order—last names go last. Use the wife's married name, unless the form asks specifically for her maiden name, or unless she used her maiden name during the marriage.

## Court address

Call the County Clerk's Office, Civil Filings desk, and ask which branch you should file in and the name and address for that branch. For a list of California Superior courts, look in the Court_Addresses folder on the companion CD, or go to **www.nolodivorce.com/links** or **www.courts.ca.gov/find-my-court.htm**.

## Change of address or other contact information

Once you have filed papers in the case, if any contact information that appeared on your captions should change, it is *essential* to serve the other side (see chapter 12.3) with notice of the change. Serve them with a *copy* of form MC-040 and file the *original* with a Proof of Service (chapter 13) with the court. The form can be found in the Kit section of the companion CD, with instructions.

## Number of copies

You need the original and two copies—original for the court and copies for you and the other party, and make an extra copy while you're at it. Some counties want an extra copy of each form when you file in a branch office.

## Additional pages (illustrated on next page)

If you need more room to complete any item on a form, use the Additional Page. Identify each item being continued by labelling it, "Continuation of Item Number __." (Note that the Property Declaration (chapter 15) has its own continuation form to use.) You can also use this form to make a declaration if one is ever required.

**Computer users:** This form, provided by the Judicial Council, enters single-spaced text that is *not* lined up with numbers on the side, but their forms are like Rules of Court, so just use it as is and don't worry about trying to make the text double-spaced or lined up with the numbers.

**Short captions**, like the one in figure 7.2 below, are acceptable with names in either order, last name first or last name last. Try to be consistent, but the Judicial Council forms do it one way on some forms and the other way on others. Just go along with however they do it.

# 7.2  Privacy

Court documents are public, so you don't want Social Security or financial account numbers on view for identity thieves. So, on any document filed with the court, for account numbers use only the last four digits, preceded by a code number associated with that item. So, for example: R1 ****-5678 (or Conf. 1 ****-5678) could be your Social Security number in all documents filed with the court, and R6 ****-3210 (or Conf. 6 ****-3210) could be a Schwab account. Keep a private list of each code with the related full account number.

**But note:** Use coding only on documents filed in court. The other party has a right to all account numbers, so for any document sent to the other party

# Figure 7.2 ADDITIONAL PAGE
## Form MC-020
## (discussed on previous page)

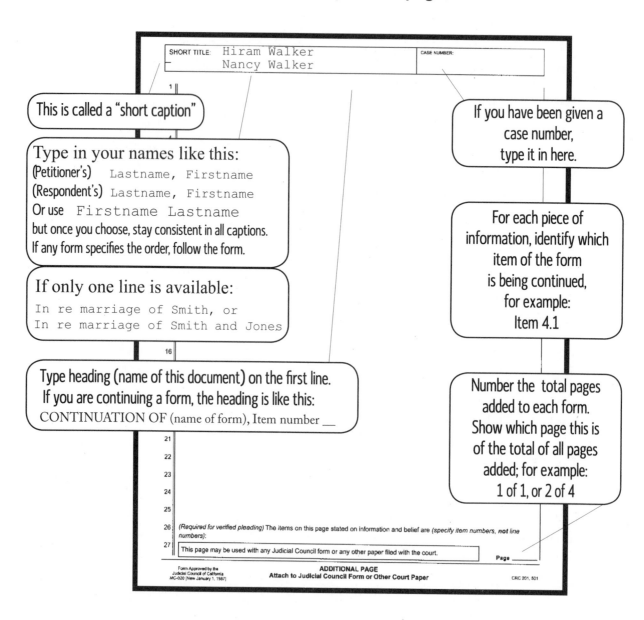

SHORT TITLE: Hiram Walker / Nancy Walker          CASE NUMBER:

This is called a "short caption"

Type in your names like this:
(Petitioner's)  Lastname, Firstname
(Respondent's)  Lastname, Firstname
Or use  Firstname Lastname
but once you choose, stay consistent in all captions.
If any form specifies the order, follow the form.

If only one line is available:
In re marriage of Smith, or
In re marriage of Smith and Jones

Type heading (name of this document) on the first line.
If you are continuing a form, the heading is like this:
CONTINUATION OF (name of form), Item number __

If you have been given a case number, type it in here.

For each piece of information, identify which item of the form is being continued, for example: Item 4.1

Number the total pages added to each form. Show which page this is of the total of all pages added; for example: 1 of 1, or 2 of 4

(Required for verified pleading) The items on this page stated on information and belief are (specify item numbers, not line numbers):

This page may be used with any Judicial Council form or any other paper filed with the court.          Page ____

Form Approved by the
Judicial Council of California
MC-020 [New January 1, 1987]

**ADDITIONAL PAGE**
**Attach to Judicial Council Form or Other Court Paper**

CRC 201, 501

that includes coded account numbers, also include a list of the actual numbers associated with each code number. If some day you are asked by the court to identify your information, you must file form MC-120 (figure 7.3). Do not file it unless asked. This form can be found on the CD that comes with this book.

**Settlement Agreements.** If you file a Settlement Agreement with the court, use your code number in place of all Social Security or financial account numbers in the copy that goes to the court.

## Figure 7.3 CONFIDENTIAL REFERENCE LIST OF IDENTIFIERS
### (Form MC-120)

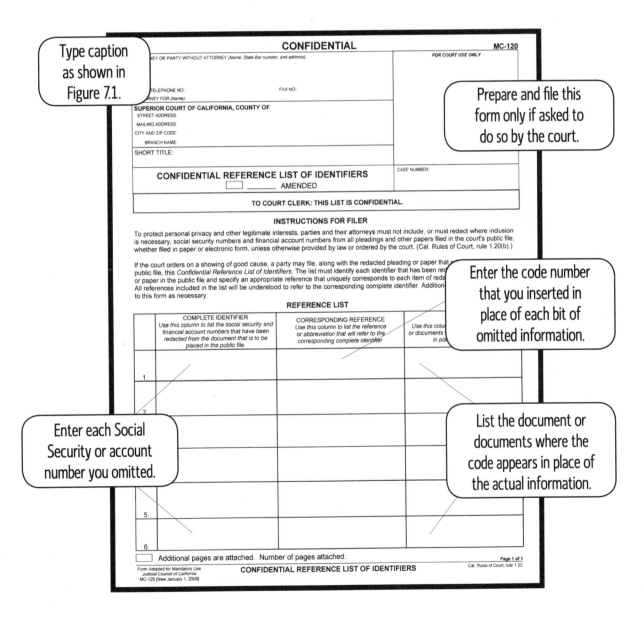

## 7.3 How to file your papers

Domestic partners can file anywhere in California, but for married people, the county in which you file is determined by the residency requirement (chapter 2.4) and must be where one of the parties lives. Before you start, call the Superior Court Clerk's office and ask some questions:

- How to find the desk at the Clerk's office where you file divorce papers?
- Is there a branch court where you can file papers that is nearer to you than the main office?
- Exactly how much are the filing fees for a dissolution, and can filing fees be paid by personal check?
- Are there any printed instructions for people filing "in pro per"?
- Are local forms required in an uncontested dissolution? Or for filing in a branch court?
- Where can you get copies of local forms (if required) ?
- How long does it take to process dissolution paperwork at each stage?

You must punch two holes, centered at the top of every sheet you file, using a standard two-hole punch. The clerks won't do it for you, but they usually have a two-hole punch at the counter. **Los Angeles County** wants an extra copy of the front page of your Petition. Humor them.

**Privacy.** Check all forms before you file them to make sure there are no complete account or Social Security numbers on them. The same goes for attachments, such as pay stubs or the settlement agreement (section 7.2). The Case Registry form is excepted, as it is not on public view.

**Filing in person.** Take your papers to the Superior Court Clerk's office, civil filings desk, and hand them over. Include all copies with the original so they can stamp them. If your county has branch courts, you can file at the main branch or at a branch where either party resides. Filing can be done by mail, but going in person is much more certain and immediate, if it is not too inconvenient for you.

**Filing by mail.** If you file by mail, be sure to include a self-addressed, stamped envelope for the return of all copies. In busy counties it can take some time to get your papers through the mill, so be patient.

When you file your first papers, you pay your filing fee (see below). The clerk will give you a case number and, from that time on, all documents you file *must* have your case number on them.

Clerks will not give you legal advice because they are not attorneys and it would be illegal for them to do so, but if they feel like it, they can help you a lot with information about the filing of papers and how matters are handled in their county. Don't be afraid to ask questions.

## SASE envelope for free document review service

A clerk recently confided that fewer than 1% of divorce papers go through the first time, so don't be surprised if yours come back with a page of notes of things they want done differently. This is great! Think of it as a free document review service and carefully do whatever they ask. This is why, when you file papers, you need to include a self-addressed, stamped envelope that is large enough and with enough postage to get all papers back. If you need your Judgment by a particular date, say to remarry or by December 31 for tax purposes, you should allow several extra weeks for this inevitable and invaluable part of the process.

## Clerk errors

Clerks make mistakes. Are you shocked? It doesn't happen every day, but now and then a clerk will send back papers that are correct or demand a fee that is not required. If this happens, the best thing would be to do whatever they ask. If you feel strongly about it, double check to make sure you followed our instructions exactly, then resubmit your papers and see if you get a different result. If you are in a hurry, take them in personally and try a different clerk or talk it over with the supervisor. However, unless you have a very important reason, it almost always works out better if you just do whatever they ask.

## Non vexas amanuensis

If you run into an unpleasant clerk, stay polite no matter what. If necessary, try to get another clerk to help you, even if you have to come back. Never, never, never piss off a clerk, even if they deserve it. *Never.* There's nothing to be gained and it can come back to haunt you if you need a clerk's cooperation some other day. By the way, the header above is Latin (so beloved in the law) for "don't irritate the clerk."

## Filing fees

Filing fees are paid when you file your first papers. It is now $435 in most counties, although a very few have bumped it to $450. Some counties will accept personal checks, otherwise fees should be paid with cash or a money order. Some counties also charge an additional fee to cover mandatory mediation services. Call the Superior Court Clerk's office to get the exact filing fee in your county.

A response fee equal to the first filing fee (above) is charged for anything filed by the Respondent. There is no charge for an Appearance & Waiver when filed by a member of the armed forces.

If filed by the Petitioner, there is no fee for filing a settlement agreement, a stipulated judgment, stipulation to the date of termination, stipulated post-judgment modification of child support, or stipulation to modify a settlement agreement. If a clerk tries to charge for any of these, refer them to Government Code § 70671.

## Waiver of fees

If you are *very* poor, you won't have to pay filing fees. You don't have to be totally destitute, but not far from it, either. Your application will be easy and you will be allowed to file for free if (1) you receive financial assistance (SSI, SSP, TANF/CalWORKS), food stamps, county relief, or general assistance), or (2) if your *gross* monthly income is less than amounts shown in the table below. These amounts are revised annually in March—check the latest form FL-001 for current amounts. In L.A., if you don't fit in category (1), you must attach a recent tax return or a letter from your employer on a company letterhead, verifying monthly wages. If you don't fit the first two categories, but your income is not enough to pay for the common necessaries of life for yourself and the people you support and also pay court fees, then you have to prove your case by filling out detailed income and expense forms. Don't be afraid to try it; you have nothing to lose but time and trouble.

| Number in family | Family income |
|---|---|
| 1 | $ 1,215.63* |
| 2 | 1,638.55 |
| 3 | 2,061.46 |
| 4 | 2,484.38 |
| 5 | 2,907.30 |
| 6 | 3,330.21 |
| Each additional | 422.92 |

You will find a set of forms to apply for a waiver of court fees, with instructions, in the Kit section of the companion CD, or you can get a set for free from the Clerk's office.

## 7.4 Local forms and rules

Some counties require local forms in addition to the official set. Look for them at your county's Superior Court web site. You can find links to each court's web site at **www.nolodivorce.com/links** and links to local rules for every county are at **www.courts.ca.gov/3027.htm**. Or, call your court clerk's office and ask what local forms they use in an uncontested dissolution and get copies. Ask if they have printed copies of local rules and/or instructions for people doing their own paperwork.

If you come across a form you can't figure out, just mail us two blank copies with a **stamped, self-addressed envelope** and we will send instructions.

**Branch courts and cover sheets.** If you file your first papers in a branch instead of the main office, some counties want a Certificate or Declaration of Assignment (Alameda, Riverside, San Bernardino, San Mateo, Ventura). Los Angeles County want a cover sheet in every case, even if you file in the main branch. On the next page, we show you the L.A. form as an example, but note that forms from other counties look different. They all want to know what court district you are filing in and the reason, which is invariably because you or Respondent reside in that district. So if you are asked, check a box or write: "Petitioner (or Respondent) resides in said district at (enter the address). The time for trial, if requested, would be about 15 minutes."

**ADR information packet.** Many counties now require a notice about Alternative Dispute Resolution (ADR) with the Petition and Response. This form explains the advantages of mediation, arbitration, and possibly other alternatives to taking your case to court. Check local rules or your Superior Court Clerk's office.

**L.A. wants a Family Law Worksheet** for every case filed in the Central District. Some counties require attendance at a program for parties with children and will probably require you to serve notice of the program on Respondent. Santa Barbara also wants an extra $50 with the filing fee to cover the cost of the program. They'll tell you what they want and give you papers for it when the Petition is filed.

The next time you are likely to meet a local form is when you request a hearing. This is described in chapter 20.2 with an example at figure 20.4.

## Figure 7.4  **FAMILY LAW COVER SHEET** (Certificate of Assignment)
### (Los Angeles County)

> Fill in the caption as shown in Fig 7.1 and enter Petitioner's and Respondent's names and addresses where requested.

NAME, ADDRESS, AND TELEPHONE NUMBER OF ATTORNEY OR PARTY WITHOUT ATTORNEY:   STATE BAR NUMBER   Reserved for Clerk's File Stamp

ATTORNEY FOR (Name):

**SUPERIOR COURT OF CALIFORNIA, COUNTY OF LOS ANGELES**
COURTHOUSE ADDRESS:

PETITIONER/PLAINTIFF:

RESPONDENT/DEFENDANT:

FAMILY LAW CASE COVER SHEET
CERTIFICATE OF GROUNDS FOR ASSIGNMENT TO DISTRICT   CASE NUMBER:

> Your case number.

**Case Filing Instructions**

This cover sheet is required so that the court can assign your case to the correct court district for filing and hearing. It satisfies the requirement for a certificate authorizing filing in the district, as set forth in Los Angeles Superior Court Rules 2(d) and 5.2. It must be completed and submitted to the court along with the original Complaint or Petition in ALL Family cases filed in any district of the Los Angeles County Superior Court. This form is not required in Abandonment & Emancipation cases, which are to be filed at Children's Court.

I. Fill in the requested information.

a) Enter address of Petitioner
ADDRESS:   CITY:   STATE   ZIP CODE

b) Enter address of Respondent. **DO NOT COMPLETE THIS ITEM IF THIS IS A MINOR'S CONTRACT**
ADDRESS:   CITY:   STATE

MINOR CHILDREN INVOLVED?   ☐ YES   HOW MANY? _____   ☐ NO

> Indicate if minors involved and, if so, how many.

II. Select the correct district:

a.   Under Column 1 below, check the one type of action which best describes the nature of this case.
b.   In Column 2 below, circle the reason for your choice of district that applies to the type of action.

**Applicable Reason for Choosing District (See Column 2 below)**

1.  May be filed in Central District.
2.  District where one or more of the parties reside.
3.  Child resides within the district.
4.  District where Petitioner resides.

> Items 2 - 4 are reasons for filing in a branch court.

| **1** TYPE OF ACTION (Check only one) (Continued) | **2** APPLICABLE REASONS (See above) |
|---|---|
| ☐ A5520   Dissolution of Marriage | 1. 2 |
| ☐ A5525   Summary Dissolution of Marriage | 1. 2 |
| ☐ A5521   Dissolution of Domestic Partnership | 1. 2 |
| ☐ A5530   Nullity of Void or Voidable Marriage | 1. 2 |
| ☐ A5531   Nullity of Void or Voidable Domestic Partnership | 1. 2 |

FAM 020
(Rev 11/11)   FAMILY LAW CASE COVER SHEET
CERTIFICATE OF GROUNDS FOR ASSIGNMENT TO DISTRICT

> Check box to show what kind of case you have and circle number 1 or 2 or both to show the reason(s) case to be filed in the court indicated at item IV.

## Second page

Enter short caption as shown in Fig. 7.2. Enter address of minor child (if any) at item III, and at item IV enter the name of the branch court where you wish to file your papers. Date and sign the form.

**Note.** You can download this form at **www.lacourt.org/forms/familylaw**.

# CHECKLIST

The checklist on the next page is your "How to Do It" guide; a step-by-step list that shows you what to do and when to do it, with references to the chapters where you will find detailed information about each step.

As you will see from the checklist on the next page, you only have to go through four steps to get your dissolution:

| Step | Task | Chapters |
|---|---|---|
| One | File the Petition or Response | 9–11 |
| Two | Serve papers on your spouse | 12–13 |
| Three | Declarations of Disclosure | 14 |
| Four | Get your Judgment | 15–21 |

Each step has a choice to make, a few forms to fill out, and a task to perform. You only need to use the chapters and the forms that apply to your own case. While doing the forms is not the easiest or most fun thing you will ever do, no case uses all the forms in this book, so don't be put off by the number and variety that you see on these pages.

## More help

You should also take a look at forms FL-107 and FL-182, which were developed by the Judicial Council to help people doing their own divorces understand and correctly complete their paperwork. They are on the CD in the Forms folder.

# CHECKLIST

Check each item as you progress

■ = a form to fill out     ▶ = a decision to make

**1**
- ☐ ■ **SUMMONS** (chapter 9)
- ☐ ■ **PETITION** (chapter 10)
- ☐ ■ **DECLARATION UNDER UCCJEA** (if there are minor children of this marriage) (chapter 10)
- ☐ ■ Local form required in some counties when filing in a branch court. Ask the clerk (chapter 7.4)
- ☐ **Optional:** Do Preliminary Disclosure documents now (step 3 below; chapter 14) and serve them with the documents above.
- ☐ **Task:** File papers with Clerk (chapter 7.3). If you are very poor, read chapter 7.3 and consider applying for waiver of fees.
- ☐ ■ **JOINDER.** If you need to join a retirement plan or fund (see chapter 3.6(b)), now is the best time to do it. If pressed for time, you can do the joinder shortly after filing the Petition, which requires additional Proofs of Service. Sooner is better.

**2**
- ☐ ▶ **Decision:** How to serve papers? Read chapter 12. Prepare additional forms as required by your method of service.
  **Option:** File the Response now or the A&W (chapter 12.7) and skip this step.

| Personal Service | Acknowledgment | Certified Mail |
|---|---|---|
| (chapter 12.4)<br>no other forms | ■ **ACKNOWLEDGMENT**<br>(chapter 12.5) | (Return receipt comes<br>from the Post Office) |

- ☐ ■ **PROOF OF SERVICE** (ch. 13) Attach the original Summons and forms required by your method of service, as above.
- ☐ **Task:** Get papers served (chapter 12). Make sure Proof of Service is filled out correctly and signed by person serving papers.
  **Task:** File the Proof of Service with any attachments required by your method of service.
  **Note:** Some counties (like Santa Clara) want these papers and all the rest (steps 2–4) filed at one time when you are ready to complete your case and get your Judgment. It is permitted and convenient to do this in any county.

**3**
- ☐ ■ **PRELIMINARY DECLARATION OF DISCLOSURE** (chapter 14) Petitioner must, Resp. should. Served, not filed in court.
- ☐ ■ **LIST OF ASSETS & DEBTS** (chapter 14) Served, not filed in court.
- ☐ ■ **INCOME & EXPENSE DECLARATIONS** (chapter 16) Served, not filed in court.
- ☐ ■ **DECLARATION RE SERVICE OF DISCLOSURE** (figure14.3) This is filed in court with a Proof of Service (chapter 14.2).
- ☐ **Task:** Have someone serve the Preliminary Declaration of Disclosure on Respondent, preferably within 60 days of service of the Summons. That person then signs either a Proof of Service by Mail (figure 13.3) or Proof of Personal Service (figure 13.4).

**4**
- ☐ ■ **JUDGMENT** If you have an agreement, attach it to Judgment with other Judgment attachments as required (chapter 18)
- ☐ **File with Judgment if you have child or spousal support**

| File with Judgment if you have child or spousal support | If you have a minor child, also file |
|---|---|
| ■ **WAGE ASSIGNMENT ORDER** (figure 19.1 or 19.2)<br>■ **REQUEST FOR HRG. RE WAGE ASSIGNMENT** (blank) | ■ **NOTICE OF RIGHTS & RESPONSIBILITIES** (ch. 18.4)<br>■ **INFORMATION SHEET RE CHANGES OF SUPPORT**<br>■ **CHILD SUPPORT CASE REGISTRY** (chapter 18.4) |

- ▶ Decision: Will you go to a hearing or get your Judgment by mail? Read chapter 20.

| ▶ ☐ **IF A RESPONSE WAS FILED** | ☐ **IF NO RESPONSE WAS FILED** |
|---|---|
| ■ **APPEARANCE & WAIVER** (A&W) (chapter 12.7) Signed by both parties. If Proof of Service of Summons not previously filed, be sure to return original Summons with your papers at this time. | ■ **REQUEST FOR DEFAULT** (chapter 17) with a stamped envelope addressed to Respondent's last known address with court Superior Court Clerk's return address. |

| ▶ ☐ **CASES WITH A SETTLEMENT AGREEMENT (SA)** | ☐ **CASES WITH NO SETTLEMENT AGREEMENT** |
|---|---|
| ■ **INCOME & EXPENSE FORMS** (chapter 16)<br>(Only a few counties want the I&E if you have a SA)<br>■ **DECLARATION RE SERVICE OF DISCL.** (figure 14.3)<br>■ **PROOF OF SERVICE** (of disclosure) (figure 13.3 or 13.4)<br>**Note:** You need to show that both Preliminary and Final Disclosures were served on each other. The Final can be waived if both parties file FL-144 with this set of papers. | ■ **PROPERTY DECLARATION** (chapter 15)<br>■ **INCOME & EXPENSE FORMS** (chapter 16)<br>■ **DECLARATION RE SERVICE OF DISCL.** (14.3)<br>■ **PROOF OF SERVICE** (of disclosure) (fig 13.3 or 13.4)<br>**Note:** Petitioner can waive the Final Declaration of Disclosure in the Declaration for Default Dissolution (ch. 20.1) or at a hearing. |

| ▶ ☐ **JUDGMENT BY MAIL** (chapter 20.1) | ☐ **GOING TO A HEARING** (chapter 20.3) |
|---|---|
| ■ **DECL. FOR DEFAULT DISSOLUTION** (ch. 20.1)<br><br>**Task:** Mail to Clerk together with other all papers in step 4. Include **original** Summons if not filed already. (ch. 7.3) | **Task:** Get a date for your court hearing.<br>■ Local form required in some counties to request hearing.<br>**Task:** Go to the hearing and take all Step 4 papers with you. |

- ☐ ■ **NOTICE OF ENTRY OF JUDGMENT** (chapter 21) and stamped envelopes addressed to each party, clerk's return address.

**Task:** If Judgment orders support or anything to be done in the future, have your Ex served personally (ch. 13) withl a copy of the Judgment and file a Proof of Service with the court to prove that it was done.

When you get the signed Judgment and the Notice of Entry back . . . **CELEBRATE !!**

# THE SUMMONS

## What it is

The Summons is a message from the court to the Respondent. It states that a Petition has been filed that concerns the Respondent, and that if there is no written Response within 30 days, the court may go ahead and grant the Petitioner what has been asked for. A copy of the Summons has to be served on Respondent along with the Petition (chapter 12). To make the Summons less upsetting to your spouse when served, see page 1 of chapter 7.

## Restraining orders

The back of the Summons contains restraining orders directed to *both* parties that go into effect immediately when the Summons is served (chapter 2.7). Be sure to read them, and be careful that you live within those rules until the Judgment is entered. Don't forget and transfer funds or let the kids go visiting outside California without the required notice.

When you file your first papers (chapter 8, step 1), the clerk should keep the original Summons. When you serve the first set of papers, you will include a *copy* of the Summons. However, if you happen to get the original Summons back, take very good care not to lose it, because you *must* return it when you file the Proof of Service of the Summons (chapter 13).

## How to fill it out

Fill out the Summons as shown in figure 9.1 on the next page. Prepare the original and make three copies.

**Note:** If you lose or misplace your original Summons, you are in for extra trouble because you will have to prepare and file a Declaration of Service of Lost Summons. If this misfortune happens to you, look in the Kit section in the Forms folder on the companion CD for the Lost Summons form and instructions.

## Figure 9.1  SUMMONS
### Form FL-110

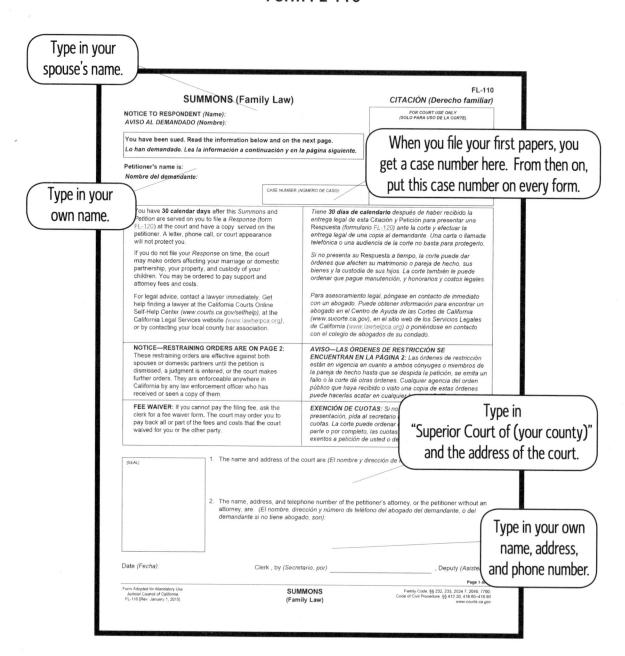

# THE PETITION

## What it is

The Petition states basic information about your union and tells the court what you want done. When it is served on Respondent (chapter 8, step 2), it gives notice of what's happening in court. If Respondent sees the Petition and declines to respond, then the judge is free to assume Respondent has no objection to letting the case go by default. See the introduction to chapter 7 for suggestions about how to defuse the effect of serving the Petition on Respondent.

## How to fill it out

Prepare the original and three copies. L.A. County wants an extra copy of the front of the Petition. If you need more space for any item, use an Additional Page form (figure 7.2) with the heading "Continuation of Petition." For each item continued, type a sub-heading that reads "Attachment n" (n = the number of the item being continued), and complete your list. The Additional Page becomes part of the Petition, so staple the original and copies to each copy of your Petition.

## NOTES FOR THE PETITION

**Item 3a or 3b.** The date of your separation is the last day you were living together as husband and wife or partners. If there is any question in your mind about what date to use, read about date of separation in chapter 3.1. If you still don't have an exact date, just get as close as you can. If you separated several times, use the most recent date. Merely sleeping together does not affect separation or dissolution.

**Item 5.** Check box 5a and 5a(1) to indicate that you want a divorce on grounds of irreconcilable differences. If you want to use other grounds or ask for a Nullity (annulment) you will require professional assistance.

**Item 8. Spousal support.** You must check a box at item 8.

**Item 8a.** To request spousal support, check box 8a and check a box to show who will receive the support you are requesting, Petitioner or Respondent.

# Figure 10.1  PETITION
## Form FL-100 (page 1)

Type caption as shown in figure 7.1.

Check this box.

Check a box to show if married or domestic partners.

Check box to show who satisfies the residency requirement. If both do, check both.

Read text note 4. Check 4a if no minor children. If there are minor children, check 4b and fill in requested information for each child and attach the Declaration re Minors (figs. 10.4 & 10.5).

Check box to show if dissolving a marriage or domestic partnership.

Dates of marriage and separation and years & months duration. Re: date of separation, see text note for item 3a.

ATTORNEY OR PARTY WITHOUT ATTORNEY (Name, State Bar number, and address):

FOR COURT USE ONLY

TELEPHONE NO.:
E-MAIL ADDRESS:
ATTORNEY FOR (Name):

FAX NO.:

**SUPERIOR COURT OF CALIFORNIA, COUNTY OF**
STREET ADDRESS:
MAILING ADDRESS:
CITY AND ZIP CODE:
BRANCH NAME:

PETITIONER:
RESPONDENT:

**PETITION FOR**

☐ AMENDED

CASE NUMBER:

|  | | |
|---|---|---|
| Dissolution (Divorce) of: | ☐ Marriage | ☐ Domestic Partnership |
| Legal Separation of: | ☐ Marriage | ☐ Domestic Partnership |
| Nullity of: | ☐ Marriage | ☐ Domestic Partnership |

1. **LEGAL RELATIONSHIP** (check all that apply):
   a. ☐ We are married.
   b. ☐ We are domestic partners and our domestic partnership was established in California.
   c. ☐ We are domestic partners and our domestic partnership was NOT established in California.

2. **RESIDENCE REQUIREMENTS** (check all that apply):
   a. ☐ Petitioner ☐ Respondent has been a resident of this state for at least six months and of this county for at least three months immediately preceding the filing of this Petition. (For a divorce, at least one person in the legal relationship described in items 1a and 1c must comply with this requirement.)
   b. ☐ We are the same sex and were married in California but are not residents of California. Neither of us lives in a state or nation that will dissolve the marriage. This case is filed in the county in which we married. Petitioner's residence (state or nation):        Respondent's residence (state or nation):
   c. ☐ Our domestic partnership was established in California. Neither of us has to be a resident or have a domicile to dissolve our partnership here.

3. **STATISTICAL FACTS**
   a. ☐ (1) Date of marriage (specify):        (2) Date of separation (specify):
       (3) Time from date of marriage to date of separation (specify):   Years   Months
   b. ☐ (1) Registration date of domestic partnership with the California Secretary of State or other state equivalent
       (2) Date of separation (specify):
       (3) Time from date of registration of domestic partnership to date of separation (specify):   Years   Months

4. **MINOR CHILDREN** (children born before (or born or adopted during) the marriage or domestic partnership):
   a. ☐ There are no minor children.
   b. ☐ The minor children are:

   | Child's name | Birthdate | Age | Sex |
   |---|---|---|---|
   | | | | |

   (1) ☐ continued on Attachment 4b.
   (2) ☐ a child who is not yet born.
   c. ☐ If there are minor children of Petitioner and Respondent, a completed Declaration Under Uniform Child Custody Jurisdiction and Enforcement Act (UCCJEA) (form FL-105) must be attached.
   d. ☐ Petitioner and Respondent signed a voluntary declaration of paternity. A copy ☐ is ☐ is not attached.

Page 1 of 3

Form Adopted for Mandatory Use
Judicial Council of California
FL-100 [Rev. January 1, 2015]

**PETITION—MARRIAGE/DOMESTIC PARTNERSHIP**
(Family Law)

Family Code, §§ 297, 299, 2320, 2330, 3409;
www.courts.ca.gov

**Item 8b Terminate spousal support.** Check 8b to ask the court to terminate spousal support, both now and in the future, and check a box to show whose right is to be terminated: Petitioner's or Respondent's or both. Or . . .

**Item 8c Reserve the matter of spousal support** for a future determination. Check a box to show whose right is to be reserved: Petitioner or Respondent or both. Or ...

**Item 8c Other.** If you have or expect to have an agreement, check here and enter "To be determined in a written agreement."

**Item 12. Restraining Orders.** Read the back of the Summons carefully; don't take the kids out of state without written permission, and don't transfer funds or do any of those other things "by accident."

## CASES WITH CHILDREN

**Item 4b.** The children listed here will include only those who are currently under 18 (or 18, enrolled full-time in high school and not self-supporting) who were born to or adopted by both you and your spouse. Don't include stepchildren who have not been formally adopted. If the wife is pregnant, include the unborn child by putting "one unborn" in the space provided for the name of child.

**Item 4c.** Fill out FL-105 Declaration Under UCCJEA as shown in figures 10.4 and 10.5 and attach it to the Petition. If you have more than two children, attach copies of form 105(A) to add more.

**Item 4d.** Refers to the Voluntary Declaration of Paternity available in many hospitals. If you happen to have one, check this box.

**Items 6a–c, Custody and Visitation.** Read chapter 4.

- To request pure joint custody, check 6a and 6b at the boxes under the "Joint" column.
- To request joint legal custody with sole physical custody to one parent, check 6a under the "Joint" column and check 6b to indicate who is to have primary physical custody.
- To request sole custody (both legal and physical) for one parent, check both 6a and 6b under the column that indicates who is to have custody.
- Check 6c to indicate which parent is to have a visitation schedule.
  > **Optional attachments:** Specifying custody or visitation arrangements in detail in the Petition is not generally necessary, but if you plan to ask for something unusual, Respondent has a right to know about it,

## Figure 10.2 PETITION
### Form FL-100 (page 2)

**Type in caption as shown in figure 7.2**

**Check boxes 5a and 5a(1).**

**If you have children, check boxes for 6a, 6b, and 6c to show what you request (see text notes on cases with children).**

**Read text note on item 8 about spousal support and fill this out accordingly.**

**Read text note on item 9 and fill this in accordingly.**

---

FL-100

PETITIONER:

RESPONDENT:

CASE NUMBER:

Petitioner requests that the court make the following orders:

5. **LEGAL GROUNDS** (Family Code sections 2200–2210, 2310–2312)

a. ☐ Divorce or ☐ Legal separation of the marriage or domestic partnership based on *(check one)*:
   (1) ☐ irreconcilable differences. (2) ☐ permanent legal incapacity to make decisions.

b. ☐ Nullity of void marriage or domestic partnership based on:
   (1) ☐ incest. (2) ☐ bigamy.

c. ☐ Nullity of voidable marriage or domestic partnership based on:
   (1) ☐ petitioner's age at time of registration of domestic partnership or marriage. (4) ☐ fraud.
   (2) ☐ prior existing marriage or domestic partnership. (5) ☐ force.
   (3) ☐ unsound mind. (6) ☐ physical incapacity.

6. **CHILD CUSTODY AND VISITATION (PARENTING TIME)**

| | Petitioner | Respondent | Joint | Other |
|---|---|---|---|---|
| a. Legal custody of children to | ☐ | ☐ | ☐ | ☐ |
| b. Physical custody of children to | ☐ | ☐ | ☐ | ☐ |
| c. Child visitation (parenting time) be granted to | ☐ | ☐ | | ☐ |

As requested in: ☐ form FL-311 ☐ form FL-312 ☐ form FL-341(C)
☐ form FL-341(D) ☐ form FL-341(E) ☐ Attachment 6c(1)

d. ☐ Determine the parentage of children born to Petitioner and Respondent before the marriage or domestic partnership.

7. **CHILD SUPPORT**

a. If there are minor children born to or adopted by Petitioner and Respondent before or during this marriage or domestic partnership, the court will make orders for the support of the children upon request and submission of financial forms by the requesting party.

b. An earnings assignment may be issued without further notice.

c. Any party required to pay support must pay interest on overdue amounts at the "legal" rate, which is currently 10 percent.

d. ☐ Other *(specify)*:

8. **SPOUSAL OR DOMESTIC PARTNER SUPPORT**

a. ☐ Spousal or domestic partner support payable to ☐ Petitioner ☐ Respondent

b. ☐ Terminate (end) the court's ability to award support to ☐ Petitioner ☐ Respondent

c. ☐ Reserve for future determination the issue of support payable to ☐ Petitioner ☐ Res

d. ☐ Other *(specify)*:

9. **SEPARATE PROPERTY**

a. ☐ There are no such assets or debts that I know of to be confirmed by the court.

b. ☐ Confirm as separate property the assets and debts in ☐ *Property Declaration* (form FL-160) ☐ Attachment 9b
   ☐ the following list. Item Confirm to

FL-100 [Rev. January 1, 2015]
**PETITION—MARRIAGE/DOMESTIC PARTNERSHIP**
(Family Law)
Page 2 of 3

in which case check a box or boxes below 6c and attach one of the forms listed there. They are on the companion CD. Take a look at these forms to see what's possible.  **Note:** FL-312 is a request for orders to prevent the abduction of a child, which is not something you should try to do yourself. If you face this threat, get help from a family law attorney.

**Item 6d—Determine parentage.** If a child of the parties was born before the marriage, you *must* check 6d. When you file your Judgment, you must attach a declaration stating facts that establish who the biological parents are. A form for this declaration, Nolo-1, is included in the companion CD in the Forms folder.

## ASSETS and DEBTS

In the Petition, you tell the court and the other party what you plan to do about your separate property (item 9) and community property (item 10). Read chapter 3 carefully, and remember that "property" includes both assets and debts.  For each kind of property, you can:

- indicate that there is none, or
- list everything on form FL-160, or
- list everything right there in the Petition (if you don't have many items), or
- list everything on an attachment (see figure 7.2), or
- you can type in "to be determined in a written agreement."

### Agreement coming?

If you plan to have a settlement agreement or have promised Respondent that you won't proceed without one, then instead of listing property, you enter "To be determined by written agreement." Doing this should make your Ex feel secure because your case can't go forward unless you present the court with a written agreement or file and serve Respondent with an Amended Petition. This way, there can be no tricks or surprises and your Ex is under no pressure to file a Response or get an attorney while you work on getting an agreement.

**Amended Petition.** If you do *not* get an agreement, then to move your case forward you have to file an Amended Petition. To do this, prepare another Petition, but this time check the "AMENDED" box in the caption, and list your assets and debts at items 9 and 10 as instructed below. File the Amended Petition with a new Summons with the words "FOR FIRST AMENDED PETITION" typed under the title "SUMMONS," have the papers served on Respondent as you did the first time, then file the new Proof of Service, as before. This might cost you an additional filing fee of about $75 and it takes more time. This is not a terrible burden, but if in doubt about getting an agreement and you don't need to soothe Respondent, then list your assets and debts in the Petition.

### Item 9, Separate Property.

- If neither spouse has any separate assets or debts, check box 9a.

- If you want anything confirmed as the separate asset or debt of you or your spouse, you need to list each item and indicate to whom it is to be confirmed (Petitioner or Respondent). If you have only a few items, check the box for "the following list" and enter your items directly on the Petition. If there's not enough room for all your items, either (a) check the box for "Property Declaration" and use form FL-160 (chapter 15), or (b) check the box for "Attachment 9b" and enter your list on an Additional Page form (figure 7.2) with the heading "Attachment 9b."

- Be sure to include any retirement plan or fund if no part was earned between marriage and separation. Do *not* list community property that has already been informally divided by the spouses—it is not separate until divided by the court and must be listed under item 10.

- **Option.** If you expect to work out a settlement agreement, check box 9(b) and check "the following list," then type in, "To be determined by written agreement of the parties."

### Item 10, Community Property.

**10a. There are no such assets or debts to be divided by the court.** Check this box only if there is *truly* no property or so little that it just doesn't matter. Property and debts of any significance *must* be dealt with under 10b even if you have already divided it, because it remains community property and you both own it as tenants-in-common until it is divided by court order. Do *not* check this box if there is or may *ever* be a disagreement about some item that you care about, or where there is any real estate, or if there is a community interest in a pension plan (chapter 3.6(b)). When you check box 10a, the court will not inquire about your community property or debst or make orders about it.

**Option—To be divided by written agreement.** If you have a settlement agreement or expect to get one, check 10b and the box "as follows," then enter "To be determined by written agreement of the parties."

# Figure 10.3  PETITION
## Form FL-100 (page 3)

Type in caption as shown in figure 7.2

Read text notes on item 10, then check 10a or 10b.

To restore Petitioner's former name, check box 11b and type in the new name exactly as she wishes it to be.

Date of signing.

Type your name.

Type "In Pro Per."

Your signature.

**10b.** Check box 10b if you have community property or debts that need to be divided in your Judgment and you do not have a written agreement. You can still work out a settlement agreement later and present it to the court when you get your Judgment. Remember, if your community estate is worth more than $5,000 net (assets minus debts) and you want an *unequal* division of it (say, all or most to one party), you *must* have a written agreement.

### List all property

If you decide to list your community assets and debts, there are three ways to do it:

- **In Property Declaration (form FL-160).** Check this box, then fill out and attach the completed Property Declaration form (chapter 15).

- **In Attachment 10b.** Check this box and use the Additional Page form (figure 7.2). Type in a heading, "Attachment 10b." Review the Property Declaration to see how items should be grouped and as a checklist for your assets and debts. Major items should be individually listed, such as cars, bank accounts, pension plans, stocks, accumulated vacation pay, trusts, and things of special importance to you. Real estate is identified by its common address and assessor's parcel number. Household goods and appliances can simply be lumped together as such.

- **As follows.** If you have only a few items, check the "as follows" box and enter your list right on the Petition. Most people need more space and will use either of the previous two options.

## Case Management or Status Conference (CMC) ?

If a Response is filed, the court is likely to start scheduling hearings to find out what's going on with your case. These are called Case Management or Status Conferences. See the last page of chapter 11 for more details.

## Family Centered Case Resolution (FCCR)?

Even if no Response has been filed, the court might require a hearing if your case does not move along efficiently. You could be required to file form FL-172, (on the companion CD). The Judicial Council suggests a timeline for dissolutions, but we don't know how closely any court will follow it.

(A) After filing the Petition, a proof of service of summons and petition should be filed within 60 days of filing the Petition;

(B) If no response has been filed, and the parties have not agreed on an extension of time to respond, a request to enter default should be submitted within 60 days after the date the response was due (90 days from filing the Petition);

(C) The petitioner's preliminary declaration of disclosure should be served within 60 days of the filing of the petition;

(D) When a default has been entered, a Judgment should be submitted within 60 days of the entry of default;

(E) When the parties have notified the court that they are actively negotiating or mediating their case, a written agreement for Judgment should be submitted within six months of the date the petition was filed, or the date that a request for a trial date is submitted.

# Notes for filling out FL-105
## (next page)

### Dealing with limited space

Detailed information about each child is required, but the space provided makes it almost impossible to complete the form on the form itself. Give it a try, but if your information doesn't fit, and it probably won't, here's what you do:

- At item 3a, if you have only one child enter "See attachment 3." If you have more than one child, enter, "All info for all minors on attachment 3."
- Use an Additional Page form (Figure 7.2), give it the heading "Attachment 3," and enter every bit of the required information for each child, following the same order and language used on the form. Now you have plenty of room.
- At the bottom of page 2, enter the total number of pages attached.

### More than two children

If you have more than two minor children and all of your information for the first two children miraculously fit on FL-105, then add additional children on form FL-105A. However, if your information did not fit and you used an Additional Page form, simply enter the information for all children on the additional pages.

### Keeping addresses secret

If there is a threat of violence or harassment in your case, you can keep your address(es) secret. Check the box at item 2, and for each child who lives with you, check the "confidential" box in the address column and do not give your address. There is a slight chance this will cause you to be called in for a hearing when you apply to get your Judgment by mail (chapter 20).

## Figure 10.4  DECLARATION UNDER UCCJEA
### Form FL-105  (page 1)

**Type in caption as shown in figure 7.1.**

**Name, place of birth, date of birth, and sex of first child.**

**Child's present address (city and state). Enter name, address, and relationship of child's custodian.**

**Child's addresses and custodian(s) for past five years.**

**If there are more than two children, check this box and give same info for each child on form FL-105(A) (on the CD).**

**Number of minor children of this marriage at time of filing (spell out the number).**

**If there's a second child, type in name, birthplace, birth date, and sex.**

**If residence info is same as for first child, check box, otherwise type it in below.**

**If a child lived in more than four places in five years, check this box and continue on an additional page (see Fig. 7.2).**

FL-105/GC-120

ATTORNEY OR PARTY WITHOUT ATTORNEY (Name, State Bar number, and address):

FOR COURT USE ONLY

TELEPHONE NO.:  FAX NO. (Optional):
E-MAIL ADDRESS (Optional):
ATTORNEY FOR (Name):

SUPERIOR COURT OF CALIFORNIA, COUNTY OF
STREET ADDRESS:
MAILING ADDRESS:
CITY AND ZIP CODE:
BRANCH NAME:

PETITIONER: (This section applies only to family law cases.)
RESPONDENT:
OTHER PARTY:

GUARDIANSHIP OF (Name): (This section applies only to guardianship cases.)
Minor

CASE NUMBER:

**DECLARATION UNDER UNIFORM CHILD CUSTODY JURISDICTION AND ENFORCEMENT ACT (UCCJEA)**

1. I am a party to this proceeding to determine custody of a child.
2. [ ] My present address and the present address of each child residing with me is confidential under Family Code section 3429 as I have indicated in item 3.
3. There are (specify number):  minor children who are subject to this proceeding, as follows:
(Insert the information requested below. The residence information must be given for the last FIVE years.)

| a. Child's name | Place of birth | Date of birth | Sex |
| --- | --- | --- | --- |

| Period of residence | Address | Person child lived with (name and complete current address) | Relationship |
| --- | --- | --- | --- |
| to present | [ ] Confidential | [ ] Confidential | |
| to | Child's residence (City, State) | Person child lived with (name and complete current address) | |
| to | Child's residence (City, State) | Person child lived with (name and complete current address) | |
| to | Child's residence (City, State) | Person child lived with (name and complete current address) | |

| b. Child's name | Place of birth | Date of birth |
| --- | --- | --- |

[ ] Residence information is the same as given above for child a.
(If NOT the same, provide the information below.)

| Period of residence | Address | Person child lived with (name and complete current address) |
| --- | --- | --- |
| to present | [ ] Confidential | [ ] Confidential |
| to | Child's residence (City, State) | Person child lived with (name and complete current address) |
| to | Child's residence (City, State) | Person child lived with (name and complete current address) |
| to | Child's residence (City, State) | Person child lived with (name and complete current address) |

c. [ ] Additional residence information for a child listed in item a or b is continued on attachment 3c.
d. [ ] Additional children are listed on form FL-105(A)/GC-120(A). (Provide all requested information for addit

Form Adopted for Mandatory Use
Judicial Council of California
FL-105/GC-120 [Rev. January]

DECLARATION UNDER UNIFORM CHILD CUSTODY

Probate Code, §§ 1510(f), 1512

# Figure 10.5 DECLARATION UNDER UCCJEA
## Form FL-105 (page 2)

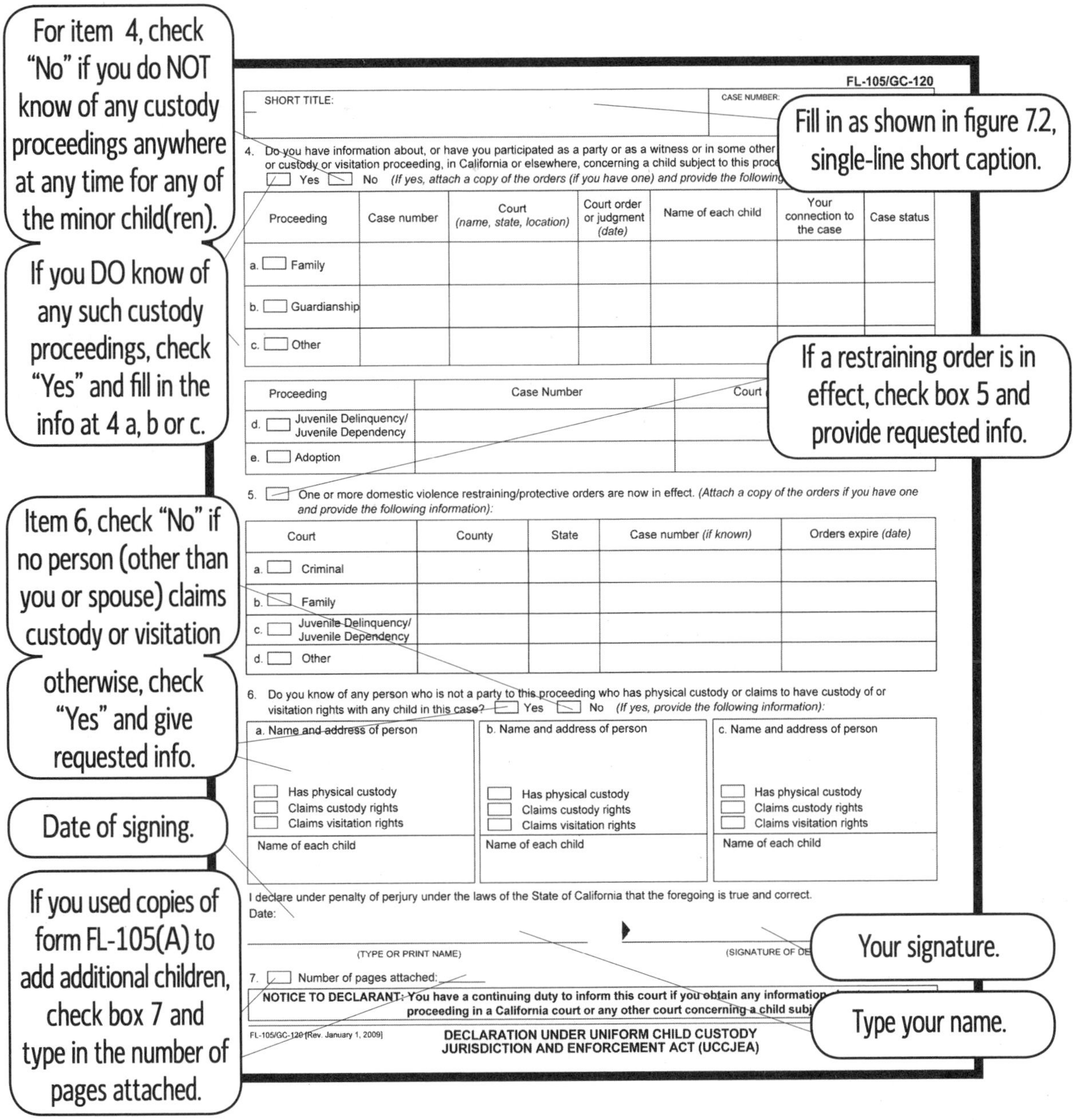
For item 4, check "No" if you do NOT know of any custody proceedings anywhere at any time for any of the minor child(ren).
If you DO know of any such custody proceedings, check "Yes" and fill in the info at 4 a, b or c.
Item 6, check "No" if no person (other than you or spouse) claims custody or visitation
otherwise, check "Yes" and give requested info.
Date of signing.
If you used copies of form FL-105(A) to add additional children, check box 7 and type in the number of pages attached.
Fill in as shown in figure 7.2, single-line short caption.
If a restraining order is in effect, check box 5 and provide requested info.
Your signature.
Type your name.

FL-105/GC-120

SHORT TITLE: | CASE NUMBER:

4. Do you have information about, or have you participated as a party or as a witness or in some other ... or custody or visitation proceeding, in California or elsewhere, concerning a child subject to this proc...
☐ Yes ☐ No *(If yes, attach a copy of the orders (if you have one) and provide the following ...*

| Proceeding | Case number | Court *(name, state, location)* | Court order or judgment *(date)* | Name of each child | Your connection to the case | Case status |
|---|---|---|---|---|---|---|
| a. ☐ Family | | | | | | |
| b. ☐ Guardianship | | | | | | |
| c. ☐ Other | | | | | | |

| Proceeding | Case Number | Court ... |
|---|---|---|
| d. ☐ Juvenile Delinquency/ Juvenile Dependency | | |
| e. ☐ Adoption | | |

5. ☐ One or more domestic violence restraining/protective orders are now in effect. *(Attach a copy of the orders if you have one and provide the following information):*

| Court | County | State | Case number *(if known)* | Orders expire *(date)* |
|---|---|---|---|---|
| a. ☐ Criminal | | | | |
| b. ☐ Family | | | | |
| c. ☐ Juvenile Delinquency/ Juvenile Dependency | | | | |
| d. ☐ Other | | | | |

6. Do you know of any person who is not a party to this proceeding who has physical custody or claims to have custody of or visitation rights with any child in this case? ☐ Yes ☐ No *(If yes, provide the following information):*

| a. Name and address of person | b. Name and address of person | c. Name and address of person |
|---|---|---|
| ☐ Has physical custody<br>☐ Claims custody rights<br>☐ Claims visitation rights | ☐ Has physical custody<br>☐ Claims custody rights<br>☐ Claims visitation rights | ☐ Has physical custody<br>☐ Claims custody rights<br>☐ Claims visitation rights |
| Name of each child | Name of each child | Name of each child |

I declare under penalty of perjury under the laws of the State of California that the foregoing is true and correct.
Date:

(TYPE OR PRINT NAME) ▶ (SIGNATURE OF DE...

7. ☐ Number of pages attached: ____

**NOTICE TO DECLARANT: You have a continuing duty to inform this court if you obtain any informatio... proceeding in a California court or any other court concerning a child subj...**

FL-105/GC-120 [Rev. January 1, 2009]

**DECLARATION UNDER UNIFORM CHILD CUSTODY JURISDICTION AND ENFORCEMENT ACT (UCCJEA)**

# THE RESPONSE

## About the Response

The Response lets everyone know that you have officially joined the case. Depending on how you fill it out, it might also give notice that you want some separate property confirmed to you, or have a different view of the basic facts or the ultimate outcome. Once the Response is filed and served, you and Petitioner are exact equals in the legal proceedings and have equal ability to go ahead with any legal procedure.

**Time to file.** Once you are served with the Petition, you have 30 days to file your Response. However, if Petitioner sends you a letter stating that you can have a specific amount of extra time, or better, that he/she will not proceed in the case without giving you 30 days' written notice to respond, then you can put off filing the Response and concentrate on getting an agreement worked out.

## Study the Summons and Petition

**Restraining orders.** Once you are served, you and Petitioner are bound by the restraining orders on the back of the Summons (chapter 2.7). Examine them carefully. Until the Judgment, do not take the kids out of state without written permission and don't transfer funds or do any of those other things "by accident."

**Facts.** Check every fact stated in the Petition. You get to state your version of facts in your Response.

**Property.** If assets and debts are actually listed on the Petition or on an attached list, then Petitioner will be able to go to court and get a Judgment if you do not respond in time. **However,** if items 9 or 10 say "to be determined by written agreement," or something similar, this means Petitioner can't get a Judgment without your written agreement, so you can decide not to respond and focus on working out an agreement, because the case can't go forward without either an agreement or until an Amended Petition listing all property is filed and served on you, giving you another chance to respond.

## What to do

First, read Part One of this book and decide what you want to accomplish. If you want to enter the case, prepare the original and three copies of the Response. L.A. County wants an extra copy of the front. If you need more space to complete any item, use an Additional Page form (figure 7.2) with the heading "Continuation of Response." For each item continued, type a sub-heading that reads "Attachment n" (n = the number of the item being continued), and complete your list. The Additional Page becomes part of the Response, so staple the original and copies to each copy of your Response.

**Amended Response.** If, for some reason, you need to file an amended Response to correct any errors or make changes, it must be done before the case is "at issue" or trial date is set. Prepare another Response, but this time check the "AMENDED" box in the caption, fill it out with the changed information, file it with the court and have the papers served on Petitioner as you did the first time, then file the new Proof of Service, as before.

# NOTES FOR THE RESPONSE

**Caption.** If the Petition asks for Legal Separation and you want a divorce, check the boxes "and Request For," and "Dissolution of Marriage." Also check boxes 5c and 5c(1). Divorce trumps separation; you will almost certainly get it. If you want to ask for a Nullity (annulment) you will require professional assistance.

**Item 3a or 3b.** The date of your separation is the last day you were living together as husband and wife or partners. If there is any question in your mind about what date to use, read about date of separation in chapter 3.1. If you still don't have an exact date, just get as close as you can. If you separated several times, use the most recent date. Merely sleeping together does not affect separation or dissolution.

**Item 5.** Most people should check 5(c)(1) to request a divorce on the grounds of "irreconcilable differences." If one party asks for a legal separation and the other asks for a divorce, the divorce wins. It's hard to stop a divorce if one party wants it. Do *not* check any of the other boxes without legal advice and assistance.

**Item 8   Spousal support.** You must check a box at item 8.

Item 8a. If spousal support is requested, check box 8a and check a box to show who will receive the support you are requesting, Petitioner or Respondent.

## Figure 11.1 RESPONSE
### Form FL-120 (page 1)

**Type caption as shown in figure 7.1.**

**Check this box.**

**Check a box to show if married or domestic partners.**

**Check box to show who satisfies the residency requirement. If both do, check both.**

**Read text note 4. Check 4a if no minor children. If there are minor children, check 4b and fill in requested information for each child and attach the Declaration re Minors (figs. 10.4 & 10.5).**

**Check box to show if dissolving a marriage or domestic partnership.**

**Dates of marriage and separation and years & months duration. Re: date of separation, see text note for item 3a.**

---

FL-120

ATTORNEY OR PARTY WITHOUT ATTORNEY *(Name, State Bar number, and address):*

FOR COURT USE ONLY

TELEPHONE NO.:          FAX NO.:
E-MAIL ADDRESS:
ATTORNEY FOR *(Name):*

SUPERIOR COURT OF CALIFORNIA, COUNTY OF
STREET ADDRESS:
MAILING ADDRESS:
CITY AND ZIP CODE:
BRANCH NAME:

PETITIONER:
RESPONDENT:

| RESPONSE | ☐ AND REQUEST FOR | ☐ AMENDED | CASE NUMBER: |
|---|---|---|---|
| ☐ Dissolution (Divorce) of: | ☐ Marriage | ☐ Domestic Partnership | |
| ☐ Legal Separation of: | ☐ Marriage | ☐ Domestic Partnership | |
| ☐ Nullity of: | ☐ Marriage | ☐ Domestic Partnership | |

1. **LEGAL RELATIONSHIP** *(check all that apply):*
   a. ☐ We are married.
   b. ☐ We are domestic partners and our domestic partnership was established in California.
   c. ☐ We are domestic partners and our domestic partnership was NOT established in California.

2. **RESIDENCE REQUIREMENTS** *(check all that apply):*
   a. ☐ Petitioner ☐ Respondent has been a resident of this state for at least six months and of this county for at least three months immediately preceding the filing of this *Petition*. (For a divorce, at least one person in the legal relationship described in items 1a and 1c must comply with this requirement.)
   b. ☐ We are the same sex and were married in California but are not residents of California. Neither of us li[...] nation that will dissolve the marriage. This case is filed in the county in which we married.
      Petitioner's residence *(state or nation):*          Respondent's residence *(state or nation):*
   c. ☐ Our domestic partnership was established in California. Neither of us has to be a resident or have a [...] to dissolve our partnership here.

3. **STATISTICAL FACTS**
   a. ☐ (1) Date of marriage *(specify):*          (2) Date of separation *(specify):*
      (3) Time from date of marriage to date of separation *(specify):*          Years          Months
   b. ☐ (1) Registration date of domestic partnership with the California Secretary of State or other state e[...]
      (2) Date of separation *(specify):*
      (3) Time from date of registration of domestic partnership to date of separation *(specify):*          Yea[...]

4. **MINOR CHILDREN** (children born before (or born or adopted during) the marriage or domestic partnership):
   a. ☐ There are no minor children.
   b. ☐ The minor children are:
      Child's name          Birthdate          Age          Sex

   (1) ☐ continued on Attachment 4b.
   (2) ☐ a child who is not yet born.
   c. If there are minor children of Petitioner and Respondent, a completed *Declaration Under Uniform Child Custody Jurisdiction and Enforcement Act (UCCJEA)* (form FL-105) must be attached.
   d. ☐ Petitioner and Respondent signed a voluntary declaration of paternity. A copy ☐ is ☐ is not attached.

Page 1 of 3

Form Adopted for Mandatory Use
Judicial Council of California
FL-120 [Rev. January 1, 2015]

**RESPONSE—MARRIAGE/DOMESTIC PARTNERSHIP**
**(Family Law)**

Family Code, § 2020
www.courts.ca.gov

## Figure 11.2  RESPONSE
### Form FL-120 (page 2)

**Type in caption as shown in figure 7.2**

**Type in case number.**

PETITIONER:

RESPONDENT:

CASE NUMBER:

Respondent requests that the court make the following orders:

5.  **LEGAL GROUNDS** (Family Code sections 2200–2210; 2310–2312)

a. ☐ **Respondent contends** that the parties never legally married or registered a domestic partnership.

b. ☐ **Respondent denies** the grounds set forth in item 5 of the petition.

c. ☑ **Respondent requests**

**Check boxes 5c and 5c(1).**

(1) ☐ divorce  ☐ legal separation  of the marriage or domestic partnership based on

    (a) ☐ irreconcilable differences.  (b) ☐ permanent legal incapacity to make decisions.

(2) ☐ nullity of void marriage or domestic partnership based on

    (a) ☐ incest.  (b) ☐ bigamy.

(3) ☐ nullity of voidable marriage or domestic partnership based on

    (a) ☐ respondent's age at time of registration of domestic partnership or marriage.  (d) ☐ fraud.

    (b) ☐ prior existing marriage or domestic partnership.  (e) ☐ force.

    (c) ☐ unsound mind.  (f) ☐ physical incapacity.

**If you have children, check boxes for 6a, 6b, and 6c to show what you request (see text notes on cases with children).**

6.  **CHILD CUSTODY AND VISITATION (PARENTING TIME)**

|  | | Petitioner | Respondent | Joint | Other |
|---|---|---|---|---|---|
| a. | Legal custody of children to | ☐ | ☐ | ☐ | ☐ |
| b. | Physical custody of children to | ☐ | ☐ | ☐ | ☐ |
| c. | Child visitation (parenting time) be granted to | ☐ | ☐ | ☐ | ☐ |

As requested in: ☐ form FL-311  ☐ form FL-312  ☐ form FL-341(C)

☐ form FL-341(D)  ☐ form FL-341(E)  ☐ Attachment 6c(1)

d. ☐ Determine the parentage of children born to Petitioner and Respondent before the marriage or domestic partnership.

7.  **CHILD SUPPORT**

a. If there are minor children born to or adopted by Petitioner and Respondent before or during this marriage or domestic partnership, the court will make orders for the support of the children upon request and submission of financial forms by the requesting party.

b. An earnings assignment may be issued without further notice.

c. Any party required to pay support must pay interest on overdue amounts at the "legal" rate, which is currently 10 percent.

d. ☐ Other (specify):

8.  **SPOUSAL OR DOMESTIC PARTNER SUPPORT**

a. ☐ Spousal or domestic partner support payable to  ☐ Petitioner  ☐ Respondent

b. ☐ Terminate (end) the court's ability to award support to  ☐ Petitioner  ☐ Respondent

c. ☐ Reserve for future determination the issue of support payable to  ☐ Petitioner  ☐ Res

d. ☐ Other (specify):

**Read text note on item 8 about spousal support and fill this out accordingly.**

9.  **SEPARATE PROPERTY**

a. ☐ There are no such assets or debts that I know of to be confirmed by the court.

b. ☐ Confirm as separate property the assets and debts in  ☐ Property Declaration (form FL-160)  ☐ Attachment 9b

    ☐ the following list.  Item  Confirm to

**Read text note on item 9 and fill this in accordingly.**

FL-120 [Rev. January 1, 2015]  **RESPONSE—MARRIAGE/DOMESTIC PARTNERSHIP**  (Family Law)  Page 2 of 3

**Item 8b Terminate spousal support.** Check 8b to ask the court terminate spousal support, both now and in the future, and check a box to show whose right is to be terminated: Petitioner's or Respondent's or both. Or . . .

**Item 8c  Reserve the matter of spousal support** for a future determination. Check a box to show whose right is to be reserved: Petitioner's or Respondent's or both. Or ...

**wwItem 8c  Other.** If you have or expect to have an agreement, check here and enter "To be determined in a written agreement."

## CASES WITH CHILDREN

**Item 4b.**  The children listed here include only those who are currently under 18 (or 18, enrolled full-time in high school and not self-supporting) who were born to or adopted by both you and your spouse. Don't include stepchildren who have not been formally adopted. If the wife is pregnant, include the unborn child by putting "one unborn" in the space provided for the name of child.

**Item 4c.** Fill out FL-105 Declaration Under UCCJEA as shown in figures 10.4 and 10.5 and attach it to the Response.  If you have more than two children, attach copies of form FL-105(A) to add more.

**Item 4d.** Refers to the Voluntary Declaration of Paternity available in many hospitals. If you happen to have one, check this box.

**Items 6a–d, Custody and Visitation.** Read chapter 4.

- To request pure joint custody, check 6a and 6b at the boxes under the "Joint" column.
- To request joint legal custody with sole physical custody to one parent, check 6a under the "Joint" column and check 6b to indicate who is to have primary physical custody.
- To request sole custody (both legal and physical) for one parent, check both 6a and 6b under the column that indicates who is to have custody.
- Check 6c to indicate which parent is to have a visitation schedule.

    **Optional attachments:** Specifying custody or visitation arrangements in detail in the Response is not generally necessary, but if you plan to ask for something unusual, Respondent has a right to know about it, in which case check a box or boxes below 6c and attach one of the forms listed there. They are on the companion CD. Take a look at these forms to see what's possible. **Note:** FL-312 is a request for orders to prevent the abduction of a child, which is not something you should try to do yourself. If you face this threat, get help from a family law attorney.

- **Determine parentage.** If a child of the parties was born before the marriage, you *must* check 6d for a determination of parentage. When you apply for your Judgment, you will have to attach a declaration stating facts that establish who the biological parents are. Nolo-1, a form for your declaration, is on the CD in the Forms folder.

# ASSETS and DEBTS

Read chapter 3 carefully. Remember that "property" includes assets and debts.

**Item 9, Separate Property.**

- If neither spouse has any separate assets or debts, check box 9a.

- If you want anything confirmed as the separate asset or debt of you or your spouse, you need to list each item and indicate to whom it is to be confirmed (Petitioner or Respondent). If you have only a few items, check the box for "the following list" and enter your items directly on the Response. If there's not enough room for all your items, either (a) check the box for "Property Declaration" and use form FL-160 (chapter 15), or (b) check the box for "Attachment 9b" and enter your list on an Additional Page form (figure 7.2) with the heading "Attachment 9b."

- Be sure to include any retirement plan or fund if no part was earned between marriage and separation. Do *not* list community property that has already been informally divided by the spouses—it is not separate until divided by the court and must be listed under item 10.

- **Option.** If you expect to work out a settlement agreement, check "the following list," then type in, "To be determined by written agreement of the parties."

**Item 10, Community Property.**

**10a. There are no such assets or debts subject to disposition by the court in this proceeding.** Check this box only if there is truly no property or so little that it just doesn't matter. When you check box 10a, the court will not inquire about

# Figure 11.3  RESPONSE
## Form FL-120 (page 3)

**Type in caption as shown in figure 7.2**

**Read text notes on item 10, then check 10a or 10b.**

PETITIONER:

RESPONDENT:

CASE NUMBER:

**10. COMMUNITY AND QUASI-COMMUNITY PROPERTY**

a. ☐ There are no such assets or debts that I know of to be divided by the court.

b. ☐ Determine rights to community and quasi-community assets and debts. All such assets and debts are listed
   ☐ in *Property Declaration* (form FL-160)   ☐ in Attachment 10b.
   ☐ as follows (*specify*):

**11. OTHER REQUESTS**

a. ☐ Attorney's fees and costs payable by   ☐ Petitioner   ☐ Respondent

b ☐ Respondent's former name be restored to (*specify*):

c. ☐ Other (*specify*):

**To restore Respondent's former name, check box 11b and type in the new name exactly as she wishes it to be.**

☐ Continued on Attachment 11c.

I declare under penalty of perjury under the laws of the State of California that the foregoing is true and correct.

Date:

_____
(TYPE OR PRINT NAME)

▶ _____
(SIGNATURE OF RESPONDENT)

Date:

_____
(TYPE OR PRINT NAME)

▶ _____
(SIGNATURE OF ATTORNEY FOR RESPONDENT)

**NOTICE:** You may redact (black out) social security numbers from any written material filed with the court in this case other than a form used to collect child, spousal or partner support.

**NOTICE—CANCELLATION OF RIGHTS:** Dissolution or legal separation may automatically cancel the rights of a domestic partner or spouse under the other domestic partner's or spouse's will, trust, retirement plan, power of attorney, pay-on-death bank account, survivorship rights to any property owned in joint tenancy, and any other similar thing. It does not automatically cancel the right of a domestic partner or spouse as beneficiary of the other partner's or spouse's life insurance policy. You should review these matters, as well as any credit cards, other credit accounts, insurance polices, retirement plans, and credit reports, to determine whether they should be changed or whether you should take any other actions. Some changes may require the agreement of your partner or spouse or a court order.

**The original response must be filed in the court with proof of service of a copy on Petitioner.**

FL-120 [Rev. January 1, 2015]

**RESPONSE—MARRIAGE/DOMESTIC PARTNERSHIP**
(Family Law)

Page 3 of 3

**Date of signing.**

**Type your name.**

**Type "In Pro Per."**

**Your signature.**

your community property or make orders about it. Property of any significance *must* be listed. Even if you have already divided your community property, legally it is still community property and technically you both own it all as tenants-in-common until it is divided by a court order. Do *not* check this box if there is or may *ever* be a disagreement between you about some item of property that you care about, or where there is any real estate, or if there is a community interest in a pension plan (chapter 3.6(b)).

**10b.** Check this box if you have property or debts that have not yet been divided in a written agreement. You can still put together a settlement agreement with your spouse at a later time and present it to the court when you get your Judgment.

**Agreement coming.** If the Petition, at either item 9 or 10, indicates that property and debts will be determined in a written agreement, and if you, too, are reasonably sure you will have one, check boxes for "10b" and "as follows" then type in, "To be determined by written agreement." If both you and Petitioner do this, the case cannot move forward without an agreement unless either an Amended Petition or an Amended Response is filed listing all property and debts.

**Listed.** If you decide to list all community assets and debts, you have three ways to do it:

— **As follows.** If you have only a few items, you can check this box and enter your list right on the Response. Most people need more space and will use either of the next two options.

— **In Property Declaration (form FL-160).** Check this box, then fill out and attach the Property Declaration form (chapter 15).

— **In Attachment 10b.** Check this box and use the Additional Page form (figure 7.2). Type in a heading, "Attachment 10b." Review the Property Declaration to see how items should be grouped. Major items should be individually listed, such as cars, bank accounts, pension plans, stocks, accumulated vacation pay, trusts, and things of special importance to you. Real estate is identified by its common address and assessor's parcel number. Household goods and appliances can simply be lumped together as such.

## What next?

- Serve the Response on Petitioner by mail (chapter 12.6) along with a copy of the Proof of Service by Mail (FL-335, chapter 13, figure 13.3).
- Once the papers have been mailed, the server signs the Proof of Service by Mail, then you file the Response and the Proof of Service with the court along with the Response filing fee (chapter 7.3).
- Respondent is now on equal footing with Petitioner and can do any of the things Petitioner can do described in this book or in *How to Solve Divorce Problems* to move the case toward completion.
- If you have trouble settling issues in your divorce, you should both read my book *Make Any Divorce Better* and learn how to reduce upset, talk to your spouse, and negotiate a settlement. If your case seems headed to court anyway, get *How to Solve Divorce Problems*, and learn how to use the legal process to reach your goals or supervise your attorney if you decide to retain one.

## Case Management or Status Conference?

Courts are very concerned with the management of their case loads and they worry about the large number of cases in their files that are inactive for long periods of time. If a Response is filed, many counties will start scheduling hearings to find out what's going on with your case. These are called Case Management Conferences or Status Conferences. Typically, they will send you a form to gather information about your case. Somewhere in there you can tell them you are currently in negotiation or mediation and expect to settle everything by agreement. For example, if they ask you to list the issues, you can check a box for "other" and type in, "None—the parties are in mediation," or "None—the parties are negotiating a settlement." This will usually get you a continuance for a few months, at which time you might have to repeat the process if your case is not yet moving toward Judgment.

## Family Centered Case Resolution

Similar to the Case Management Conference, this is another procedure the court might use to keep dissolution cases moving along efficiently. For details and the suggested timeline, see chapter 10 at page 127.

# HOW TO SERVE PAPERS

Giving formal notice to the other side is called "service of process." To start a case, the Petition and other papers must be correctly served on the other spouse. If a Response is filed, it must be served on Petitioner. As the case progresses, there will be a few times when you have to give formal notice of some step to the other side. If your case moves into legal conflict, serving papers will happen many times. We will tell you each time when service is required. In this chapter, we explain the general rules for getting it done.

## 12.1  Who serves whom and when

**Who can serve?** Papers must be served by someone who is at least 18 years old and not a party to the action, so neither spouse can do it, but almost anyone else can. A relative can do it, but it would look better if the person were unrelated. You can hire a professional process server (see yellow pages) but don't use a Sheriff, Marshal, or Constable if you are in a hurry, or if it might take diligence to find your spouse. Being a citizen is not a requirement. Each time papers are served, the person who does it must sign a Proof of Service form so you can prove when, where, how, and by whom it was done.

**Who gets served?** The Summons and Petition set is always served directly on the spouse. For everything else, papers are always served on the "attorney of record." Look on the caption of the most recent court document you received (if any) from your spouse and the name that appears there is the "attorney of record." If you were never served with court documents, keep serving your spouse directly. Just because your Ex consulted an attorney does *not* make that attorney "of record" unless his/her name appears on a court document that is served on you. Whoever is "of record," your spouse or your spouse's attorney, you *must* use that name and address on all your Proofs of Service, *exactly* as it appears in the captions.

**Order of events.** For the first step—the Summons, Petition, and related documents—you need to file your papers first, then have the papers served, then file your Proof of Service.

## 12.2 Serving the Petition

You *must* serve your spouse with:

- A *copy* (not the original) of the Summons,
- A copy of the file-stamped Petition, plus any attachments you filed with it, e.g., FL-105, the Declaration Re: Minors (Fig. 10.4), and
- A blank Response form.

**Got kids?** In addition to FL-105, some counties might require you to also serve either FL-313 or 314. These information sheets are discussed on the second page of chapter 4. Both are on the CD and you can choose to send one or the other to the other parent even if your county court doesn't require it. Take a look.

**Optional:** This is the ideal time to include copies of joinder documents, if needed in your case (see chapter 3.6(b)). This can be done later, but sooner is better.

**Optional:** Serve your Preliminary Disclosure papers at this time (Checklist, step 3; chapter 14). This saves you having to serve them later by mail and having to do another Proof of Service for them. However, don't unduly delay filing your Petition in order to do this step, too.

**Recommended:** Unless your spouse is an abuser/controller, consider also sending a cover letter with the papers being served saying there's no hurry to Respond, that you want to work out an agreement and won't go further in the case without giving 30 days' written notice. Consider sending copies of this book and a copy of *Make Any Divorce Better*. This is all designed to reduce chances for conflict.

**Recommended:** This is a logical time to get Respondent involved with the Declarations of Disclosure (chapter 14). In a separate envelope, send blanks of the Declaration of Disclosure, the Declaration Re: Service, the Income and Expense Forms, and a copy of chapter 14. Send a note explaining that Respondent's rights will best be protected and the case will go easier if Respondent completes first the Preliminary and, later, the Final Declarations of Disclosure and files a Declaration that it was done. If you like, you can offer to help Respondent fill out the forms.

## 12.3 Choosing the method of service

### The Summons and Petition (first set)

1. If your spouse is located inside California:
   - Personal service (section 12.4), or
   - Service by Notice and Acknowledgment (section 12.5).

2. If your spouse is located outside California:
   - Any of the methods above (section 12.4 or 12.5), or
   - Service by certified or registered mail (section 12.6).

   **Note: important!** See chapter 2.6. The court's power (jurisdiction) to order your spouse to pay support or to do or not do certain acts (hand over property or not to harass you, for example) is most clear when your spouse (a) files a Response or the Appearance and Waiver, or (b) is served personally inside California. If neither of these is possible, the court's jurisdiction to make orders against your spouse *might* be limited. What to do? Use one of the other methods and hope for the best or consult an attorney, or call Divorce Helpline for advice.

3. The Appearance and Waiver—for cooperative and military spouses:

   If your spouse is on *active* military duty, you *cannot* use any other method—you *must* use the Appearance and Waiver and your spouse must be willing to sign it. If your spouse is on active military duty and will not sign and return this form, you should consult an attorney.

4. If your spouse cannot be located anywhere:

   If you can't find your spouse, serving your papers becomes much more difficult. You are required to try *very* hard to locate your spouse. Get the most recent address you can and try serving papers by mail as described in section 12.5 or 12.6—maybe they will get through. If that fails, try to contact relatives and friends who might know where your spouse is, the last-known employer, and the County Tax Assessor. If nothing works, you can proceed by publishing or posting your Summons.

   **Kit for publishing or posting.** You will find forms and instructions for publishing or posting your Summons in the Kits folder (in Forms folder) in the companion CD. Call Divorce Helpline if you need more information, advice, or help with serving papers.

Look over the various methods and decide which to use. If your spouse will be cooperative, then service by Notice and Acknowledgment (section 12.5) is easiest and cheapest, but it does not clearly give the court personal jurisdiction to make enforceable support and other orders against your spouse. If your spouse is out-of-state and will not try to avoid a certified letter, service by certified or registered mail (section 12.6) is good. If you know where your spouse is located, but aren't sure how much cooperation you will get, then personal service (section 12.4) is most certain. It's okay to try one method, then another if the first fails.

### All other papers

The Summons and Petition can be served as decribed above. If your spouse has **not** appeared in the case by filing a document with the court and serving you with it, all other papers should be served personally (section 12.4). If your spouse **has** appeared in the case, you can serve all other papers personally or by mail (section 12.6) sent to the attorney of record (your spouse or your spouse's attorney, see section 12.1), using the name and address exactly as it appears in the caption on the most recent court documents. Personal service on a licensed attorney is easier than on a non-attorney. Following Code of Civil Procedure 1011, the server can simply (1) go to the attorney's office any time it is open and hand an envelope containing the papers, with the attorney's name on the envelope, to a receptionist or any adult in charge, or (2) from 9 a.m. to 5 p.m., if nobody is there, leave the envelope in a conspicuous place. Where the Proof of Personal Service form asks for the name of the person served, type in "Receptionist at the office of Attorney (name)." Instead of "receptionist" you could also use "adult in charge." If no one was present, type in "Attorney (name), papers left at address in conspicuous place."

## 12.4 Personal service

If you know where your spouse can be located, you can have papers served personally. This means that some person (over 18 and not a party to the action) must personally hand your spouse the package of papers being served.

Whoever is going to serve your spouse must be given the following items:

1. For servers who don't know your spouse personally, a photo and description of your spouse.

2. Complete information about where your spouse can be found, including work schedules, and home and work addresses.

3. The papers to be served (for the Petition, those listed in section 12.2).

4. The Proof of Service form, filled out, to be signed by the person who serves the papers:

> **When serving the Petition and papers along with it:** use the Proof of Service of Summons form (figure 13.1).

> **When serving other papers at other times:** use the Proof of Personal Service form (figure 13.4)

If you want to use a professional process server, use Google or other search engine to find a process server near your spouse. Also try Yelp.com to see if any have been rated by others. You could also look in the yellow pages of the phone book for the area near your spouse (big libraries and some phone companies keep national sets of phone books), or check with a process server near you to see if they can recommend someone near your spouse. Call around for the best price. Call the one you select and discuss delivery of papers and the items they want sent.

If you are in *no* hurry, it might be cheaper to use a Sheriff, Marshal, or Constable. Just mail the items listed above to one of those officials nearest your spouse, and request that they serve him/her. Include a money order for $20 with a request to refund any unused portion. Be prepared to wait patiently.

If you decide to have a friend or relative make service, deliver the items listed above and explain that all they have to do is to personally hand the package of papers being served to your spouse. If your spouse might be tricky to serve, the process server should know this: Once your spouse has been located and identified, the server should say, "I have court papers for you." If your spouse won't open the door, or if he turns and runs, or in any other way tries to avoid service, the server can just put the papers in the nearest convenient spot where they can be picked up, then leave, and service will have been effectively completed.

Make sure the Proof of Service is filled out properly (chapter 13). If service is made outside California, it must be proved by a sworn and notarized affidavit, so do not send FL-115 Proof of Service. Use only a professional or an official and request that they send an affidavit of service to you and file that as your Proof of Service.

## 12.5 Service by Notice and Acknowledgment

This is only for the first set of papers: Summons, Petition and others papers that might be served with them. If you know your spouse's address, and if your Ex will cooperate to the extent of signing an Acknowledgment, then your job is easy.

A copy of papers to be served (section 12.2) should be mailed by first class mail, postage prepaid, to your spouse, together with the original and one copy of the Acknowledgment *and* a return envelope, postage prepaid, addressed to the sender. You can't send or recieve this yourself; someone over 18 must do it for you. Fill it out as shown in figure 13.2 and make three copies.

All your spouse needs to do is enter the date papers were received (which *must* be after the date the Summons was filed), then date and sign the original Acknowledgment and return it to the sender. It is not necessary for Respondent to fill out, file, or return any of the other papers that were sent. The sender then completes the Proof of Service (chapter 13) and the job is complete. Be sure to attach the original Acknowledgment to the original Proof of Service when you file it. Service by this method is effective on the date the papers are signed by your spouse.

## 12.6  Service by mail

### The Petition

If you know your spouse's address and it is *outside* California, you can have the server mail papers to be served (section 12.2) along with a copy of the Proof of Service by Mail (figure 13.3), by registered or certified mail, with a return receipt requested. Make sure the sender indicates "restricted delivery" or "deliver to addressee only" on the post office form. When the return receipt comes back with your spouse's signature, it must be filed as a part of the Proof of Service of Summons (figure 13.1), which must be signed by the person who mailed the papers. When using this method, the effective date of service is the 10th day after mailing. Use that date as the "date of service" on forms and in court.

### All other papers

Once a party has made a general appearance—that is, filed a Petition or Response or the Appearance and Waiver form (next page) with item 1 checked—then you can serve all documents other than a Summons by ordinary mail, addressed exactly as the name appears on the caption of the most recent court documents you received from your spouse. When you serve by mail, you *must* always include a copy of the Proof of Service by Mail (figure 13.3) with the papers served. The copy served must be completely filled out, though it need not be signed. This is so the recipient knows the date, time, and manner papers were mailed. The person who did the mailing must sign a Proof of Service by Mail (figure 13.3) immediately after posting the papers.

If your spouse has *not* made a general appearance, everything should be served personally (section 12.4).

## 12.7 Appearance, Stipulations, and Waivers

This form is signed by both parties and is used in either of two situations:

- **Respondent is on active military duty.** You can proceed *only* if Respondent will sign at least the military waiver portion of this form, which means you check box 1(c) and attach form FL-130(A), filled out as described below.

- **A Response has been filed.** Your case can proceed only by trial or by agreement. After you work out a written settlement agreement, one party files this form to allow the other party to get the Judgment.

**Good news.** If Respondent makes an appearance with this form (by checking box 1a), the need for service of process is eliminated, just as would be the case if a Response were filed. It also eliminates having to file the Request for Default, and avoids the 30 days' wait before you can go on to the next steps.

**Less-good news.** The Response filing fee (chapter 7.3) will be charged if it hasn't already been paid for filing a Response. However, no fee can be charged for filing the Appearance and Waiver if the form is used solely as a military waiver, that is, if under item 1 *only* box c is checked.

**Caution!** In cases with property, support, or unresolved issues, Respondent should hesitate to waive rights *before* a settlement agreement has been signed. If a settlement agreement has not yet been signed, Respondent should file a Response within 30 days of being served, or any time before a Request for Default is filed by Petitioner, and file this A&W form *after* the agreement is completed.

**How to fill out the A&W form.** Fill it out using figure 12.1 as a guide. Prepare the original and three copies. You can prepare and file the form if Respondent just signs it. Send all but one copy to Respondent with a copy of the Petition and a self-addressed, stamped envelope. Respondent dates and signs the original and one copy—exactly as his or her name appears in the caption—and returns them to you, keeping one copy.

**Military Waiver—FL-130(A).** To accomplish the military waiver, you check box 1(c) and also attach form FL-130(A). This form is found on the CD that comes with this book but is not illustrated as it is so easy to fill out. Just complete the caption as shown in Figure 7.2 and check one of the boxes under item 2. The military waiver is conditional, meaning it is only valid if the Judgment contains the terms of an existing settlement agreement or stipulated Judgment (page 187), so the usual way to proceed would be to check box 2a if you have a stipulated Judgment, or box 2b if you have a settlement agreement. If you can't get either one of those, you have to wait for Respondent to leave active duty or get help from a family law attorney. Call Divorce Helpline.

**How to file it.** Return the *original* Summons to the court when this Waiver form is filed. No Proof of Service is necessary and no Request for Default is necessary. Service by this method is effective on the date the A&W is filed with the court, which will show on the file stamp when the clerk returns stamped copies to you.

**Note:** The date of Respondent's signature must be *after* the date your Petition was filed. Respondent keeps a copy of the A&W form and the copy of the Petition, but has no further responsibility in the case except for completing a Declaration of Disclosure (chapter 14).

**Note:** Once either a Response has been filed or Respondent makes a general appearance with the A&W, the parties are equal, so either spouse can take care of the business of finishing the case.

# Figure 12.1  APPEARANCE, STIPULATIONS, AND WAIVERS
## Form FL-130

**Type in caption as shown in figure 7.1.**

**Type in your case number.**

**If a Response was filed, check box 1b, otherwise check box 1a.**

**If Respondent is on active military duty, check this box.**

**Check boxes 2a, 2b & 2c. See caution note in section 12.7.**

**Check this box. If the judge doesn't approve your SA as written, the case goes back to the parties for further discussion.**

**Check box 2d if there is a written settlement agreement (SA).**

**Type in name of Petitioner.**

**Date of signature, signature of Petitioner.**

**Date of signature, signature of Respondent.**

**Type in name of Respondent.**

**Type in "In Pro Per."**

FL-130

ATTORNEY OR PARTY WITHOUT ATTORNEY (Name, State Bar number, and address):

FOR COURT USE ONLY

TELEPHONE NO.:                FAX NO. (Optional):
E-MAIL ADDRESS (Optional):
ATTORNEY FOR (Name):

SUPERIOR COURT OF CALIFORNIA, COUNTY OF
STREET ADDRESS:
MAILING ADDRESS:
CITY AND ZIP CODE:
BRANCH NAME:

PETITIONER:

RESPONDENT:

APPEARANCE, STIPULATIONS, AND WAIVERS

CASE NUMBER:

1. **Appearance by respondent** (you must choose one):
   a. ☐ By filing this form, I make a general appearance.
   b. ☐ I have previously made a general appearance.
   c. ☐ I am a member of the military services of the United States of America. I have completed and att Declaration and Conditional Waiver of Rights Under the Servicemembers Civil Relief Act of 2003

2. **Agreements, stipulations, and waivers** (choose all that apply):
   a. ☐ The parties agree that this cause may be decided as an uncontested matter.
   b. ☐ The parties waive their rights to notice of trial, a statement of decision, a motion for new trial, and
   c. ☐ This matter may be decided by a commissioner sitting as a temporary judge.
   d. ☐ The parties have a written agreement that will be submitted to the court, or a stipulation for judg the court and attached to Judgment (Family Law) (form FL-180).
   e. ☐ None of these agreements or waivers will apply unless the court approves the stipulation for judgment or incorporates the written settlement agreement into the judgment.
   f. ☐ This is a parentage case, and both parties have signed an Advisement and Waiver of Rights Re: Relationship (form FL-235) or its equivalent.

3. **Other** (specify):

Date: _____
_____
(TYPE OR PRINT NAME)                ► _____
                                      (SIGNATURE OF PETITIONER)

Date: _____
_____
(TYPE OR PRINT NAME)                ► _____
                                      (SIGNATURE OF RESPONDENT)

Date: _____
_____
(TYPE OR PRINT NAME)                ► _____
                                      (SIGNATURE OF ATTORNEY F

Date: _____
_____
(TYPE OR PRINT NAME)                ► _____
                                      (SIGNATURE OF ATTORNEY FOR RESPONDENT)

Page 1 of 1

Form Approved for Optional Use
Judicial Council of California
FL-130 [Rev. January 1, 2011]

APPEARANCE, STIPULATIONS, AND WAIVERS
(Family Law—Uniform Parentage—Custody and Support)

Government Code, § 70673
www.courtinfo.ca.gov

**Note:** Check box 2c unless you have some special reason not to. You have a right to demand a judge, but you also don't want to upset the system without a good reason.

# PROOF OF SERVICE

## What they are

A Proof of Service (POS) is a declaration swearing that certain steps were carried out to serve papers on the other side. This is so the court is certain that notice of the action was actually given correctly.

1. The Proof of Service of Summons (figure 13.1) is used after the Summons and Petition have been served.

2. The Notice and Acknowledgment of Receipt (figure 13.2) is used with the POS above when you have a cooperative spouse who will sign this form and return it to the sender.

3. The Proof of Service by Mail (figure 13.3) is used when serving any documents (other than the Summons and Petition) by mail.

4. The Proof of Personal Service (figure 13.4) is used when serving any documents (other than the Summons and Petition) personally.

## How to fill them in

Fill out forms as shown in figures 13.1–13.4. Prepare the original and two copies. The form can be filed immediately, but if you are doing an uncontested dissolution with no motions or other legal action, some courts want you to wait and file all papers at once, when you file for your Judgment (chapter 20). That's also more convenient, but be sure to keep all papers safe until filed.

**Note on personal service** (chapter 12.4). If service is done by a friend, you can fill out the Proof of Service, but he or she must sign it. If service is made in California by an official or a professional, send the Proof of Service form for them to fill out and return. If service is made outside California by an official or professional, simply request that they send you their notarized affidavit of service and file that as your Proof of Service.

## Summons: the Effective Date of Service

1. Personal Service (chapter 12.4) becomes effective on the date papers were handed to Respondent.

2. Service by Notice and Acknowledgment (chapter 12.5) becomes effective on the date Respondent signs the papers. Attach the original Acknowledgment to the Proof of Service.

3. Service by certified or registered mail (chapter 12.6) becomes effective on the 10th day after the date mailed. Attach the returned signature receipt to the Proof of Service.

4. The Appearance and Waiver (chapter 12.7) becomes effective on the date it is filed.

5. Service by publication or posting becomes effective at the end of the 28th day after the first date of publication or posting (so use the 29th day).

## Figure 13.1  PROOF OF SERVICE OF SUMMONS
### Form FL-115  (page 1)

Type in the caption as shown in figure 7.1.

Your case number.

Check box 1a.

If you have children or serve Disclosure or other forms with the Petition, check box 1d and . . .

Check boxes to show what other forms were served with the Petition.

In every case, type address where Respondent was served.

If Respondent was served personally (ch. 12.4), check box 3a and type in date and time of delivery.

---

FL-115

ATTORNEY OR PARTY WITHOUT ATTORNEY *(Name, State Bar number, and address)*:

FOR COURT USE ONLY

TELEPHONE NO.:          FAX NO.:
E-MAIL ADDRESS:
ATTORNEY FOR *(Name)*:

**SUPERIOR COURT OF CALIFORNIA, COUNTY OF**
STREET ADDRESS:
MAILING ADDRESS:
CITY AND ZIP CODE:
BRANCH NAME:

PETITIONER:

RESPONDENT:

| PROOF OF SERVICE OF SUMMONS | CASE NUMBER: |
|---|---|

1. At the time of service I was at least 18 years of age and not a party to this action. **I served the respondent**
    a. ☐ Family Law—Marriage/Domestic Partnership: *Petition—Marriage/Domestic Partnership* (form FL-100), *Summons* (form FL-110), and blank *Response—Marriage/Domestic Partnership* (form FL-120)
    —or—
    b. ☐ Uniform Parentage: *Petition to Establish Parental Relationship* (form FL-200), *Summons* (form FL-210), and blank *Response to Petition to Establish Parental Relationship* (form FL-220)
    —or—
    c. ☐ Custody and Support: *Petition for Custody and Support of Minor Children* (form FL-260), *Summons* (form FL-210), and blank *Response to Petition for Custody and Support of Minor Children* (form FL-270)
    **and**
    d. ☐ (1) ☐ Completed and blank *Declaration Under Uniform Child Custody Jurisdiction and Enforcement Act* (form FL-105)
        (2) ☐ Completed and blank *Declaration of Disclosure* (form FL-140)
        (3) ☐ Completed and blank *Schedule of Assets and Debts* (form FL-142)
        (4) ☐ Completed and blank *Income and Expense Declaration* (form FL-150)
        (5) ☐ Completed and blank *Financial Statement (Simplified)* (form FL-155)
        (6) ☐ Completed and blank *Property Declaration* (form FL-160)
        (7) ☐ *Request for Order* (form FL-300) and blank *Responsive Declaration* to *Request for Order* (form FL-320)
        (8) ☐ Other *(specify)*:

2. Address where respondent was served:

3. I served the respondent by the following means *(check proper boxes)*:
    a. ☐ **Personal service.** I personally delivered the copies to the respondent (Code Civ. Proc., § 415.10)
        on *(date)*:                at *(time)*:
    b. ☐ **Substituted service.** I left the copies with or in the presence of *(name)*:
        who is *(specify title or relationship to respondent)*:
        (1) ☐ **(Business)** a person at least 18 years of age who was apparently in charge at the office or usual place of business of the respondent. I informed him or her of the general nature of the papers.
        (2) ☐ **(Home)** a competent member of the household (at least 18 years of age) at the home of the respondent. I informed him or her of the general nature of the papers.
        on *(date)*:                at *(time)*:
        I thereafter mailed additional copies (by first class, postage prepaid) to the respondent at the place where the copies were left (Code Civ. Proc., § 415.20b) on *(date)*:
        A **declaration of diligence** is attached, stating the actions taken to first attempt personal service.

Page 1 of 2

Form Approved for Optional Use
Judicial Council of California
FL-115 [Rev. January 1, 2015]

**PROOF OF SERVICE OF SUMMONS**
**(Family Law—Uniform Parentage—Custody and Support)**

Code of Civil Procedure, § 417.10
www.courts.ca.gov

## Figure 13.1a  PROOF OF SERVICE OF SUMMONS
### Form FL-115  (page 2)

If Respondent was served by Notice & Acknowledgment (ch. 12.5), check box 3c and type in date and place of mailing.

Check box 3c(1) and attach the completed Acknowledgment form.

Check this box if you used method 12.6. Enter "CCP 415.40" and attach the return receipt.

Type in caption as shown in figure 7.2.

If a friend serves or mails papers for you, type in his/her name, address, and phone at item 4, check box 4b, type "none" at 4d, and check box 5.

Date of signing.

If friend or other non-professional served Respondent, type server's name here.

Server's signature.

PETITIONER:

RESPONDENT:

CASE NUMBER:

3. c. ☐ **Mail and acknowledgment service.** I mailed the copies to the respondent, addressed as shown in item 2, by first-class mail, postage prepaid, on *(date):*                    from *(city):*

    (1) ☐ with two copies of the *Notice and Acknowledgment of Receipt* (form FL-117) and a postage-paid return envelope addressed to me. **(Attach completed *Notice and Acknowledgment of Receipt* (form FL-117).)** (Code Civ. Proc., § 415.30.)

    (2) ☐ to an address outside California (by registered or certified mail with return receipt requested). **(Attach signed return receipt or other evidence of actual delivery to the respondent.)** (Code Civ. Proc., §§ 415.40, 417.20.)

  d. ☐ **Other** *(specify code section):*
    ☐ Continued on Attachment 3d.

4. **Person who served papers**
   Name:
   Address:

   Telephone number:

   This person is
  a. ☐ exempt from registration under Business and Professions Code section 22350(b).
  b. ☐ not a registered California process server.
  c. ☐ a registered California process server: ☐ an employee or ☐ an independent contractor.
    (1) Registration no.:
    (2) County:
  d. **The fee for service was** *(specify):* $

5. ☐ I declare under penalty of perjury under the laws of the State of California that the foregoing is true and
                              –or–
6. ☐ **I am a California sheriff, marshal, or constable,** and I certify that the foregoing is true and correct.

Date:

▶

_____
(NAME OF PERSON WHO SERVED PAPERS)

_____
(SIGNATURE OF PERSON WHO SERVED PAPERS)

FL-115 [Rev. January 1, 2015]

**PROOF OF SERVICE OF SUMMONS**
(Family Law—Uniform Parentage—Custody and Support)

Page 2 of 2

## Figure 13.2  NOTICE AND ACKNOWLEDGMENT OF RECEIPT
### Form FL-117

**Type in caption as shown in figure 7.1.**

**Petitioner's name.**

**Respondent's name.**

**Name and signature of sender and date of mailing.**

**Check this box.**

**This part is completed by Respondent before returning form to sender. Make sure it is filled out correctly before filing it.**

**Type in case number.**

**If you have minor children check these boxes.**

**Check boxes to show what other forms were served with the Petition.**

---

FL-117

ATTORNEY OR PARTY WITHOUT ATTORNEY *(Name, State Bar number, and address):*

FOR COURT USE ONLY

TELEPHONE NO.:
FAX NO.:
E-MAIL ADDRESS:
ATTORNEY FOR *(Name):*

SUPERIOR COURT OF CALIFORNIA, COUNTY OF
STREET ADDRESS:
MAILING ADDRESS:
CITY AND ZIP CODE:
BRANCH NAME:

PETITIONER:

RESPONDENT:

NOTICE AND ACKNOWLEDGMENT OF RECEIPT

CASE NUMBER:

*(Sender completes items 1 through 4 and signs before mailing. Recipient completes items 5 and 6, signs, the*

1. To *(name of individual being served):*

**NOTICE**

The documents identified below are being served on you by mail with this acknowledgment form. You must personally sign, or a person authorized by you must sign, this form to acknowledge receipt of the documents.

If the documents described below include a summons and you fail to complete and return this acknowledgment form to the sender within 20 days of the date of mailing, you will be liable for the reasonable expenses incurred after that date in serving you or attempting to serve you with these documents by any other methods permitted by law.  If you return this form to the sender, service of a summons is deemed complete on the date you sign the acknowledgment of receipt below. This is **not** an answer to the action. If you do not agree with what is being requested, you must submit a completed *Response* form to the court within 30 calendar days.

2. Date of mailing *(specify):*

3. _____
(TYPE OR PRINT SENDER'S NAME)
(SIGNATURE OF SENDER—MUST NOT BE A PARTY IN THIS CASE AND MUST BE 18 YEARS OR OLDER)

**ACKNOWLEDGMENT OF RECEIPT**

4. I agree I received the following:
   a. ☐ Family Law: *Petition—Marriage/Domestic Partnership* (form FL-100), *Summons* (form FL-110), *Marriage/Domestic Partnership* (form FL-120)
   b. ☐ Uniform Parentage: *Petition to Establish Parental Relationship* (form FL-200), *Summons* (form FL-210), and blank *Response to Petition to Establish Parental Relationship* (form FL-220)
   c. ☐ Custody and Support: *Petition for Custody and Support of Minor Children* (form FL-260), *Summons* (form FL-210), and blank *Response to Petition for Custody and Support of Minor Children* (form FL-270)
   d. ☐ (1) ☐ Completed and blank *Declaration Under Uniform Child Custody Jurisdiction and Enforcement Act* (form FL-105)
      (2) ☐ Completed and blank *Declaration of Disclosure* (form FL-140)
      (3) ☐ Completed and blank *Schedule of Assets and Debts* (form FL-142)
      (4) ☐ Completed and blank *Property Declaration* (form FL-160)
      (5) ☐ Completed and blank *Declaration* (form FL-
      (6) ☐ Completed and blank *(Simplified)* (form FL-
      (7) ☐ *Request for Order* (for *Responsive Declaration* (form FL-320)
      (8) ☐ Other *(specify):*

5. Recipient signed this acknowledgment on *(specify date):*

6. _____
(TYPE OR PRINT NAME OF PERSON ACKNOWLEDGING RECEIPT)
(SIGNATURE OF PERSON ACKNOWLEDGING RECEIPT)

Page 1 of 1

Form Approved for Optional Use
Judicial Council of California
FL-117 [Rev. January 1, 2015]

**NOTICE AND ACKNOWLEDGMENT OF RECEIPT**
**(Family Law)**

Code of Civil Procedure, § 415.30, 417.10
www.courts.ca.gov

---

**Note:** When you use this method, the server must also send a self-addressed, stamped envelope for Respondent to return the form to the server, who will then pass them to you.

# Figure 13.3 PROOF OF SERVICE BY MAIL
## Form FL-335

Note: Always include a copy of this form along with whatever papers are being served. The copy must be completely filled out but need not be signed. This is to give the other side notice of the time, place, and manner of mailing.

**\* Note.** When this form is used by Respondent for the Declarations of Disclosure (chapter 14), if Respondent is not filing any papers other than this form, you can improve chances for not paying the Response fee if you (or Respondent) will put Petitioner's name and address in the caption and have Petitioner file it. In other words, although signed by Respondent, this can be considered just another document in Petitioner's case.

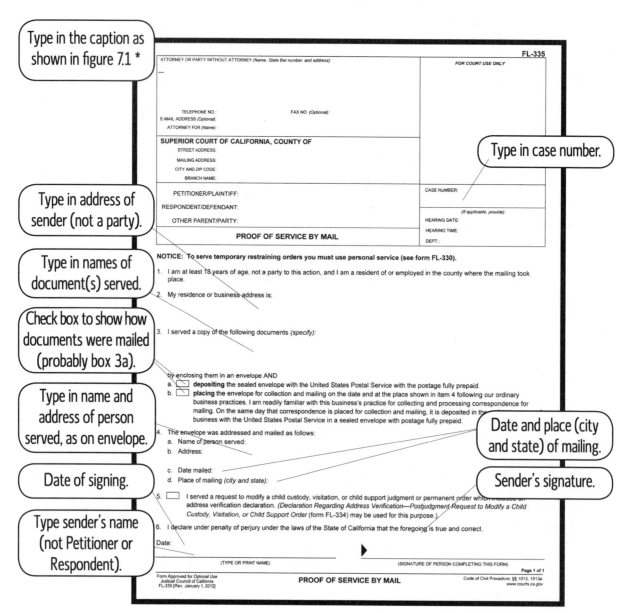

# Figure 13.4  PROOF OF PERSONAL SERVICE
## Form FL-330

Type in the caption as shown in figure 7.1.

Type in case number.

Type in name of person served.

Type in name(s) of document(s) served.

Type in date and time papers were served and the address where they were served.

Check boxes 5a and 7.

Type in name, address, and phone number of sender (not a party).

Date of signing.

Type sender's name (not Petitioner or Respondent).

Sender's signature.

---

**FL-330**

ATTORNEY OR PARTY WITHOUT ATTORNEY OR GOVERNMENTAL AGENCY (under Family Code, §§ 17400, 17406) (Name, State Bar number, and address):

*FOR COURT USE ONLY*

TELEPHONE NO.:          FAX NO.:

ATTORNEY FOR (Name):

**SUPERIOR COURT OF CALIFORNIA, COUNTY OF**

STREET ADDRESS:

MAILING ADDRESS:

CITY AND ZIP CODE:

BRANCH NAME:

PETITIONER/PLAINTIFF:

RESPONDENT/DEFENDANT:

OTHER PARENT/PARTY:

**PROOF OF PERSONAL SERVICE**

CASE NUMBER:

(If applicable, provide):

HEARING DATE:

HEARING TIME:

DEPT.:

1. I am at least 18 years old, not a party to this action, and not a protected person listed in any of the orders.
2. Person served (name):
3. I served copies of the following documents (specify):

4. By personally delivering copies to the person served, as follows:
   a. Date:                          b. Time:
   c. Address:

5. I am
   a. ☑ not a registered California process server.
   b. ☐ a registered California process server.
   c. ☐ an employee or independent contractor of a registered California process server.
   d. ☐ exempt from registration under Business & Profession Code section 22350(b).
   e. ☐ a California sheriff or marshal.

6. My name, address, and telephone number, and, if applicable, county of registration and number (specify):

7. ☐ I declare under penalty of perjury under the laws of the State of California that the foregoing is true and correct.
8. ☐ I am a California sheriff or marshal and I certify that the foregoing is true and correct.

Date:

▶

_____
(TYPE OR PRINT NAME OF PERSON WHO SERVED THE PAPERS)

_____
(SIGNATURE OF PERSON WHO SERVED THE PAPERS)

Form Approved for Optional Use
Judicial Council of California
FL-330 [Rev. January 1, 2012]

**PROOF OF PERSONAL SERVICE**

# DECLARATIONS OF DISCLOSURE

To get a divorce, both spouses *must* exchange Declarations of Disclosure listing all information about their property, debts, income, and expenses. This is an extension of the fiduciary duty (discussed in chapters 3.2 and 3.3) requiring spouses to always be completely open and honest in their dealings with each other. Keep in mind that any property or important information about property that is concealed, misrepresented, or mistakenly overlooked can result in your agreement or Judgment being set aside, even years after you think the divorce is over, and penalties can be imposed. One woman lost her entire $1.3 million lottery prize because she intentionally failed to disclose it. Another Judgment was set aside because the Disclosure stated "unknown" for the value of one spouse's pension. So be very careful.

## 14.1  The law and how it works

### The disclosure law

1.  **Preliminary Declaration of Disclosure** (PD). When the Petition is filed or within 60 days thereafter, Petitioner *must* serve Respondent with a Preliminary Declaration of Disclosure, which consists of (1) a list of all assets and debts in which the spouse has or may have an interest, including both community and separate property, no matter where located, along with (2) a completed Income and Expense Declaration (I&E) and all tax returns filed in the previous two years. **Note:** The PD can't be waived—Petitioner *must* do it, although there is no automatic penalty for being late. Respondent must serve Petitioner with a PD upon filing a Response or within 60 days thereafter.

2.  **Final Declaration of Disclosure** (FD). At or before the time you enter into a settlement agreement, each spouse must serve the other with a Final Declaration of Disclosure. The FD must include "all material facts and information" regarding the character of each asset or debt (whether community or separate), the value of community assets and debts, and a completed I&E form (FL-150, ch. 16).

3. Each spouse has a *continuing* duty to update information so the other spouse has accurate information whenever support or the division of property is settled by written agreement or by Judgment. The duty continues as to each asset or debt until it has in fact been divided by the parties.

4. In addition, each party must disclose in writing any income-producing opportunities that arise after separation which result directly from the income-producing activities of either spouse during the marriage. The disclosure must be in time to allow the other spouse to decide whether to participate in the opportunity.

5. **Waiver of FD.** In a default case (ch. 20) the Final Disclosure (FD) can be waived by Petitioner unilaterally if there is *no* settlement agreement and Respondent has not filed a Response. If there *is* an agreement, both parties can mutually agree to waive the FD with form FL-144 (on the CD in the forms folder but not illustrated as it is so easy to fill out). However, if you have significant assets or debts, we recommend that you do not waive the FD.

## How it works

• Disclosures are served but *not* filed with the court. Only the parties see the disclosures. The court sees only proofs of service.

• If a declaration is incomplete or inadequate, the other party can object in court, either immediately or in the future.

• Omitted community property is owned by the spouses as tenants in common and can be divided later by the court, whenever the omission is discovered. A party who makes incorrect or inadequate disclosure risks having the case reopened in the future, perhaps *much* later (chapter 2.9). However, it takes time, money and energy to do this, so it has to be worth the effort. Therefore, the risk created by inadequate disclosure increases with the value of the property and the degree of upset involved.

• Assuming all of the required information is included, it is okay for one spouse to prepare lists and documents for the other spouse to sign, or to make one set of documents to satisfy both the Preliminary and Final Disclosures, serve them, and file one Declaration Re Service (figure 14.3) to cover both.

1. **If Respondent *will* participate:**

   - If you had no significant property or debts to divide when you separated, no minor children, and no spousal support to be arranged, there is no advantage to having the other spouse pay a filing fee to enter the case formally as Respondent. Go to item 2, below.

   - If you have significant property or debts to divide, or minor children, or spousal support to be arranged, you should make a written settlement agreement to settle all issues. Both parties should complete Preliminary and Final Declarations of Disclosure, and file a Proof of Service for each one to prove they were delivered, along with a Declaration Re Service of Disclosure (figure 14.3).

2. **If Respondent will *not* participate:**

Petitioner *must* serve the Preliminary Declaration on Respondent in every case.

   - If there is no settlement agreement, Petitioner can complete the case by default (chapter 17) and waive the Final Disclosure on FL-170 Declaration for Default Dissolution (figure 20.1) by checking box 5(b).

   - If you will have a settlement agreement, try *very* hard to get your spouse to sign a Final Disclosure beforehand or at the same time, even if you have to prepare it yourself. If he/she will not sign it, you have a problem. In order to complete your case, you must *both* waive Final Disclosure by signing form FL-144 (not recommended in cases with significant property because you *want* the other party's sworn info before you sign). You will also check box 5(c) in the Declaration for Default Dissolution (figure 20.1).

   - If you want to *force* compliance and go for your other remedies, you will need an attorney.

## 14.2 Doing the declarations

### The Preliminary Declaration

The Preliminary Declaration (PD) includes the Declaration of Disclosure, the Schedule of Assets and Debts, and the Income and Expense Declarations. Petitioner serves these documents on Respondent either along with the Summons and Petition or soon afterward. If possible, Respondent should also complete the PD and have someone mail it to Petitioner and file a Proof of Service by Mail (figure 13.3) with the court.

# Figure 14.1  DECLARATION OF DISCLOSURE
## Form FL-140

In the instructions below,  PD = Preliminary Declaration,  FD = Final Declaration

**Type in the caption as shown in figure 7.1.**

**Check whose declaration this is.**

**Check box 1.**

**Check box 2 & 3 for the PD. Check box 2 for the FD if updated I&E forms are included.**

**Check boxes 4, 5 & 6 when making a Final Declaration.**

**Type in date and name.**

**Check this box for the PD.**

**Check this box for the FD.**

**You can type very brief statements here, or enter "see attachment for (item number)".**

**Your signature.**

---

FL-140

ATTORNEY OR PARTY WITHOUT ATTORNEY (Name, State Bar number, and address):

TELEPHONE NO.:                    FAX NO.:
E-MAIL ADDRESS:
ATTORNEY FOR (Name):

SUPERIOR COURT OF CALIFORNIA, COUNTY OF
STREET ADDRESS:
MAILING ADDRESS:
CITY AND ZIP CODE:
BRANCH NAME:

PETITIONER:
RESPONDENT:
OTHER PARENT/PARTY:

**DECLARATION OF DISCLOSURE**            CASE NUMBER:

☐ Petitioner's        ☐ Preliminary
☐ Respondent's       ☐ Final

**DO NOT FILE DECLARATIONS OF DISCLOSURE OR FINANCIAL ATTACHMENTS WITH THE COURT**

In a dissolution, legal separation, or nullity action, both a preliminary and a final declaration of disclosure must be served on the other party with certain exceptions. Neither disclosure is filed with the court. Instead, a declaration stating that service of disclosure documents was completed or waived must be filed with the court (see form FL-141).

• In summary dissolution cases, each spouse or domestic partner must exchange preliminary disclosures as described in Summary Dissolution Information (form FL-810). Final disclosures are not required (see Family Code section 2109).

• In a default judgment case that is not a stipulated judgment or a judgment based on a marital settlement agreement, only the petitioner is required to complete and serve a preliminary declaration of disclosure. A final disclosure is not required of either party (see Family Code section 2110).

• Service of preliminary declarations of disclosure may not be waived by an agreement between the parties.

• Parties who agree to waive final declarations of disclosure must file their written agreement with the court (see form FL-144).

The petitioner must serve a preliminary declaration of disclosure at the same time as the Petition or within 60 days of filing the Petition. The respondent must serve a preliminary declaration of disclosure at the same time as the Response or within 60 days of filing the Response. The time periods may be extended by written agreement of the parties or by court order (see Family Code section 2104(f)).

**Attached are the following:**

1. ☐ A completed Schedule of Assets and Debts (form FL-142) or ☐ A Property Declaration (form FL-160) for (specify):
   ☐ Community and Quasi-Community Property  ☐ Separate Property.

2. ☐ A completed Income and Expense Declaration (form FL-150).

3. ☐ All tax returns filed by the party in the two years before the date that the party served the disclosure documents.

4. ☐ A statement of all material facts and information regarding valuation of all assets that are community [property or in which the] community has an interest (not a form).

5. ☐ A statement of all material facts and information regarding obligations for which the community is lia[ble] (not a form).

6. ☐ An accurate and complete written disclosure of any investment opportunity, business opportunity, or [other income-producing] opportunity presented since the date of separation that results from any investment, significant busin[ess, or other income-] producing opportunity from the date of marriage to the date of separation (not a form).

I declare under penalty of perjury under the laws of the State of California that the foregoing is true and correct.
Date:

_____          ▶  _____
(TYPE OR PRINT NAME)                             SIGNATURE

Form Adopted for Mandatory Use              **DECLARATION OF DISCLOSURE**       Page 1 of 1
Judicial Council of California                      **(Family Law)**               Family Code, §§ 2102, 2104,
FL-140 [Rev. July 1, 2013]                                                          2105, 2106, 2112
                                                                                    www.courts.ca.gov

**How to do it:**

- Complete the Declaration of Disclosure (figure 14.1) and attach to it the following:

- Schedule of Assets and Debts (figure 14.2). List *all* of your property and debts. It is not necessary *at this time* to list values, indicate whether the property is separate, or provide attachments, but you can if you wish. List separately major items or any that have some special significance to you, and items that have title documents (land, cars) or account numbers. Include account or ID numbers, wherever applicable.

- Complete a set of Income and Expense forms (chapter 16).

## The Final Declaration

The Final Declaration should be completed before you sign your settlement agreement. If no agreement, do it before you file the final papers. The FD includes statements of "all material facts and information regarding . . ." (a) the value of all community assets and debts; and (b) the character of each asset or debt. So for every item of significant value, you must indicate whether you think it is separate (in which case, who it belongs to) or community property. If property is mixed, a brief statement of facts should be added to clarify its mixed character and what part belongs to each.

Who knows exactly what "all material facts" includes? You don't have to do any guessing, but if you *do* know something that might even *possibly* make a difference, you'd better write it down and include it in your disclosure.

**How to do it:**

- Complete the Declaration of Disclosure (figure 14.1) and attach to it the following:

- The Schedule of Assets and Debts (figure 14.2) with all columns completed and indicate the character of each asset and debt (whether community, separate, or mixed).

- Attach an updated Income and Expense form (chapter 16) if anything has changed since the Preliminary Declaration.

**Statements** *must* be made in *every* case for items 3 and 4 on the Declaration of Disclosure (figure 14.1). Minimum statements can be typed on the face of the Declaration form. A minimum statement for item 3 or 4 would be, "Regarding item __, I know of no special facts or other information regarding this subject other than what is contained in the Schedule of Assets and Debts attached to this Final Declaration." To be safe, some corporate officers might have occasion to state, "Certain information cannot be disclosed due to SEC rules against insider trading."

**More than minimum information.** If you *do* have some "material facts or information" to disclose about any item, it should be typed on an Additional Page form (figure 7.2) with the heading, "Statement Regarding Item __ of the (Schedule of Assets and Debts) (or Declaration of Final Disclosure)." Use any number of pages to be complete.

## Service and Proofs of Service

**Preliminary Disclosure.** Each party should have someone serve the PD on the other party, by mail or personally, then sign either a Proof of Service by Mail (figure 13.3) or Proof of Personal Service (figure 13.4). Optionally, Petitioner can include the PD with the first papers served and enter it on the Proof of Service of Summons. Also complete the Declaration Re Service of Declaration of Disclosure (figure 14.3) and file it along with the Proof of Service.

**Final Disclosure.** Each party should have someone serve the FD on the other party, by mail or personally, then sign either a Proof of Service by Mail (figure 13.3) or a Proof of Personal Service (figure 13.4). Option: some counties are satisfied if you state in your settlement agreement that the Final Disclosures were served. We suggest you do both. Each party signs a Declaration Regarding Service of Declaration of Disclosure (figure 14.3), which should then be filed with the court along with the Proofs of Service.

**If Summons was published or posted.** This is discussed in the instructions for service by publication or posting, in the Forms folder > Kits folder in the CD.

## 14.3  Schedule of Assets and Debts

### When to use it

This form is used as part of the Preliminary and Final Declarations of Disclosure. It is also used as part of formal discovery when you need to formally demand information from the other side (see chapter 17 in Book 2, *How to Solve Divorce Problems*).

## How to fill it out

Make extra copies of the blank form to use as work sheets. Fill it out as shown in figures 14.2. Prepare the original and make three copies. Don't guess about anything; if you don't know some piece of information, put "Unknown."

**Listing property.** Type entries to show what assets and debts you or your spouse have or might have, individually or together. List separately any items that have title documents, registration numbers or account numbers, special personal importance to you, or high monetary value. For information you don't have access to, put "Known only to my spouse." On the Preliminary Disclosure, if you have no other choice, put "To be provided on the Final Disclosure" in place of identifying numbers that you haven't been able to determine.

If you run out of room in any asset category, use another sheet and type in "Continuation of item __." On the Schedule form, put in a line "Value from continuation sheet" and include the value from the continuation for that item. At item 27 on page 4, type in the number of all continuation pages attached.

**Attachments.** Many items on this form request attachments to document the items entered. These are *required* for purposes of discovery (Book 2, chapter 17) but not, strictly speaking, required as part of disclosure. However, it would be a good idea to attach whatever documents you can get in order to inspire trust and to avoid giving the other side a good reason to start formal discovery procedures.

**Completing the columns.** The Preliminary Declaration requires only a simple list, but for the Final Declaration, you must complete the columns:

> **Sep Prop.** For each item that you believe to be separate property, enter a P for Petitioner or R for Respondent in this column. If the separate interest is partial or shared, indicate a percentage for one party (e.g., P 50%). For some items, it might help to attach an explanatory note, but if you do this, enter "See attached note." in the left column (Assets Description).

> **Date acquired.** This is an important indicator of the character of an asset or debt. For each item or group, give the date if you can, otherwise enter "UNK" if you don't know. They should have asked if it was acquired before marriage, during the marriage, or after separation (which is what really counts) or over a period of time covering two or more of those periods. Here again, in order to be clear, you might want to attach an explanatory note, in the same manner as described above.

## Figure 14.2  SCHEDULE OF ASSETS AND DEBTS
### Form FL-142

Fill out the caption as shown in figure 7.1

Check box to show whose list this is.

**THIS FORM SHOULD NOT BE FILED WITH THE COURT**   FL-142

ATTORNEY OR PARTY WITHOUT ATTORNEY *(Name and Address):*   TELEPHONE NO.:

ATTORNEY FOR *(Name):*

SUPERIOR COURT OF CALIFORNIA, COUNTY OF

PETITIONER:

RESPONDENT:

SCHEDULE OF ASSETS AND DEBTS         CASE NUMBER
☐ Petitioner's    ☐ Respondent's

Enter case number.

All columns need to be completed, but only for the Final Declaration.

— INSTRUCTIONS —

List all your known community and separate assets or debts. Include assets even if they are in the possession of another person, including your spouse. If you contend an asset or debt is separate, put P (for Petitioner) or R (for Respondent) in the first column (separate property) to indicate to whom you contend it belongs.

All values should be as of the date of signing the declaration unless you specify a different valuation date with the description. For additional space, use a continuation sheet numbered to show which item is being continued.

| ITEM NO. | ASSETS DESCRIPTION | SEP. PROP | DATE ACQUIRED | CURRENT GROSS FAIR MARKET VALUE | AMOUNT OF MONEY OWED OR ENCUMBRANCE |
|---|---|---|---|---|---|
| 1. | REAL ESTATE *(Give street addresses and attach copies of deeds with legal descriptions and latest lender's statement.)* | | | $ | $ |
| 2. | HOUSEHOLD FURNITURE, FURNISHINGS, APPLIANCES *(Identify.)* | | | | |
| 3. | JEWELRY, ANTIQUES, ART, COIN COLLECTIONS, etc. *(Identify.)* | | | | |

Column totals are entered on page 3 at item 18.

For real estate, give address or location plus name and account number of mortgages.

Pages 2 and 3 are not illustrated. They are much like this section and easy to follow.

List separately items that have title documents, account or registration numbers, or that have special personal significance or high money value.

Form Approved for Optional Use
Judicial Council of California
FL-142 [Rev. January 1, 2005]

**SCHEDULE OF ASSETS AND DEBTS**
(Family Law)

Page 1 of 4
Code of Civil Procedure, §§ 2030(c), 2033.5
www.courtinfo.ca.gov

Bottom of page 4

| 25. TOTAL DEBTS FROM CONTINUATION SHEET | | |
|---|---|---|
| 26. TOTAL DEBTS | | $ |

27. ☐ *(Specify number):*_____ pages are attached as continuation sheets.

Enter totals.

I declare under penalty of perjury under the laws of the State of California that the foregoing is true and correct.

Date:

Type date signed.

Type your name.

_____        ►  _____
(TYPE OR PRINT NAME)                (SIGNATURE OF DECLARANT)

Your signature.

**Gross fair market value.** This is what the item could get on the open market if sold right now. Put down what you know or believe to be the value, but don't just guess, because you might be held responsible for it later. Get a professional appraisal on major items, talk to dealers, scan the want ads, try to estimate what you could get. If you simply don't know, put "Unknown."

**Money owed.** Make an entry for each item, either a value, $0 if nothing owed, or "Unknown" if you don't know and can't easily find out. If you can find out with a phone call, do it.

**Totals.** When finished, total the columns at items 18 and 26.

**Explain contradictions.** For example, if an asset was acquired during marriage, but you believe it is separate or partly separate, attach a note explaining why.

# Notes for FL-141 (next page)

## Item 4 — Waiving the Final Disclosure

Petitioner *must* serve the Preliminary Disclosure (PD) documents, but as discussed in section 14.1 (item 5), the parties can mutually agree to waive Final Disclosure (FD) by filing FL-144, or by using similar language in a settlement agreement. In a default case (chapter 20) where there is no written agreement and Petitioner has served the PD, then Petitioner alone can waive the FD requirement.

Check box 4 and also check a box to show whose FD is being waived: Petitioner's, Respondent's, or both. Also check a box to show that it is the Final Declaration that is being waived.

Item 4a. Check this box if FD waived by both parties in FL-144 or a written agreement and enter the date FL-144 or your agreement was filed with the court.

Item 4b. You check this box only if the court issued an order on a motion to allow the moving party to waive PD or FD disclosure requirements.

Item 4c. Check this box if Petitioner alone is waiving the FD requirement in a default proceeding (ch. 20) where there is no agreement and Petitioner has served the Preliminary Disclosure as shown in item 2 of this form.

PD and FD documents can be served at different times or the same time, but any disclosure documents not waived must be served before an agreement is signed or Judgment can be granted, and one or more FL-141 forms must be filed to swear that required documents were served.

## Figure 14.3 DECLARATION RE SERVICE OF DECLARATION OF DISCLOSURE

### Form FL-141

**Note:** If filed on behalf of Respondent, and if Respondent is not filing any papers other than this form, you can avoid the chance of being asked to pay a response filing fee if you put Petitioner's name and address in the caption and have Petitioner file it. In other words, although signed by Respondent, this form should be treated as just another document in Petitioner's case.

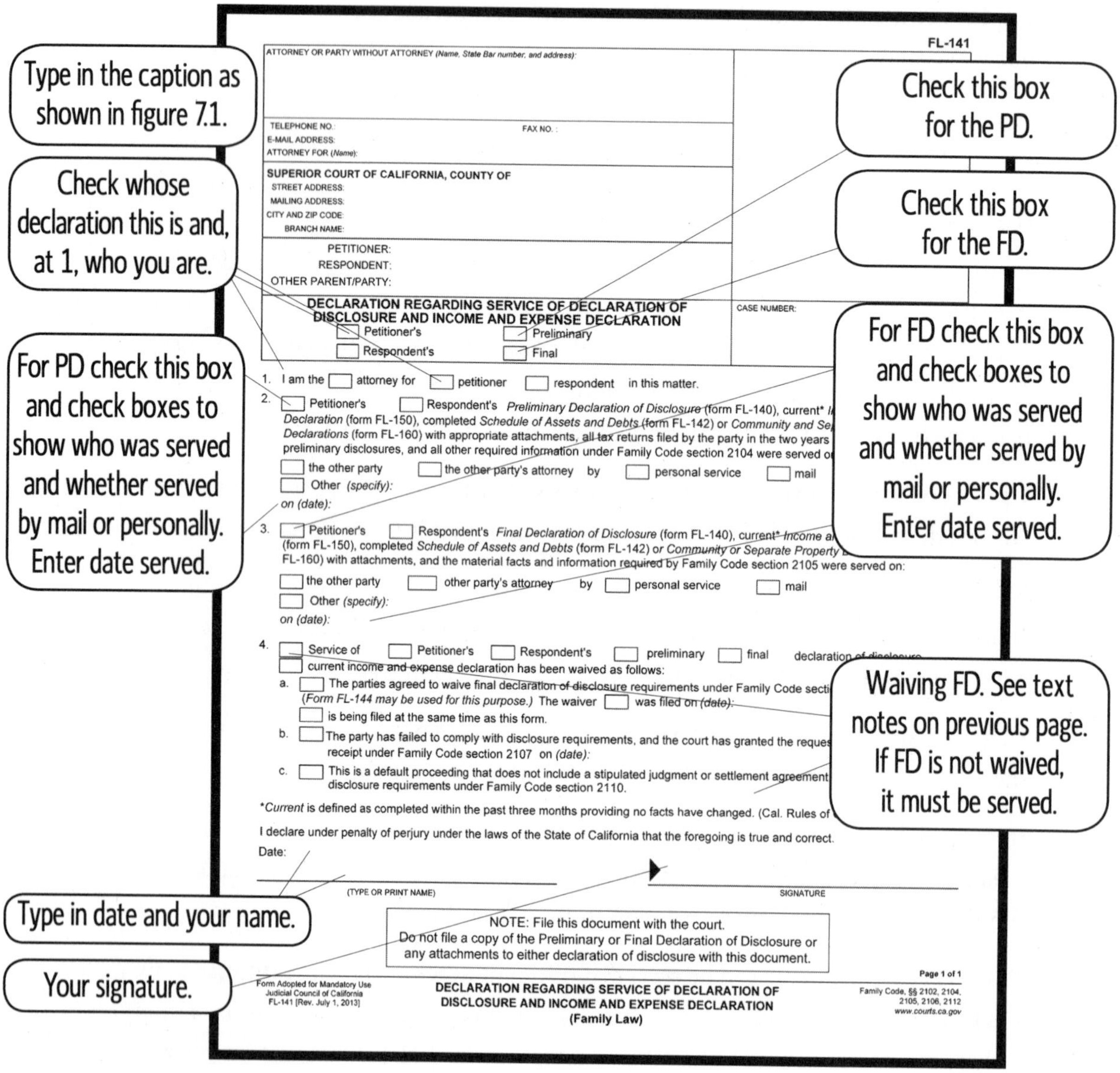

FL-141

ATTORNEY OR PARTY WITHOUT ATTORNEY (*Name, State Bar number, and address*):

TELEPHONE NO.: FAX NO.:
E-MAIL ADDRESS:
ATTORNEY FOR (*Name*):

SUPERIOR COURT OF CALIFORNIA, COUNTY OF
STREET ADDRESS:
MAILING ADDRESS:
CITY AND ZIP CODE:
BRANCH NAME:

PETITIONER:
RESPONDENT:
OTHER PARENT/PARTY:

DECLARATION REGARDING SERVICE OF DECLARATION OF DISCLOSURE AND INCOME AND EXPENSE DECLARATION
☐ Petitioner's ☐ Preliminary
☐ Respondent's ☐ Final

CASE NUMBER:

1. I am the ☐ attorney for ☐ petitioner ☐ respondent in this matter.
2. ☐ Petitioner's ☐ Respondent's *Preliminary Declaration of Disclosure* (form FL-140), current* *I… Declaration* (form FL-150), completed *Schedule of Assets and Debts* (form FL-142) or *Community and Se… Declarations* (form FL-160) with appropriate attachments, all tax returns filed by the party in the two years… preliminary disclosures, and all other required information under Family Code section 2104 were served o…
☐ the other party ☐ the other party's attorney by ☐ personal service ☐ mail
☐ Other (*specify*):
*on (date)*:
3. ☐ Petitioner's ☐ Respondent's *Final Declaration of Disclosure* (form FL-140), current* *Income a…* (form FL-150), completed *Schedule of Assets and Debts* (form FL-142) or *Community or Separate Property…* FL-160) with attachments, and the material facts and information required by Family Code section 2105 were served on:
☐ the other party ☐ other party's attorney by ☐ personal service ☐ mail
☐ Other (*specify*):
*on (date)*:
4. ☐ Service of ☐ Petitioner's ☐ Respondent's ☐ preliminary ☐ final declaratio…
☐ current income and expense declaration has been waived as follows:
a. ☐ The parties agreed to waive final declaration of disclosure requirements under Family Code secti… (*Form FL-144 may be used for this purpose.*) The waiver ☐ was filed on (*date*):
☐ is being filed at the same time as this form.
b. ☐ The party has failed to comply with disclosure requirements, and the court has granted the reque… receipt under Family Code section 2107 on (*date*):
c. ☐ This is a default proceeding that does not include a stipulated judgment or settlement agreement… disclosure requirements under Family Code section 2110.

**Current* is defined as completed within the past three months providing no facts have changed. (Cal. Rules of…

I declare under penalty of perjury under the laws of the State of California that the foregoing is true and correct.
Date:

(TYPE OR PRINT NAME) SIGNATURE

NOTE: File this document with the court.
Do not file a copy of the Preliminary or Final Declaration of Disclosure or any attachments to either declaration of disclosure with this document.

Page 1 of 1

Form Adopted for Mandatory Use
Judicial Council of California
FL-141 [Rev. July 1, 2013]

DECLARATION REGARDING SERVICE OF DECLARATION OF DISCLOSURE AND INCOME AND EXPENSE DECLARATION
(Family Law)

Family Code, §§ 2102, 2104, 2105, 2106, 2112
www.courts.ca.gov

# THE PROPERTY DECLARATION

## What it is

The Property Declaration is a detailed list and valuation of your property, designed to give you, your spouse, and the court a good idea of what you have, how much you owe, and how you would like things to be divided.

## When required

If you have community property and/or debts to be divided or separate property to confirm, you *must* file a Property Declaration with your Request to Enter Default (chapter 17) *unless* you have a settlement agreement or unless you listed everything in the tiny spaces provided on the Petition form itself at items 4 and 5.

## How to fill it out

Make extra copies of the *blank* form to use as worksheets.

**Community and separate property.** If you have both types of property, you must put community and separate property on two separate forms.

**Read page 4** of this form carefully and follow those instructions. Fill it out as shown in figures 15.1 and 15.2 below. Prepare the original and make three copies.

**Listing property.** List separately any major items or items with title; minor things can go in a group, like "household goods." If you have no property in a category, put "none." Don't guess about anything! If you don't know some piece of information, put "unknown."

**Need more room?** If you run out of room for an item, use form FL-161 Continuation of Property Declaration (on the companion CD in the forms folder).

**Values on Property Declaration.** In column C, you *must* value each item or group of items so the judge can divide your property. The "fair market value" of an item or group is the amount you could get if sold on the open market. Put down what you know or believe to be the value, but don't just guess, because you might be held responsible later. If you don't know, put "unknown." Get a professional appraisal on major items, talk to dealers, scan the want ads, try to estimate what you could get. The judge might ask how you arrived at your figures. In column D, put the amount of any debt owed on that item or group, deduct it from the amount in column C and enter the balance in column E.

**Division of community property (CP).** On the form listing your CP, in columns, E and F show the value of each item listed and how you wish it to be divided between you and Respondent.

The total *net* value of the proposed division of community property, considering all CP assets and debts, should come out so that each spouse gets about the same *net* value, unless your total net CP property value is under $5,000 or you have a written agreement for an unequal division.

# Figure 15.1 PROPERTY DECLARATION
## Form FL-160 (page 1)

Fill in caption as shown in figure 7.1.

Check box to show whose declaration this is.

Check first box if list is community property, second box if list is separate property. Use separate forms for separate property and community property.

Enter requested information for each item. (see text notes).

Enter case no. if you have one.

If attached to Petition or Response, complete columns A and F on pages 1 and 2 and A and D on page 3.

For Declaration of Disclosure, complete columns A - E on pages 1 and 2 and A - C on page 3. Attach copies of supporting documents: i.e., deeds, vehicle titles, latest account statements, contracts, etc. See form page 4.

If attached to Request to Enter Default or Judgment, complete all columns.

FL-160

ATTORNEY OR PARTY WITHOUT ATTORNEY (Name, State Bar number, and address):

TELEPHONE NO.: FAX NO.:
E-MAIL ADDRESS:
ATTORNEY FOR (Name):

SUPERIOR COURT OF CALIFORNIA, COUNTY OF
STREET ADDRESS:
MAILING ADDRESS:
CITY AND ZIP CODE:
BRANCH NAME:

PETITIONER:
RESPONDENT:
OTHER PARENT/PARTY:

☐ PETITIONER'S ☐ RESPONDENT'S
☐ COMMUNITY AND QUASI-COMMUNITY PROPERTY DECLARATION
☐ SEPARATE PROPERTY DECLARATION

CASE NUMBER:

See *Instructions* on page 4 for information about completing this form. For additional space, use *Continuation of Property Declaration* (form FL-161).

| A ITEM NO. BRIEF DESCRIPTION | B DATE ACQUIRED | C GROSS FAIR MARKET VALUE | - D AMOUNT OF DEBT | = E NET FAIR MARKET VALUE | F PROPOSAL FOR DIVISION Award or Confirm to: PETITIONER RESPONDENT |
|---|---|---|---|---|---|
| 1. REAL ESTATE | | $ | $ | $ | $ |
| 2. HOUSEHOLD FURNITURE, FURNISHINGS, APPLIANCES | | | | | |
| 3. JEWELRY, ANTIQUES, ART, COIN COLLECTIONS, etc. | | | | | |
| 4. VEHICLES, BOATS, TRAILERS | | | | | |
| 5. SAVINGS ACCOUNTS | | | | | |
| 6. CHECKING ACCOUNTS | | | | | |

Form Approved for Mandatory Use
Judicial Council of California
FL-160 [Rev. July 1, 2013]

PROPERTY DECLARATION
(Family Law)

## Figure 15.2 PROPERTY DECLARATION
### Form FL-160 (page 2)

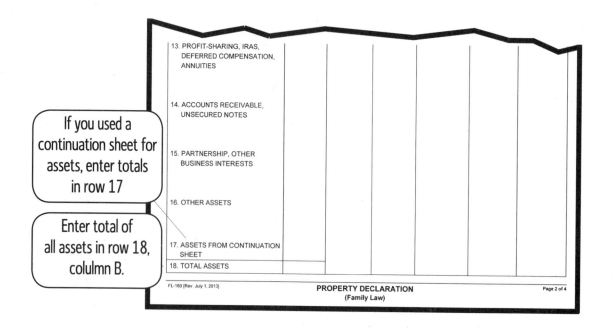

If you used a continuation sheet for assets, enter totals in row 17

Enter total of all assets in row 18, colulmn B.

## Figure 15.3 PROPERTY DECLARATION
### Form FL-160, (page 3)

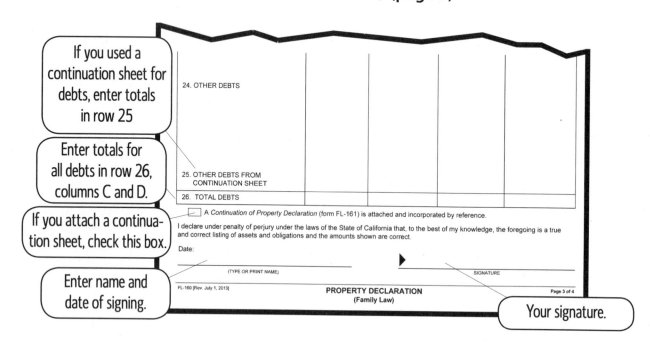

If you used a continuation sheet for debts, enter totals in row 25

Enter totals for all debts in row 26, columns C and D.

If you attach a continuation sheet, check this box.

Enter name and date of signing.

Your signature.

# THE INCOME AND EXPENSE DECLARATION

## What it is

The Income and Expense Declaration structures a detailed look at your income and expenses. There are four pages to this form (figures 16.1 to 16.4), each of which is a different financial statement.

## When the Income and Expense Declaration is required

**Child support information.** The fourth page (figure 16.4) is specifically about child support. If you have minor children, you *must* complete this page; otherwise, you do not complete it.

**The Income and Expense Declaration** is used in *every* case as part of the Declaration of Disclosure (chapter 14). Don't forget, disclosures are served on your spouse but not filed with the court. However, if your case involves any kind of support, you have to file this form with the court *unless* you have a settlement agreement. Even if you have an agreement, some counties (Alameda, Contra Costa, Monterey, San Francisco, Santa Clara, Solano) want it anyway. If required in your county, include it when you mail your papers for the Judgment (chapter 20.1) or take it with you if you go to a hearing (chapter 20.2). Don't forget, if you have minor children, you *must* also include the fourth page, Child Support Information.

## How to fill it out

Make a *blank* copy of the form to use as a worksheet and another to give to your spouse to complete and return to you as part of mandatory disclosure.

Prepare the original and make three copies. Read the instructions on each page *very* carefully and follow them *exactly*. Every blank should have an entry. Either put down the information or figure requested, "zero" or "none" if not any, "not applicable" if the item is not relevant according to previous answers, "est." where you are estimating, or "unknown" if you have no idea at all.

**Privacy.** If filed with the court, this form will be a public record, so you should use a code for any Social Security or financial account numbers. This is true wherever such information appears in any document filed with the court or on any document attached to a form filed in court. Instructions for how to do this can be found in chapter 7.2.

**Need more space?** If more information is requested than will fit on the page, use the Additional Page form (figure 7.2). Type the heading, "Continuation Sheet for (name of form)," and identify each item with the heading, "Continuation of Item Number ___." At the bottom of page one, in the space provided, enter the total number of extra pages attached to the form.

**Your spouse's figures.** The judge needs information about your spouse's income, mandatory deductions, and hardship expenses, if any. You are entitled by law to get this information in your spouse's disclosures. You are also entitled by law to see your spouse's current pay stubs, the last two state income tax returns, and other relevant documents.

If you do *not* get information voluntarily from your spouse, make estimates based on whatever you know from past records or past experience and mark these entries "est." If you have no figures at all and no facts from the past to use for a guess, put "unknown" wherever necessary, then go to a hearing with blanks left in the orders for support and let the judge decide the amount for support.

In Book 2, *How to Solve Divorce Problems,* chapters 8, 17, and 18 tell you how to get information from your spouse, either with or without court action.

## Financial Statement (Simplified) FL–155

If you are eligible, you might want to use the simplified form instead of the more detailed Income and Expense Declaration illustrated in this chapter. You are not eligible to use the simplified form if either party is asking for spousal support or attorney fees, if you have any self-employment income, or if you receive *any* money from *any* source other than: salary or wages, interest, welfare, disability, unemployment, worker's compensation, Social Security, or retirement income. We recommend the longer version illustrated here for most people, but if you want to take a look, you will find the simplified form on the companion CD in the Forms folder.

## Figure 16.1  INCOME AND EXPENSE DECLARATION
### Form FL-150 (page 1)

**Fill in caption as shown in figure 7.1.**

**Your case number.**

**Enter personal and financial information requested in these items.**

**See note on previous page, "Your spouse's figures."**

**Number of extra pages attached to this form, if any.**

**Your signature.**

**Type in your name and the date.**

---

FL-150

ATTORNEY OR PARTY WITHOUT ATTORNEY (Name, State Bar number, and address):

FOR COURT USE ONLY

TELEPHONE NO.:
E-MAIL ADDRESS (Optional):
ATTORNEY FOR (Name):

SUPERIOR COURT OF CALIFORNIA, COUNTY OF
STREET ADDRESS:
MAILING ADDRESS:
CITY AND ZIP CODE:
BRANCH NAME:

PETITIONER/PLAINTIFF:
RESPONDENT/DEFENDANT:
OTHER PARENT/CLAIMANT:

INCOME AND EXPENSE DECLARATION

CASE NUMBER

1. **Employment** (Give information on your current job or, if you're unemployed, your most recent job.)

*Attach copies of your pay stubs for last two months (black out social security numbers).*

   a.  Employer:
   b.  Employer's address:
   c.  Employer's phone number:
   d.  Occupation:
   e.  Date job started:
   f.  If unemployed, date job ended:
   g.  I work about    hours per week.
   h.  I get paid $    gross (before taxes) ☐ per month ☐ per week ☐ per hour.

**(If you have more than one job, attach an 8½-by-11-inch sheet of paper and list the same information as above for your other jobs. Write "Question 1—Other Jobs" at the top.)**

2. **Age and education**
   a.  My age is (specify):
   b.  I have completed high school or the equivalent: ☐ Yes ☐ No  If no, highest grade completed (specify):
   c.  Number of years of college completed (specify):   ☐ Degree(s) obtained (specify):
   d.  Number of years of graduate school completed (specify):   ☐ Degree(s) obtained (specify):
   e.  I have: ☐ professional/occupational license(s) (specify):
          ☐ vocational training (specify):

3. **Tax information**
   a.  ☐ I last filed taxes for tax year (specify year):
   b.  My tax filing status is ☐ single ☐ head of household ☐ married, filing separately
          ☐ married, filing jointly with (specify name):
   c.  I file state tax returns in ☐ California ☐ other (specify state):
   d.  I claim the following number of exemptions (including myself) on my taxes (specify):

4. **Other party's income.** I estimate the gross monthly income (before taxes) of the other party in this case This estimate is based on (explain):

**(If you need more space to answer any questions on this form, attach an 8½-by-11-inch sheet of paper and write the question number before your answer.)** Number of pages attached: _____

I declare under penalty of perjury under the laws of the State of California that the information contained on all pages of this form and any attachments is true and correct.

Date:

_____
(TYPE OR PRINT NAME)

▶ _____
(SIGNATURE OF DECLARANT)

Form Adopted for Mandatory Use
Judicial Council of California
FL-150 [Rev. January 1, 2007]

INCOME AND EXPENSE DECLARATION

Page 1 of 4
Family Code, §§ 2030–2032,
2100–2113, 3552, 3620–3634,
4050–4076, 4300–4339
www.courtinfo.ca.gov

## Figure 16.2  INCOME AND EXPENSE DECLARATION
## (Income)
### Form FL-150 (page 2)

**Type in names as shown in figure 7.2.**

**Type in your case number.**

**FL-150**

PETITIONER/PLAINTIFF:
RESPONDENT/DEFENDANT:
OTHER PARENT/CLAIMANT:

CASE NUMBER:

Attach copies of your pay stubs for the last two months and proof of any other income.  Take a copy of your latest federal tax return to the court hearing. *(Black out your social security number on the pay stub and tax return.)*

5.   **Income** *(For average monthly, add up all the income you received in each category in the last 12 months and divide the total by 12.)*

Last month | Average monthly

a.  Salary or wages (gross, before taxes) . . . . . . . . . . . . . . . . . . . . . . . . . . . . . . . . . . . . . . . $_____  _____
b.  Overtime (gross, before taxes) . . . . . . . . . . . . . . . . . . . . . . . . . . . . . . . . . . . . . . . . . . . . $_____  _____
c.  Commissions or bonuses . . . . . . . . . . . . . . . . . . . . . . . . . . . . . . . . . . . . . . . . . . . . . . . . . $_____  _____
d.  Public assistance (for example: TANF, SSI, GA/GR) ☐ currently receiving . . . . . . . . . . . . . . . . . $_____  _____
e.  Spousal support ☐ from this marriage ☐ from a different marriage . . . . . . . . . . . . . . $_____  _____
f.  Partner support ☐ from this domestic partnership ☐ from a different domestic partnership $_____  _____
g.  Pension/retirement fund payments . . . . . . . . . . . . . . . . . . . . . . . . . . . . . . . . . . . . . . . . . . $_____  _____
h.  Social security retirement (not SSI) . . . . . . . . . . . . . . . . . . . . . . . . . . . . . . . . . . . . . . . . . $_____  _____
i.  Disability: ☐ Social security (not SSI) ☐ State disability (SDI) ☐ Private insurance . $_____  _____
j.  Unemployment compensation . . . . . . . . . . . . . . . . . . . . . . . . . . . . . . . . . . . . . . . . . . . . . . $_____  _____
k.  Workers' compensation . . . . . . . . . . . . . . . . . . . . . . . . . . . . . . . . . . . . . . . . . . . . . . . . . . . $_____  _____
l.  Other (military BAQ, royalty payments, etc.) *(specify):* . . . . . . . . . . . . . . . . . . . . . . . . . $_____  _____

6.   **Investment income** *(Attach a schedule showing gross receipts less cash expenses for each piece of property.)*
a.  Dividends/interest . . . . . . . . . . . . . . . . . . . . . . . . . . . . . . . . . . . . . . . . . . . . . . . . . . . . . . . $_____  _____
b.  Rental property income . . . . . . . . . . . . . . . . . . . . . . . . . . . . . . . . . . . . . . . . . . . . . . . . . . . $_____  _____
c.  Trust income . . . . . . . . . . . . . . . . . . . . . . . . . . . . . . . . . . . . . . . . . . . . . . . . . . . . . . . . . . . . $_____  _____
d.  Other *(specify):* . . . . . . . . . . . . . . . . . . . . . . . . . . . . . . . . . . . . . . . . . . . . . . . . . . . . . . . . $_____  _____

7.   **Income from self-employment, after business expenses for all businesses** . . . . . . . . . . . . . . . . $_____
I am the ☐ owner/sole proprietor ☐ business partner ☐ other *(specify):*
Number of years in this business *(specify):*
Name of business *(specify):*
Type of business *(specify):*

Attach a profit and loss statement for the last two years or a Schedule C from your last federal tax return.  Black out your social security number.  If you have more than one business, provide the information above for each of your businesses.

8.  ☐  **Additional income.** I received one-time money (lottery winnings, inheritance, etc.) in the last 12 months *(specify source and amount):*

9.  ☐  **Change in income.** My financial situation has changed significantly over the last 12 months because *(specify):*

10.  **Deductions**

Last month

a.  Required union dues . . . . . . . . . . . . . . . . . . . . . . . . . . . . . . . . . . . . . . . . . . . . . . . . . . . . . . $_____
b.  Required retirement payments (not social security, FICA, 401(k), or IRA) . . . . . . . . . . . . . . . . . . . . . $_____
c.  Medical, hospital, dental, and other health insurance premiums *(total monthly amount)* . . . . . . . . . . . $_____
d.  Child support that I pay for children from other relationships . . . . . . . . . . . . . . . . . . . . . . . . . . $_____
e.  Spousal support that I pay by court order from a different marriage . . . . . . . . . . . . . . . . . . . . . . $_____
f.  Partner support that I pay by court order from a different domestic partnership . . . . . . . . . . . . . . . . . . $_____
g.  Necessary job-related expenses not reimbursed by my employer *(attach explanation labeled "Question 10g")* . . . . . $_____

11.  **Assets**

Total

a.  Cash and checking accounts, savings, credit union, money market, and other deposit accounts . . . . . . . . . . . . . . . $_____
b.  Stocks, bonds, and other assets I could easily sell . . . . . . . . . . . . . . . . . . . . . . . . . . . . . . . . . . $_____
c.  All other property, ☐ real and ☐ personal *(estimate fair market value minus the debts you owe)* . . . . $_____

FL-150 [Rev. January 1, 2007]      **INCOME AND EXPENSE DECLARATION**      Page 2 of 4

**Enter the income information requested in items 5—10 and asset info at item 11.**

**For wage earners, amounts for items 10(a)—(c) will be on paycheck stubs.**

*Additional page for expenses pg. 110 Figure 1.2* (handwritten)

## Figure 16.3 INCOME AND EXPENSE DECLARATION
### (Expenses)
### Form FL-150 (page 3)

**Type in names as shown in figure 7.2.**

**Type in your case number.**

FL-150

PETITIONER/PLAINTIFF:
RESPONDENT/DEFENDANT:
OTHER PARENT/CLAIMANT:

CASE NUMBER:

**12. The following people live with me:**

| Name | Age | How the person is related to me? (ex: son) | That person's gross monthly income | Pays some of the household expenses? |
|------|-----|-----|-----|-----|
| a. | | | | Yes ☐ No ☐ |
| b. | | | | Yes ☐ No ☐ |
| c. | | | | Yes ☐ No ☐ |
| d. | | | | Yes ☐ No ☐ |
| e. | | | | Yes ☐ No ☐ |

**For each person, indicate income from all sources, not just work and wages.**

**13. Average monthly expenses** ☐ Estimated expenses ☐ Actual expenses ☐ Proposed needs

a. Home:
  (1) ☐ Rent or ☐ mortgage... $ _____
  If mortgage:
    (a) average principal: $ _____
    (b) average interest: $ _____
  (2) Real property taxes ............. $ _____
  (3) Homeowner's or renter's insurance (if not included above) ........... $ _____
  (4) Maintenance and repair .......... $ _____
b. Health-care costs not paid by insurance...$ _____
c. Child care ......................... $ _____
d. Groceries and household supplies....... $ _____
e. Eating out.......................... $ _____
f. Utilities (gas, electric, water, trash)...... $ _____
g. Telephone, cell phone, and e-mail...... $ _____

h. Laundry and cleaning ................ $ _____
i. Clothes .......................... $ _____
j. Education ........................ $ _____
k. Entertainment, gifts, and vacation........ $ _____
l. Auto expenses and transportation (insurance, gas, repairs, bus, etc.) ....... $ _____
m. Insurance (life, accident, etc.; do not include auto, home, or health insurance)... $ _____
n. Savings and investments............. $ _____
o. Charitable contributions................ $ _____
p. Monthly payments listed in item 14 (itemize below in 14 and insert total here).. $ _____
q. Other (specify):.................... $ _____

r. **TOTAL EXPENSES** (a–q) (do not add in the amounts in a(1)(a) and (b)) $ _____

s. **Amount of expenses paid by others** $ _____

**Total for item 13 expenses.**

**14. Installment payments and debts not listed above**

| Paid to | For | Amount | Balance | Date of last payment |
|---------|-----|--------|---------|----------------------|
| | | $ | $ | |
| | | $ | $ | |
| | | $ | $ | |
| | | $ | $ | |
| | | $ | $ | |
| | | $ | $ | |

**If not enough room for all of payments, on last line enter "Continued on attached page." See figure 7.2 for how to add Additional Page.**

**15. Attorney fees** (This is required if either party is requesting attorney fees.):
  a. To date, I have paid my attorney this amount for fees and costs (specify): $
  b. The source of this money was (specify):
  c. I still owe the following fees and costs to my attorney (specify total owed): $
  d. My attorney's hourly rate is (specify): $
I confirm this fee arrangement.

Date:

▶

(TYPE OR PRINT NAME OF ATTORNEY)      (SIGNATURE OF ATTORNEY)

FL-150 [Rev. January 1, 2007]      **INCOME AND EXPENSE DECLARATION**      Page 3 of 4

# Figure 16.4  INCOME AND EXPENSE DECLARATION
## (Child Support Information)
### Form FL-150 (page 4)

**Type in names as shown in figure 7.2.**

**Type in your case number.**

FL-150

PETITIONER/PLAINTIFF:
RESPONDENT/DEFENDANT:
OTHER PARENT/CLAIMANT:

CASE NUMBER:

**CHILD SUPPORT INFORMATION**
(NOTE: Fill out this page only if your case involves child support.)

**Enter number of minors.**

16.  **Number of children**
   a.  I have *(specify number)*: _____ children under the age of 18 with the other parent in this case.
   b.  The children spend _____ percent of their time with me and _____ percent of their time with the other parent.
   *(If you're not sure about percentage or it has not been agreed on, please describe your parenting schedule here.)*

**Part of child support calculation. Timeshare must add up to 100%. See chapter 5.3 and page 74.**

17.  **Children's health-care expenses**
   a.  ☐ I do   ☐ I do not   have health insurance available to me for the chil
   b.  Name of insurance company:
   c.  Address of insurance company:

   d.  The monthly cost for the **children's** health insurance is or would be *(specify):* $ _____
      *(Do not include the amount your employer pays.)*

**Read very carefully, then enter the information requested.**

18.  **Additional expenses for the children in this case**                          Amount per month
   a.  Child care so I can work or get job training. . . . . . . . . . . . . . . . . . . . .   $ _____
   b.  Children's health care not covered by insurance . . . . . . . . . . . . . . . . . .   $ _____
   c.  Travel expenses for visitation . . . . . . . . . . . . . . . . . . . . . . . . . . . . . .   $ _____
   d.  Children's educational or other special needs *(specify below):* . . . . . . . .   $ _____

19.  **Special hardships.** I ask the court to consider the following special financial circumstances
   *(attach documentation of any item listed here, including court orders):*     Amount per month    For how many months?
   a.  Extraordinary health expenses not included in 18b. . . . . . . . . . . . . . . .   $ _____   _____
   b.  Major losses not covered by insurance (examples: fire, theft, other
      insured loss) . . . . . . . . . . . . . . . . . . . . . . . . . . . . . . . . . . . . . . . .   $ _____   _____
   c.  (1)  Expenses for my minor children who are from other relationships and
           are living with me . . . . . . . . . . . . . . . . . . . . . . . . . . . . . . . . . .   $ _____   _____
      (2)  Names and ages of those children *(specify):*

      (3)  Child support I receive for those children. . . . . . . . . . . . . . . . . .   $ _____

   The expenses listed in a, b, and c create an extreme financial hardship because *(explain):*

20.  **Other information I want the court to know concerning support in my case** *(specify):*

FL-150 [Rev. January 1, 2007]          **INCOME AND EXPENSE DECLARATION**          Page 4 of 4

# THE REQUEST TO ENTER DEFAULT

## What it is

This form declares Respondent in default because no Response has been filed. After this, Respondent can no longer file legal documents in this case. If Respondent *has* filed a Response, this form is not used—proceed instead with a settlement agreement and the Appearance and Waiver form (chapter 12.7).

**When used.** When you are ready to get your Judgment, file this form along with all your other papers in chapter 8, step 4. If you wish, you can request a date for your hearing when you file this form, or at a later time. Along with this form, you must also include a stamped envelope addressed to Respondent with the Superior Court Clerk's return address.

The five parts in the Request To Enter Default form:

Item 1 requests the clerk to enter the default of Respondent.

Item 2 declares which, if any, of the Financial Declarations are attached (see note below).

Item 3 is an oath, swearing that a copy of this form and the indicated attachments were provided to the court with an envelope addressed to Respondent's last known address.

Item 4 itemizes your costs in the action. Put down "not claimed."

Item 5 is your oath that Respondent is not on active military duty. If you cannot swear to this, you cannot proceed this way (chapter 12.3(3)).

## How to fill it out

As shown in figure 17.1. Prepare the original and make three copies.

Item 2: If you have no settlement agreement, a completed Property Declaration (chapter 15) *must* be attached to the original and all copies. If support is an issue, you must also attach Income and Expense forms (chapter 16). If you do have an agreement, Santa Clara wants these forms anyway. The signature on item 2 must be dated *at least* 31 days after the effective date of service on Respondent. In fact, you should wait until you have both completed the Declarations of Disclosure (chapter 14) or until it appears certain that Respondent will not do the Declarations.

**Item 3:** With this form, include an envelope addressed to Respondent's attorney or, if no attorney, to Respondent's last known address, stamped with sufficient postage to mail the form and all attachments, return address to the Superior Court Clerk's office. If service was by publication or posting, this is not required.

# Figure 17.1  REQUEST TO ENTER DEFAULT
## Form FL-165

**Type in caption as shown in figure 7.1.**

**Check box to show whether the Income and Expense forms are attached.**

**If the I&E or Property Decl. are not attached, check a box to explain why. Check (a) if the form was already filed. Check (b) if there is a written agreement. Check (c) and/or (d) and/or (e) if you are not requesting an order that makes the omitted form relevant.**

**Type in date and name.**

**Type in case number.**

**Check box to show if the Property Declaration is attached or not (see text note).**

**Type your name and date of signing (not earlier than date next section signed).**

**Your signature.**

**If Respondent was served by publication or posting, check (a), otherwise check (b) and type in Respondent's name and last known address.**

**Your signature.**

---

FL-165

ATTORNEY OR PARTY WITHOUT ATTORNEY *(Name, State Bar number, and address):*

FOR COURT USE ONLY

TELEPHONE NO.:    FAX NO. *(Optional):*
E-MAIL ADDRESS *(Optional):*
ATTORNEY FOR *(Name):*

SUPERIOR COURT OF CALIFORNIA, COUNTY OF
STREET ADDRESS:
MAILING ADDRESS:
CITY AND ZIP CODE:
BRANCH NAME:

PETITIONER:

RESPONDENT:

REQUEST TO ENTER DEFAULT    CASE NUMBER:

1. **To the clerk:** Please enter the default of the respondent who has failed to respond to the petition.
2. A completed *Income and Expense Declaration* (form FL-150) or *Financial Statement (Simplified)* (form FL-...)
   ☐ is attached    ☐ is not attached.
   A completed *Property Declaration* (form FL-160) ☐ is attached    ☐ is not attached
   because *(check at least one of the following):*
   (a) ☐ there have been no changes since the previous filing.
   (b) ☐ the issues subject to disposition by the court in this proceeding are the subject of a written agreement.
   (c) ☐ there are no issues of child, spousal, or partner support or attorney fees and costs subject to det...
   (d) ☐ the petition does not request money, property, costs, or attorney fees. (Fam. Code, § 2330.5.)
   (e) ☐ there are no issues of division of community property.
   (f) ☐ this is an action to establish parental relationship.

Date:

(TYPE OR PRINT NAME)    ▶    (SIGNATURE OF [ATTORNEY FOR])

3. **Declaration**
   a. ☐ No mailing is required because service was by publication or posting and the address of the res...
   b. ☐ A copy of this *Request to Enter Default*, including any attachments and an envelope with sufficie...
      provided to the court clerk, with the envelope addressed as follows *(address of the respondent's attorney or, if none, the respondent's last known address):*

I declare under penalty of perjury under the laws of the State of California that the foregoing is true and correc...
Date:

(TYPE OR PRINT NAME)    ▶    (SIGNATURE OF DECLA...)

FOR COURT USE ONLY
☐ *Request to Enter Default* mailed to the respondent or the respondent's attorney on *(date):*
☐ Default entered as requested on *(date):*
☐ Default **not** entered. Reason:

Clerk, by _____, Deputy

Form Adopted for Mandatory Use
Judicial Council of California
FL-165 [Rev. January 1, 2005]

REQUEST TO ENTER DEFAULT
(Family Law—Uniform Parentage)

Family Code, § 2335.5
www.courtinfo.ca.gov

---

## How to fill out the back

**Item 4, Memorandum of Costs:** Check box 4a (costs waived). On the line for Total, type in "not claimed." Date and sign as for previous section.

**Item 5, Declaration of Nonmilitary Status:** Assuming the statement is true, date and sign as shown for previous sections.

# HOW TO FILL OUT THE JUDGMENT

## What it is

The Judgment is your most critical document. It is the final resolution of all legal issues in your case, so take your time, be careful, get it right. The Judgment does not become effective until (1) you prepare it, (2) the judge signs it, and (3) it is entered into court records. Upon *entry* of Judgment, every part of it becomes effective and the Judgment can be modified only by stipulation of the parties or after a hearing on a motion to modify the Judgment.

➔ When the Judgment is entered, the automatic restraining orders on the back of the Summons (chapter 2.7) are automatically ended.

## How to fill it out

Fill it out as shown in figures 18.1 and 18.2. Prepare an original and 3 copies.

**Date marital status ends.** The Judgment *must* specify the date your marital status will be terminated. At the earliest, this is six months plus one day after the date the service of the Summons became effective. See the second page of chapter 13 to determine your effective date of service and enter that date at item 3, then add six months plus one day and enter that date where indicated (the last line in the caption) and also at item 4(a)(1) on the Judgment. In San Mateo, do not use a holiday or weekend date! **If the date has already passed,** type in "upon entry of Judgment" except as follows: Alameda and Marin, "forthwith;" Contra Costa, "date of filing;" Santa Clara, "date Judgment is filed;" leave it blank in Fresno, Los Angeles, Orange, San Diego, San Luis Obispo, and Santa Cruz counties. If the field provided is too small, abbreviate Judgment = Jdgmt.

**Now or later?** In some cases, there might be big advantages (Social Security, military benefits, taxes, etc.) to ending the marriage at a later date. To end your marriage at some date beyond the six-month waiting period, you must either leave it to be determined later—by checking box 4(a)(2)—or by filing a stipulated Judgment (signed by your spouse as shown page 187) setting the date you want. If

# Figure 18.1 JUDGMENT
## Form FL-180 (Page 1)

See FL-182 Judgment Checklist (on the CD), which will help you make sure you have completed all documents needed to get your Judgment. It might be helpful to file it with your Judgment, but this is required only in San Francisco and Santa Clara counties.

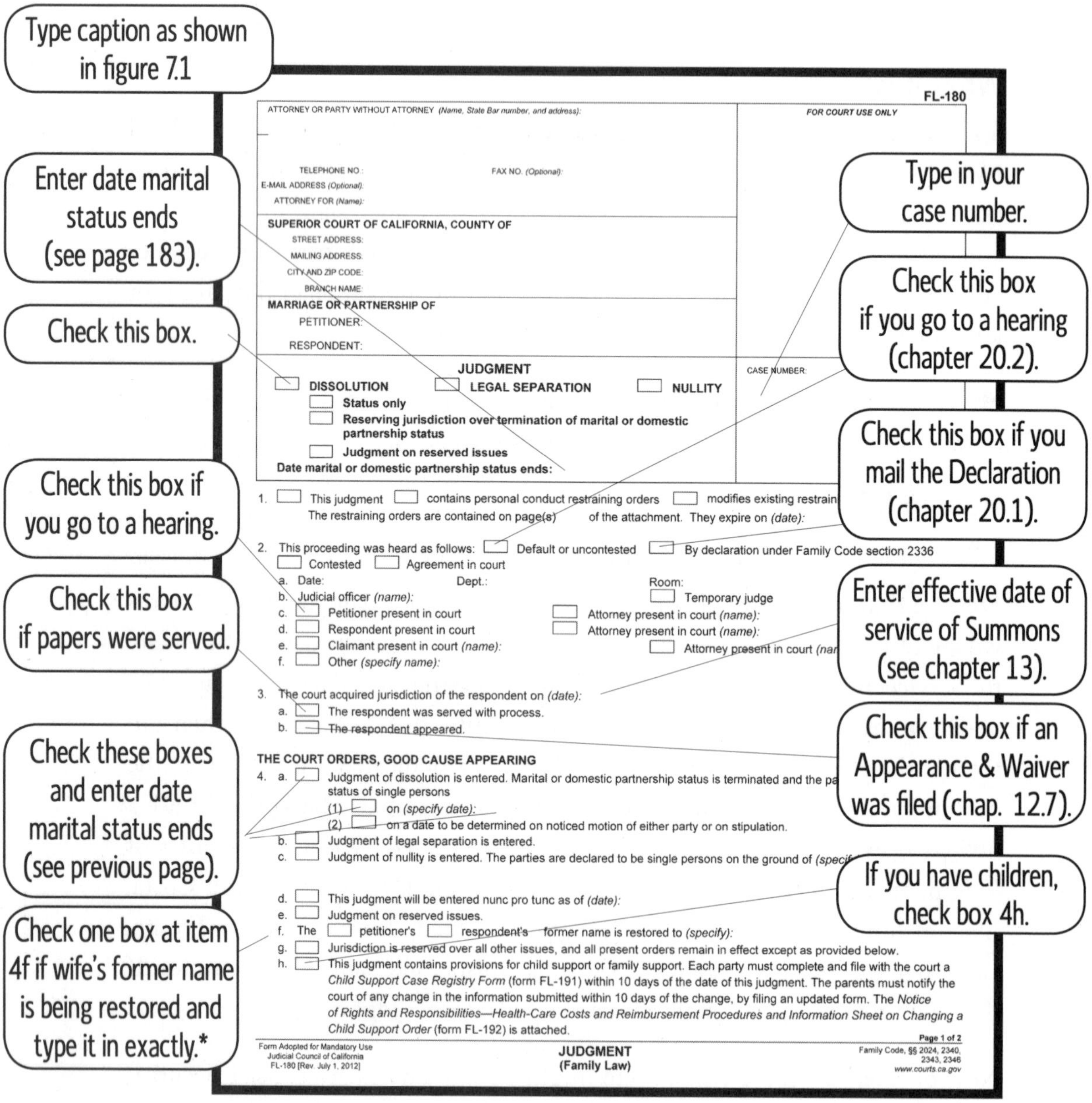
Type caption as shown in figure 7.1
Enter date marital status ends (see page 183).
Check this box.
Check this box if you go to a hearing.
Check this box if papers were served.
Check these boxes and enter date marital status ends (see previous page).
Check one box at item 4f if wife's former name is being restored and type it in exactly.*
Type in your case number.
Check this box if you go to a hearing (chapter 20.2).
Check this box if you mail the Declaration (chapter 20.1).
Enter effective date of service of Summons (see chapter 13).
Check this box if an Appearance & Waiver was filed (chap. 12.7).
If you have children, check box 4h.

FL-180

ATTORNEY OR PARTY WITHOUT ATTORNEY (Name, State Bar number, and address): | FOR COURT USE ONLY

TELEPHONE NO.: FAX NO. (Optional):
E-MAIL ADDRESS (Optional):
ATTORNEY FOR (Name):

SUPERIOR COURT OF CALIFORNIA, COUNTY OF
STREET ADDRESS:
MAILING ADDRESS:
CITY AND ZIP CODE:
BRANCH NAME:

MARRIAGE OR PARTNERSHIP OF
PETITIONER:
RESPONDENT:

JUDGMENT
☐ DISSOLUTION ☐ LEGAL SEPARATION ☐ NULLITY
☐ Status only
☐ Reserving jurisdiction over termination of marital or domestic partnership status
☐ Judgment on reserved issues
Date marital or domestic partnership status ends:

CASE NUMBER:

1. ☐ This judgment ☐ contains personal conduct restraining orders ☐ modifies existing restrain...
The restraining orders are contained on page(s) of the attachment. They expire on (date):

2. This proceeding was heard as follows: ☐ Default or uncontested ☐ By declaration under Family Code section 2336
☐ Contested ☐ Agreement in court
a. Date: Dept.: Room:
b. Judicial officer (name): ☐ Temporary judge
c. ☐ Petitioner present in court ☐ Attorney present in court (name):
d. ☐ Respondent present in court ☐ Attorney present in court (name):
e. ☐ Claimant present in court (name): ☐ Attorney present in court (na...
f. ☐ Other (specify name):

3. The court acquired jurisdiction of the respondent on (date):
a. ☐ The respondent was served with process.
b. ☐ The respondent appeared.

THE COURT ORDERS, GOOD CAUSE APPEARING
4. a. ☐ Judgment of dissolution is entered. Marital or domestic partnership status is terminated and the pa... status of single persons
(1) ☐ on (specify date):
(2) ☐ on a date to be determined on noticed motion of either party or on stipulation.
b. ☐ Judgment of legal separation is entered.
c. ☐ Judgment of nullity is entered. The parties are declared to be single persons on the ground of (speci...
d. ☐ This judgment will be entered nunc pro tunc as of (date):
e. ☐ Judgment on reserved issues.
f. The ☐ petitioner's ☐ respondent's former name is restored to (specify):
g. ☐ Jurisdiction is reserved over all other issues, and all present orders remain in effect except as provided below.
h. ☐ This judgment contains provisions for child support or family support. Each party must complete and file with the court a *Child Support Case Registry Form* (form FL-191) within 10 days of the date of this judgment. The parents must notify the court of any change in the information submitted within 10 days of the change, by filing an updated form. The *Notice of Rights and Responsibilities—Health-Care Costs and Reimbursement Procedures and Information Sheet on Changing a Child Support Order* (form FL-192) is attached.

Page 1 of 2

Form Adopted for Mandatory Use
Judicial Council of California
FL-180 [Rev. July 1, 2012]

JUDGMENT
(Family Law)

Family Code, §§ 2024, 2340, 2343, 2346
www.courts.ca.gov

*Note: If Husband is applying for the Judgment, some judges will not restore Wife's former name unless she agreed to it in the settlement agreement or has signed her consent to the Judgment (page 187).

the date is left to be determined, then when the time comes to end the marriage you will have to make a formal motion or file a stipulated Judgment signed by both parties. You can find a stipulation form in the Kits section of the companion CD.

**Very important! Serve the Judgment on Respondent.** To enforce an order, especially by using "contempt of court," you *must* be able to prove Respondent knew of the order. So if Respondent has been ordered to pay support, deliver property, or do or not do any act in the future, then once the Judgment has been signed and entered (chapter 21), it is *very* important to have a copy of the Judgment *personally* served on Respondent (chapter 12.4) and a Proof of Personal Service filed with the court (figure 13.4).

## 18.1  How to add further orders

### What they are

If you have property, debts, kids, or spousal support, you *must* attach language to your Judgment that spells out the terms of your orders on those subjects. These are called "further orders" and *must* be added if you have no settlement agreement. If you attach a settlement agreement to your Judgment, most counties don't require further orders, but a few do. So, how you present your settlement agreement and whether you add further orders to your Judgment depends on which county you are in, as explained in section 18.2 below.

### Two ways to add further orders

**A. Use Judgment attachments.** This is the preferred method. Use Judicial Council order forms that you attach to your Judgment to define your orders, mostly by checking boxes and filling in blanks. These forms are found in the Forms folder on the CD that comes with this book. The Judgment attachment forms are:

- FL-341 Child Custody and Visitation Order Attachment (used alone or attached to FL-355)
- FL-355 Stipulation and Order for Custody/Visitation, which can have the following attachments:  FL-341, 341(C), 341(D), 341(E).

  **Note:** FL-341(A) and 341(B)—supervised visitation and abduction orders—are found only in Book 2, *How to Solve Divorce Problems,* which is about cases contested in court.

- FL-342 Child Support Information and Order Attachment
- FL-342(A) Non-Guideline Child Support Findings Attachment

- FL-343 Spousal or Family Support Order Attachment
- FL-345 Property Order Attachment

Attach these forms to your Judgment, or study them for ideas for writing your own further orders, or combine the two methods. When you use these forms, then at items 4j–4m you must check boxes to show which orders have related attachments.

**B. Write your own.** While still valid, this method is not favored: courts generally prefer you to use the attachment forms. Still, there might be an occasion when adding a written order is useful, so return to these instructions if the need arises.

To add further orders that you prepare yourself, use the order language shown in various places below as a guide, mostly in sections 18.3 to 18.6. Use parts that apply to your case and change wording to fit your situation. You can also borrow language from the Judgment Attachment forms described in Method A above.

Put each written further order on an Additional Page form (figure 7.2) and use a new page to start each separate order. Type the heading: "Continuation of Judgment for Item 4j," (or 4k or 4l or 4m). Below that, type your further orders related to that item. Use as many Additional Pages as necessary. Your orders should be typed double-spaced so that your lines match the numbers on the left. However, if you're completing the form on a computer, don't worry that the lines don't match up—that's just the way the form works. Always refer to the parties as Petitioner and Respondent unless we tell you otherwise.

On the Judgment form, check box 4(o) and enter "See attached further orders."

## Adding pages to your Judgment

When attaching further orders, you must indicate at item 5 the number of pages that are attached. This means how many pages of further orders you attach, so do *not* include the pages of an attached settlement agreement—just pages that have further orders on them. Next, check the box under the judge's signature line to show that the judge's signature will now appear at the end of your further orders.

At the end of all further orders, whether you used attachment forms or prepared your own, add an Additional Page with the judge's signature line including the date and the paragraph above it, just as it appears on page 2 of the Judgment form. If you are filing a Stipulated Judgment, as shown on the next page, the judge's signature would follow that as well.

### Stipulated Judgments

Instead of a settlement agreement, you can file a Judgment that is signed by both parties, showing complete agreement not just as to terms but as to the form and content of the Judgment itself. A few counties require a stipulated Judgment if you attach a settlement agreement (see below).

**How to do it.** On the Judgment form, check the box under the judge's signature line to show that the judge's signature will now appear on an attachment page. At the end of any further orders you might have attached, add a final Additional Page form (figure 7.2) with the language shown below, followed by the Judge's signature, as described on the previous page.

The foregoing is approved as conforming to the agreement of the parties and is agreed to by:

Dated: _____

_____
Respondent, in pro per

Dated: _____

_____
Petitioner, in pro per

Dated: _____

_____
Judge of the Superior Court

## 18.2 If you have a settlement agreement

**Privacy rules.** To protect yourself, your Ex, and your children from identity theft, the copy of your agreement that is submitted to the court should be modified to have all Social Security and financial account numbers replaced with a code plus the last four digits of the account. See chapter 7.2 for details.

**Special rule for San Bernardino county.** When you file a settlement agreement in this county, both spouses must sign their approval of the Judgment as shown above, so have the Judgment ready to sign when the settlement agreement is signed. These signatures go at the very end of whatever further orders you might add, if any, and is followed only by the judge's signature section, which must be the very last thing on the Judgment. If Respondent has had his/her default taken (by filing form FL-165, chapter 17), his/her signature must be notarized, so leave several inches for this purpose between the parties' signatures and the judge's signature line. It would be a good idea to notarize both signatures in any county.

**Agreements and Judgments.** You *must* include the terms of your agreement in your Judgment. There are two ways to do this: by attaching your agreement to your Judgment, or the way San Bernardino wants it, filed as an Exhibit.

## Agreement Attached to Judgment

Almost all counties want you to attach your agreement to the Judgment and do the following:

- If you have minor children, check boxes 4(j) and 4(k) and also check the box below each of them that refers to a settlement agreement.
- If you have spousal support, check 4(l) and the box below that refers to a settlement agreement.
- If property is being divided, check 4(m) and the box below that refers to a settlement agreement.
- In **every** case, check box 4(o), enter "See attached further orders," and attach the following as a typed Further Order (as in Method B above):

> All warranties and contract remedies in the settlement agreement shall be preserved.

**Some counties also want further orders** in addition to attaching your settlement agreement. Use form FL-182 Judgment Checklist as a further guide to what forms may be required for your case.

- **Minor children.** In the following counties, attach FL-341 and 342, plus FL-342(A) if child support is below guideline: Alameda, Contra Costa, Los Angeles, Marin, Orange, Riverside, San Bernardino, San Diego, San Luis Obispo, Santa Clara, Santa Barbara, Sonoma, Solano, Sutter and Ventura. Nevada County also wants FL-350.
- **Division of property and debts.** Fresno and Sutter want FL-345.

**In counties that want further orders.** On the Judgment, check the box for each item 4(j) through 4(m) that applies to your case and also check the box below it that refers to a settlement agreement plus the box that refers to a Judgment attachment form or, if you use written orders check 4(o) "Other" and type in "See attached further orders."

# Figure 18.2  JUDGMENT
## Form FL-180  (Page 2)

**Type caption as shown in figure 7.2.**

**Minor children?** Enter their names and birth-dates. If not enough room, type in "See attachment 4i" and attach an additional page (figure 7.2). Also check 4j and 4k and complete those items.

**If you have minor children, check this box.**

**Type in your case number.**

**If you have children and a SA*, check these boxes. (not in San Bernardino –see not below)**

**If further orders are required in your county (section 18.2) check box 2 or 3 and attach the indicated form.**

**If you have a spousal support order, check this box. Check boxes (2) or (3) if they apply.**

**If you have property orders, check box m.**

**If you have a SA* also check box (4) (not in San Bernardino).**

**(not in San Bernardino) If you have a SA also check box m(1).**

**If further orders are required in your county, check box (5) and enter "as in Further Orders."**

**If further orders are required, check m(2) and attach the form, or check box m (3) and type in "as in Further Orders."**

**If you attach further orders, enter the number of pages of orders attached and check this box.**

**In San Bernardino** if you have a SA, check this box and follow the instructions on the next page.

---

FL-180

CASE NAME (Last name, first name of each party):

CASE NUMBER:

4.  i. ☐ The children of this marriage or domestic partnership are:
      (1) ☐ Name                              Birthdate

      (2) ☐ Parentage is established for children of this relationship born prior to the marriage or c
   j. ☑ Child custody and visitation (parenting time) are ordered as set forth in the attached
      (1) ☐ Settlement agreement, stipulation for judgment, or other written agreement which con required by Family Code section 3048(a).
      (2) ☐ Child Custody and Visitation Order Attachment (form FL-341).
      (3) ☐ Stipulation and Order for Custody and/or Visitation of Children (form FL-355).
      (4) ☐ Previously established in another case. Case number:              Court:
   k. ☐ Child support is ordered as set forth in the attached
      (1) ☐ Settlement agreement, stipulation for judgment, or other written agreement which con required by Family Code section 4065(a).
      (2) ☐ Child Support Information and Order Attachment (form FL-342).
      (3) ☐ Stipulation to Establish or Modify Child Support and Order (form FL-350).
      (4) ☐ Previously established in another case. Case number:              Court:
   l. ☐ Spousal, domestic partner, or family support is ordered:
      (1) ☐ Reserved for future determination as relates to    ☐ petitioner    ☐ responde
      (2) ☐ Jurisdiction terminated to order spousal or partner support to ☐ petitioner ☐
      (3) ☐ As set forth in the attached Spousal, Partner, or Family Support Order Attachment (fo
      (4) ☑ As set forth in the attached settlement agreement, stipulation for judgment, or other w
      (5) ☐ Other (specify):
   m. ☐ Property division is ordered as set forth in the attached
      (1) ☐ Settlement agreement, stipulation for judgment, or other written agreement.
      (2) ☐ Property Order Attachment to Judgment (form FL-345).
      (3) ☐ Other (specify):
   n. ☐ Attorney fees and costs are ordered as set forth in the attached
      (1) ☐ Settlement agreement, stipulation for judgment, or other written agreement.
      (2) ☐ Attorney Fees and Costs Order (form FL-346).
      (3) ☐ Other (specify):
   o. ☐ Other (specify):

Each attachment to this judgment is incorporated into this judgment, and the parties are ordered to comply with provisions. Jurisdiction is reserved to make other orders necessary to carry out this judgment.

Date:
5. Number of pages attached: _____
                                                    JUDICIAL OFFICER
                                  ☐ SIGNATURE FOLLOWS LAST ATTACHMENT

**NOTICE**
Dissolution or legal separation may automatically cancel the rights of a spouse or domestic partner under domestic partner's will, trust, retirement plan, power of attorney, pay-on-death bank account, transfer-on-death vehicle registration, survivorship rights to any property owned in joint tenancy, and any other similar property interest. It does not automatically cancel the rights of a spouse or domestic partner as beneficiary of the other spouse's or domestic partner's life insurance review these matters, as well as any credit cards, other credit accounts, insurance policies, retirement p determine whether they should be changed or whether you should take any other actions.
A debt or obligation may be assigned to one party as part of the dissolution of property and debts, but if that debt or obligation, the creditor may be able to collect from the other party.
An earnings assignment may be issued without additional proof if child, family, partner, or spousal support Any party required to pay support must pay interest on overdue amounts at the "legal rate," which is curren

FL-180 [Rev. July 1, 2012]                    **JUDGMENT**
                                               (Family Law)

---

**Note:** SA = Settlement Agreement in the instructions above.

**Note:** In San Bernardino County you do not attach your SA so you do not check any boxes to show that one is attached. Instead, you attach further orders. as described on the next page.

## The San Bernardino Method

**San Bernardino County** does not want your agreement to be attached to your Judgment. Instead, put a cover page on your agreement that says:

EXHIBIT 1
SETTLEMENT AGREEMENT

File your agreement separately with your Judgment. Do *not* check any item under 4(j) – 4(m) that indicates that you have attached a settlement agreement. They also want every term of your settlement agreement attached to your Judgment as further orders. Prepare further orders as shown in section 18.1 above, adding as many further orders as required to reflect every term of your agreement, using Judgment attachments or your own typed further orders. And both spouses *must* sign the Judgment as shown on page 187, so best to have that ready when you sign your settlement agreement. Insert the language below as your first further order.

### San Bernardino, further order for settlement agreement

The settlement agreement, received in evidence as Petitioner's Exhibit 1, is approved, ordered placed in the case file and, pursuant thereto, it is ordered as follows below.

## 18.3  Orders for cases with property and debts

1.  **None:** If you checked box 5a in the Petition, you don't need orders regarding property in your Judgment. Do not check 4(m) on your Judgment.

2.  **Divided by agreement:** If you attach a written settlement agreement to your Judgment check box 4(m) and box 4(m)(1). If further orders are required in your county even when you attach an agreement, prepare and attach them as described in the next paragraph.

3.  **Divided by the court:** If you have no settlement agreement and you listed *community* property or debts at item 5 on your Petition, you must either:
   • Check box 4(m)(2) and attach form FL-345,  or
   • Check box 4(m)(3), enter "See further order" and attach your own typed property orders using the language shown below as a guide.

## Order dividing community property and debts

> Judgment Attachment 4(m)
>
> It is further ordered that the community property and obligations of the parties, in order to effectuate a substantially equal division (if you are seeking an unequal division, say "fair division"), is divided as follows:
>
> Petitioner is awarded the following:
>
> List and describe in detail with account numbers, license and VIN for vehicles, and legal description and assessor's parcel number for real estate.
>
> Respondent is awarded the following:  (list as described above)
>
> Petitioner is ordered to pay:
>
> List and describe debts in detail—use account numbers when possible.
>
> Respondent is ordered to pay:  (list as described above)
>
> The parties are ordered to do whatever acts and sign whatever documents may be necessary to carry out these orders.

**Note about pension plans.** Read chapter 3.6(b) very carefully. If the community has an interest in a retirement fund or plan, things can go smoothly if you find a way to award it entirely to the employee-spouse, but if you **divide** a pension plan or retirement fund—401(k), 403(b), SEP IRA, Keogh, or the like—you *must* have a correctly drafted QDRO order. This is technical and difficult, so call Divorce Helpline to assist with your paperwork to make sure things are done right.

**Note about the family home.** See chapter 3.6(c). If there are minor children and you want to keep them in the house for some period of time, you can order title changed to tenants-in-common and defer the sale until all child-support obligations are terminated, or other dates or conditions. The percentage interest of each spouse would be half the community interest plus any reimbursable separate contributions divided by total equity in the house. This can get complicated, so if you have this situation, get DealMaker software (see inside front cover), or call Divorce Helpline for assistance. Ask about their special deals for DealMaker users.

**About Auto IDs.** If Respondent might not sign a pink slip to transfer ownership of an auto to Petitioner, add the VIN (vehicle identification number) to the auto's description in this order and use the Judgment to transfer the auto title.

**Awards of real estate.** After the hearing, file a copy of the Judgment, certified by the court clerk, with the County Recorder, along with the Preliminary Change of Ownership form (chapter 3.6(c)). This makes the Judgment work as a legal transfer of title. Also try to get Respondent to transfer the title by deed.

**4. Separate property:** To confirm separate property or debts to one spouse, insert the following order in your Judgment:

> It is further ordered that the following described property be confirmed as (Petitioner's/Respondent's) separate property:
>
> (list property in detail and with full legal descriptions as described in item 3 above).

## 18.4 Orders for cases with children

If you have children, your Judgment *must* include orders for their custody, support, and health insurance. If you are not attaching a settlement agreement, or if you do attach a settlement agreement and your county wants further orders regarding children anyway, then you must attach further orders to your Judgment.

The easiest way is to use Judgment attachments FL-341 and FL-342. Also use FL-342(A) if child support is below guideline. Check boxes on your Judgment at items 4(j)(2) and 4(k)(2) to show there's an attachment.

Or, you can prepare typed further orders as shown below.

**Agreement?** If you covered these subjects in an attached agreement, you need further orders only in the counties listed in section 18.2 above.

### Required language in every Judgment concerning children

**Item 4j.** The Judgment must contain certain statements about notice and jurisdiction. Therefore, at item 4j, do one of the following:

a. Check item 4(j)(2) and use FL-341 (on the CD) for custody/visitation orders (it contains required statements). This is the easiest way to go. Or,

b. If you prepare your own typed further orders, check item 4(o), and type in "See further orders," and use the language below on an Additional Page form (figure 7.2) and put it at the beginning of the other further orders for custody and visitation.

> Judgment Attachment 4(j) (Family Code Sec. 3048)
>
> Jurisdiction: This court has jurisdiction to make child custody orders in this case under the Uniform Child Custody Jurisdiction and Enforcement Act (part 3 of the California Family Code commencing with section 3400).

Notice and Opportunity to Be Heard: The responding party was given notice and opportunity to be heard as provided by the laws of the State of California.

Country of Habitual Residence: The country of habitual residence of the child or children in this case is (the United States of America) (other).

Penalties for Violating This Order: If you violate this order you may be subject to civil or criminal penalties, or both.

## Two more required forms for cases with children

- **FL-192 Notice of Rights and Responsibilities.** Attach it to the Judgment. This form contains information about health care and how to change a child support order.

- **FL-191 Case Registry form.** This form is presented along with the Judgment but *not* attached to it. Filling it out is straightforward. Do the caption like most of the other forms and enter as much of the requested personal information as you can dig up, as it may help you enforce your support order some day. This form is not on public view, so you **should** include complete Social Security numbers.

## Custody order

Judgment Attachment 4(j)

It is further ordered that the care, custody, and control of the minor child(ren) of the parties, namely: **(list full name and birthday for each child)**

    ___(name)___ , born ___(date)___
    ___(name)___ , born ___(date)___

shall be as follows (choose one): **(see chapter 4.1 for definitions of terms)**

    1) legal custody to Petitioner and Respondent jointly, with primary physical custody to Petitioner (or Respondent).

    2) legal and physical custody to Petitioner and Respondent jointly.

    3) primary legal and physical custody to Petitioner (or Respondent).

### A) If joint custody or joint legal custody is ordered, add:

The consent of both parents is required to exercise legal control of the child(ren) in the following circumstances: (state "none" or specify very exactly).

**B) If joint custody or joint physical custody is ordered, add:**

Neither parent acting alone shall do any act to deprive the other parent of physical custody for a period of more than ____ days, nor take the children out of this state without the written consent of the other parent.

**C) If physical custody or primary (sole) custody is ordered, add:**

Said custody is subject to the right of visitation which is hereby awarded to Respondent (or Petitioner, or other) according to the following terms and conditions: **(Write your visitation terms (parenting plan) very clearly and specifically. See chapter 4, especially 4.3.)**

**Note for welfare parents about custody:** If joint physical custody is awarded, you should add this language to the custody order: "It is further ordered that for the purpose of determining eligibility for public assistance, the Petitioner (or Respondent) shall be considered the primary caretaker of the child, and Petitioner's (or Respondent's) home is the primary home of the child(ren)."

### Child support order

Judgment Attachment 4(k) (Child Support)

It is further ordered that (Respondent/Petitioner) shall pay to (Petitioner/Respondent/other) as and for child support, a total of $_____ per month, payable on the ___ day of each month, beginning (some date after the hearing), and continuing until further order of this court or until said child marries, dies, is emancipated, reaches the age of 19, or reaches 18 and is not a full–time high school student, whichever occurs first. **(If more than one child, unless there's different timeshare for different children, add:)** Of the total amount ordered, the amount of support for the youngest child is $____, referred to hereafter as (CS). Support has been added for additional children as follows:

.6 times (CS) for the second youngest child, or $_____, plus

.4 times (CS) for the third youngest child, or $_____, plus

.3 times (CS) for the fourth youngest child, or $_____, plus

. . . **and so on for each additional child: .2 for the 5th child; .125 for the 6th and 7th; .063 for the 8th; .031 for the 9th and .016 for the 10th. Use as many steps as there are additional children in your case, and make sure it all adds up to the total support ordered.**

**(CS) comes from the child support guideline (chapter 5.3 and page 86). CS plus any add-on support ordered must add up to the total child support ordered.**

**If child care is being paid to allow a parent to work, add:** As additional child support, it is further ordered that (Respondent/Petitioner) shall pay to (Petitioner/Respondent) for child care, a total of $___ per month, payable on the____ day of each month, beginning on _____, 20_, and continuing as long as child care is necessary and actually being paid.

**Optional:** It is further ordered that all child support obligations shall terminate upon the death of the recipient if the payor assumes full custody of the children.

## Health insurance must be ordered!

If either parent can get it at reasonable cost (see page 75), use order A below. If health care is not available at a reasonable cost now, you *must* include the alternative order B. Also, dental and vision coverage is to be included if available.

### Support order for health insurance

It is further ordered that reasonable health expenses for the child not paid for by insurance shall be shared as follows:   Mother ____% Father ___%.
   **Must be shared equally unless parents agree to share in proportion to net incomes.**

**(A)**

It is further ordered that during the term of the support obligation for each child, (Respondent/Petitioner) shall carry and maintain health, hospital, (dental, vision) insurance for the benefit of said child.

**(B)**

It is further ordered that during the term of the support obligation for each child, should health (dental, vision) insurance coverage for the benefit of the child become available at a reasonable cost to either party, that party shall provide such coverage and notify the other party in writing.

### Optional order for life insurance

It is further ordered that during the term of the child support obligation, (Respondent/Petitioner) shall maintain a policy of insurance on his/her life in the amount of $_____ and shall name said minor child(ren) as beneficiary (beneficiaries).

# CHILD SUPPORT NOTES

**Mandatory wage assignments.** If you have a child support order, you *must* also use the wage assignment order described in section 18.6, below. You must also prepare the wage assignment form described in chapter 19 and present it along with your Judgment.

**Tax savings?** If there is a significant difference in income levels between spouses, the family as a whole can very likely save some money on taxes by combining child and spousal support and calling it "family support." This way, Uncle Sam will chip in on your support payments. An order for family support is too tricky to draft without help. You can call Divorce Helpline to order a computerized calculation of possible tax savings, or you can get your own copy of Nolo's CalSupport™ software and do it yourself.

**Changes.** If you want the amount of child support to change, you must formally modify the court order. This can be done by stipulation (agreement) or by making a motion in court.

## Public assistance cases

1) If the recipient of child support gets public assistance, child support *must* be paid to the State Disbursement Unit. Add these words at the end of the child support order: "Payments are to be made through the State Disbursement Unit, P.O. Box 989067, West Sacramento, CA 95798-9067." Your Wage Assignment Order must be made payable to the same office. Find your local DCSS at **www.nolodivorce.com/links**. Contact them well ahead of Judgment to open a file.

2) The Department of Child Support Services of the county where children are receiving aid must sign off on the proposed Judgment before you file it or take it to court. Contact them to see if they will prepare this addition to the Judgment for you. If not, prepare this as a typed further order (page 186) and add the language below after the judge's signature line, then take it in and get it signed:

The Department of Child Support Services for _____ County approves the above child support order.

Dated:_____     Signed: _____

# Stipulation to Establish Child Support

## What it is

The Stipulation to Establish Child Support is an agreement signed by both parents setting the amount of child support. It can be used to set support in cases of pure joint custody or when for any reason parents want to agree to less support than is required by state guidelines, yet do not want to go to the trouble of making a complete settlement agreement. The response fee (chapter 7.3) might be charged unless it has already been paid for filing other documents. If parents stipulate to an amount below California guidelines, no change of circumstances need be shown on a future motion to modify the support order to bring it up to guideline level.

## When required

If used at all, this form is filed when you file the Judgment. If you want to agree to an amount of child support—especially if it is less than the guideline figure—you will need either a settlement agreement (chapter 6) or the Stipulation to Establish Child Support. In fact, in at least six counties, you need the Stipulation even if you *do* have a settlement agreement: Imperial, Santa Barbara, Santa Cruz, Solano, Stanislaus—and also Alameda, if the amount is above or below the guideline.

## How to fill it out

Fill it out as shown in figures 18.3 and 18.4 below. Prepare the original and make three copies.

**Your spouse's figures** for income and deductions are taken from data you already entered in the Income and Expense Declarations, discussed in chapter 16.

**Public assistance cases.** If either spouse is receiving or has applied for public assistance for the minor children of this case, this form will have to be signed by the Department of Child Support Services in the county where your case is filed. Call for an appointment and go see them. Take this completed form with you.

Note. What used to be called AFDC is now called TANF/CalWORKS. In either case, it refers to public assistance (welfare) for children.

# Figure 18.3 STIPULATION TO ESTABLISH CHILD SUPPORT
## Form FL-350 (Page 1)

**Type captions as shown in figure 7.1.**

**Check 1a, enter net income of parties (figures from Income & Expense form) or check 1b and attach a computer calculation (see text note below).**

**Enter name of payer and amount of support required by guidelines.***

**Check 6 and 6a and enter agreed amount of support.**

**Enter details of support payment at 7a, additional support, if any, at item 7b, and total at 7c.**

**Your case number.**

**Check box 2 and enter % of time each parent has care of child(ren).**

FL-350

ATTORNEY OR PARTY WITHOUT ATTORNEY (Name, State Bar number, and address):

FOR COURT USE ONLY

TELEPHONE NO:          FAX NO. (Optional):
E-MAIL ADDRESS (Optional):
ATTORNEY FOR (Name):

SUPERIOR COURT OF CALIFORNIA, COUNTY OF
STREET ADDRESS:
MAILING ADDRESS:
CITY AND ZIP CODE:
BRANCH NAME:

PETITIONER/PLAINTIFF:
RESPONDENT/DEFENDANT:
OTHER PARENT:

STIPULATION TO ESTABLISH OR MODIFY
CHILD SUPPORT AND ORDER

CASE NUMBER:

1. a. ☐ Mother's net monthly disposable income: $
      ☐ Father's net monthly disposable income: $
   -OR-
   b. ☐ A printout of a computer calculation of the parents' financial circumstances is attached.
2. ☐ Percentage of time each parent has primary responsibility for the children: Mother: ___ %   Father: ___ %
3. a. ☐ A hardship is being experienced by the mother $         per month because of (specify):

      The hardship will last until (date):
   b. ☐ A hardship is being experienced by the father $         per month because of (specify):

      The hardship will last until (date):
4. The amount of child support payable by (name):                                    , referred to as "the parent ordered to
   pay support," as calculated under the guideline is: $              per month.
5. ☐ We agree to guideline support.
6. ☐ The guideline amount should be rebutted because of the following:
   a. ☐ We agree to child support in the amount of $            per month; the agreement is in the best interest of
      the children; the needs of the children will be adequately met by the agreed amount; and application of the guideline
      would be unjust or inappropriate in this case.
   b. ☐ Other rebutting factors (specify):
7. The parent ordered to pay support must pay child support as follows beginning (date):
   a. BASIC CHILD SUPPORT
        Child's name            Monthly amount              Payable to (name):

   Total: $              payable ☐ on the first of the month ☐ other (specify):
   b. ☐ In addition, the parent ordered to pay support must pay the following:
      (1) ☐ $       per month for child care costs to (name):                            on (date):
      (2) ☐ $       per month for health-care costs not deducted from gross income
              to (name):                                                                on (date):
      (3) ☐ $       per month for special educational or other needs of the children
              to (name):                                                                on (date):
      (4) ☐ other (specify):
   c. **Total monthly child support** payable by the parent ordered to pay support will be: $
      payable ☐ on the first of the month. ☐ other (specify):

Form Adopted for Mandatory Use
Judicial Council of California
FL-350 [Rev. July 1, 2010]

STIPULATION TO ESTABLISH OR MODIFY
CHILD SUPPORT AND ORDER

Page 1 of 2
Family Code, § 4065
www.courtinfo.ca.gov

*****Note:** A computer calculation of the guideline amount, referred to in items 1b and 4, is available from Divorce Helpline, or you can calculate it yourself with CalSupport™ software (see inside front cover), or you can try to calculate the guideline figure by hand with the formula and instructions in chapter 5.4.

# Figure 18.4 STIPULATION TO ESTABLISH CHILD SUPPORT
## Form FL-350 (Page 2)

**Type in your names.**

**Your case number.**

**Indicate who will maintain basic health insurance for kids or check box 8b.**

**If travel expenses will be shared, check box 11 and enter parent's shares.**

**Check box 12.**

**Indicate how parents will share this expense.**

**Check 16a if no parent receives or has applied for welfare. Otherwise, check 16b and DA must sign here.**

**Enter date when signing and names of parties.**

**Petitioner's signature.**

**Respondent's signature.**

PETITIONER/PLAINTIFF:

RESPONDENT/DEFENDANT:

CASE NUMBER

8. a. Health insurance will be maintained by (specify name):
The parent ordered to provide health insurance must seek continuation of coverage for the child after the child attains the age when the child is no longer considered eligible for coverage as a dependent under the insurance contract, if the child is incapable of self-sustaining employment because of a physically or mentally disabling injury, illness, or condition and is chiefly dependent upon the parent providing health insurance for support and maintenance.

b. ☐ A health insurance coverage assignment will issue if health insurance is available through employment or other group plan or otherwise is available at reasonable cost. Both parents are ordered to cooperate in the presentation, collection, and reimbursement of any medical claims.

c. Any health expenses not paid by insurance will be shared: Mother: % Father: %

9. a. An earnings assignment order is issued.
b. ☐ We agree that service of the earnings assignment be stayed because we have made the following alternative arrangements to ensure payment (specify):

10. In the event that there is a contract between a party receiving support and a private child support co... pay support must pay the fee charged by the private child support collector. This fee must not exceed amount in arrears nor may it exceed 50 percent of any fee charged by the private child support colle... created by this provision is in favor of the private child support collector and the party receiving supp...

11. ☐ Travel expenses for visitation will be shared: Mother: % Father: %

12. ☐ We agree that we will promptly inform each other of any change of residence or employment, including the employer's name, address, and telephone number.

13. ☐ Other (specify):

14. We agree that we are fully informed of our rights under the California child support guidelines.
15. We make this agreement freely without coercion or duress.
16. The right to support
a. ☐ has not been assigned to any county, and no application for public assistance is pending.
b. ☐ has been assigned or an application for public assistance is pending in (county name):
If you checked b., an attorney for the local child support agency must sign below, joining in this agreement.

Date:

(TYPE OR PRINT NAME) ▶ (SIGNATURE OF ATTORNEY FOR LO...

**Notice:** If the amount agreed to is less than the guideline amount, no change of circumstances need be shown to obtain a change in the support order to a higher amount. If the order is above the guideline, a change of circumstances will be required to modify this order. This form must be signed by the court to be effective.

Date:

(TYPE OR PRINT NAME) ▶ (SIGNATURE OF PETITIONER)

Date:

(TYPE OR PRINT NAME) ▶ (SIGNATURE OF RESPONDENT)

Date:

(TYPE OR PRINT NAME) ▶ (SIGNATURE OF ATTORNEY FOR PETITIONER)

(TYPE OR PRINT NAME) ▶ (SIGNATURE OF ATTORN...

**THE COURT ORDERS**
17. a. ☐ The guideline child support amount in item 4 is rebutted by the factors stated in item 6.
b. Items 7 through 13 are ordered. All child support payments must continue until further order of the court, or until the child marries, dies, is emancipated, or reaches age 18. The duty of support continues as to an unmarried child who has attained the age of 18 years, is a full-time high school student, and resides with a parent, until the time the child completes the 12th grade or attains the age of 19 years, whichever first occurs. Except as modified by this stipulation, all provisions of any previous orders made in this action will remain in effect.

Date:

JUDGE OF THE SUPERIOR COURT

**NOTICE:** Any party required to pay child support must pay interest on overdue amounts at the "legal" rate, which is currently 10 percent per year. This can be a large added amount.

FL-350 [Rev. July 1, 2010]

STIPULATION TO ESTABLISH OR MODIFY
CHILD SUPPORT AND ORDER

Page 2 of 2

## 18.5 Orders for spousal support

If you want orders regarding spousal support, check box 4(l) on your Judgment. If you are attaching an agreement, also check box 4(l)(4). If you are not attaching a settlement agreement, or if you do attach an agreement and your county wants further orders regarding spousal support anyway, then you must attach further orders for spousal support to your Judgment as described below.

The easiest way is to use the Judgment attachment form FL-343 and check box 4(l)(3). If you prepare your own typed further orders, do it as described in section 18.1 above, check box 4(l)(5) and enter "Further Orders," and prepare your order based on the language shown below.

**1. None:** If the right to spousal support is being reserved for either spouse, check box 4(l)(1) on your Judgment. If it is being terminated for either party, check box 4(l)(2).

If further orders are required and you prepare your own, use the language below. If no spousal support was requested or desired at this time, use option A below, but if it was waived either in open court or in writing, use option B.

### No spousal support or spousal support terminated

---

Judgment Attachment 4(l) (Spousal Support)

**A.** No spousal support shall be awarded at this time.

**B. For marriages over five years, add this before the next bit:** The parties are informed and aware that, if requested by either party, the court is required to reserve spousal support for long-term marriages of over 10 years and may choose to do so for some marriages shorter than 10 years. They each waive the right to receive spousal support now or at any time in the future.

**All cases use this:** Spousal support having been waived by Petitioner (or Respondent, or Petitioner *and* Respondent), the court hereby terminates jurisdiction therein and no court shall have jurisdiction to order spousal support in the future regardless of any circumstances that may arise.*

---

**2. Spousal support ordered:** Attach form FL-343 and check box 4(l)(3) or prepare your own further order using the language below and as described in section 18.1 and check box 4(l)(5). If you covered this in an attached settlement agreement, you need further orders only in counties that require them, listed in section 18.2 above.

### Order for spousal support

---

Judgment Attachment 4(l) (Spousal Support)

The court (also) finds that the needs of Petitioner (or Respondent) are/are not met by this order.

It is hereby ordered that Respondent (or Petitioner) shall pay to Petitioner (or Respondent) the sum of $_____ per month, as and for spousal support, payable on the __ day of each month, beginning **(some date after the hearing)**, 20_, and continuing until death or remarriage of the recipient, or until **(some specific date, and/or other specific conditions upon which payments stop)**, whichever occurs first,
  . . . or until further order of the court.
  . . . and following said time (or event), no court shall have jurisdiction to modify the (amount/duration/amount or duration) of spousal support, regardless of circumstances.*

---

*****Note:** In long marriages (roughly 10 years or more), the court *must* retain jurisdiction indefinitely unless spouses agree otherwise in a very specific writing (chapter 5.2).

**Options:** There are many possibilities for customizing spousal support to suit your needs, including automatic decreases at set times, tying the amount to either spouse's income, posting security or obtaining life insurance to benefit the recipient, and so on. If you need advice on this subject, call Divorce Helpline.

**Mandatory wage assignments.** If you have an order for spousal support, you *must* also use the assignment order described in section 18.6, below. You must also prepare the wage assignment form described in chapter 19 and present it along with your Judgment.

## 18.6 Mandatory wage assignment

### Order for wage assignment cases

If you have an order for child support or spousal support, the following order *must* be inserted in your Judgment immediately after your other orders for either child or spousal support.

> It is further ordered that, pursuant to Family Code 5230, obligor is ordered to assign to obligee that portion of (his/her) earnings sufficient to pay the amount of support ordered by the Court. The obligor is ordered to give written notice to the obligee of any change in employment within ten days of said change, together with the name and address of any new employer.

### Order staying wage assignment

If you can satisfy the requirements for a stay of the wage assignment order (chapter 19), try adding this order after the one above. It could work.

> It is further ordered that service of the Wage Assignment Order is stayed provided that the Payor is not more than ___ days late in the payment of spousal/family support.

## 18.7 Personal service of the Judgment

To enforce an order, especially by using contempt of court, you have to be able to prove Respondent had notice of the order. So if Respondent has been ordered to pay support, deliver property, or do or not do any act in the future, *and* was not personally present in court when the order was made, then once the Judgment has been signed by the judge and entered (chapter 21), it is very important to have a copy of the Judgment *personally* served on Respondent as described in chapter 12.4. The person who served the papers signs this Proof of Personal Service which you then file with the Superior Court Clerk.

# WAGE AND EARNINGS ASSIGNMENT

## What it is

The best way to make sure you get paid by an employed ex-spouse is to use the Wage Assignment Order (WAO). It is served on the employer, who must take support out of the employee's earnings and pay it directly to the recipient. In child support cases, the recipient can choose to have payments made to the State Disbursement Unit, which takes over enforcement and forwards all payments to the recipient. If public assistance is being received or has been applied for, support *must* be paid to the SDU—see the last paragraph in this chapter.

**Wage assignment is mandatory.** In any case where support is ordered, you *must* include one of the Wage Assignment Orders below with your Judgment. No exceptions. After the order is signed by the judge, you can then *choose* to have it served on the paying spouse's employer. If served, the employer will withhold up to 50% of the payer's wages at each pay period to make support payments. This is now the routine way of handling support and employers are accustomed to it. It is against the law for any employer to refuse to hire, to discipline, or to fire an employee because of a wage assignment.

The WAO is binding against present or future employers. So even if the paying spouse is unemployed or self-employed or whereabouts unknown, the order must still be issued—then you just wait until your spouse has an employer (or a big customer) you can locate, whenever that might happen.

## Staying service of the Wage Assignment Order

**Formal stay by court order** is possible if the parties make a written agreement that says the WAO will not be immediately served on the payor's employer. If support is being ordered through a county officer, this agreement must be signed by the Department of Child Support Services. If the court *does* stay the service of the wage assignment, the recipient can later terminate the stay simply and easily, just by filing a declaration under penalty of perjury that the payments are in arrears in some amount, any amount.

**Informal stay.** It is always entirely in the control of the recipient to serve the Order whenever he or she chooses to do so. If the spouses are cooperative, the Order need never be served. This understanding can be made part of a settlement agreement (chapter 6). It pays to cooperate and it pays to keep payments current.

## Which wage assignment form to use

- If there's child support, use FL-195, Order/Notice to Withhold Income For Child Support (figure 19.1). If you also have spousal support, it can be included. For help filling it out, visit your county's office of the Department of Child Support Services (DCSS). A link to DCSS local offices can be found at **www.nolodivorce.com/links**.

- Where there's spousal support alone, no child support, use the Earnings Assignment Order For Spousal Support (figure 19.2).

## How to fill out the forms

Fill the forms out as shown in figures 19.1 or 19.2. Make the original and four copies. Attach this order to the Judgment and present it for the judge's signature at the same time, in the same way. When using FL-195, a local cover sheet form is required in Santa Cruz County to act as a caption. Don't forget: you should disguise Social Security numbers on papers filed with the court (chapter 7.2), but not on copies given to the other side or served on an employer.

## Service of the Wage Assignment Order and a blank Request for Hearing

Unless there is a written agreement or an order that the wage assignment will not be served, then immediately after it is signed by the judge, you should serve the WAO on the paying spouse's employer, along with a blank copy of form FL-450 Request For Hearing Re Wage Assignment (on the CD in the Forms folder). Technically, employers are to be served personally, but most will honor papers served by mail. So unless your spouse is a big wheel in a small company, serve these documents on the employer by mail (chapter 12.6) and file a Proof of Service by Mail (figure 13.3) with the court.

Whenever the paying spouse changes jobs, the new employer must be served as soon as possible with copies of the same documents, and another Proof of Service must be filed.

## Troubleshooting

**Self-employed people.** Wage assignment is not effective against self-employed people unless they happen to have one primary client or customer, in which case the order can be served on that client or customer.

**Can't find spouse or employer?** If you don't know the location of your spouse or spouse's employer, take the Judgment and the WAO to your county Department of Child Support Services, and they will try to help you. They can conduct a parent locator search. If your spouse is working but you can't find out who the employer is, go to the DCSS office in your county.

**Problem payers.** If the payer is often unemployed, or changes jobs often, or might otherwise be difficult to chase down for *child* support payments, go to your local office of the Department of Child Support Services, open a case, and make your Wage Assignment Order payable to the State Disbursement Unit at the address below. If your order is for spousal support only, contact the local District Attorney and ask if they have a support enforcement service that can help you.

**How long does it take to get paid?** You get paid when the employee does. Most employees are paid every two weeks. Depending on the company's pay period and when in that cycle the employer receives the WAO, it could take several weeks for the order to take effect and for you to start receiving payments. If three or four weeks go by and you don't see any money, call the employer's payroll department and ask if there is a problem and when you will see your check.

**If the employer does not obey the order.** It has been known to happen that in some small companies where the employee is very important, or friends with the boss, the company will try to disregard the WAO. In that case, contact your local office of the Department of Child Support Services.

## Changes of address or employment

The recipient must notify the employer of changes in address if being paid directly, or notify the State Disbursement Unit if payments are being made through that office. If payments are undeliverable for six months because the recipient failed to provide a current address, the employer or SDU will stop making payments and refund all undelivered money to the paying spouse.

If the paying spouse terminates employment, the employer *must* notify the recipient by mail on or before the date the next payment would be due. The paying spouse must notify the recipient of any changes in employment within 10 days, and provide the name and address of the new employer.

## Payments are made through the State Disbursement Unit

Child support must be paid through the State Disbursement Unit (SDU). The address where checks are to be sent has already been entered on page 2 of the form. If there is an order for spousal support, you can choose to include it on this form and have it also paid through the SDU.

Before you submit your order, go to your county's office of the Department of Child Support Services, set up an account and request whatever information and help in completing your wage assignment order. You can find a link to the locations of DCSS offices at **www.nolodivorce.com/links**.

---

# Figure 19 • FL-195 • pages 2, 3 and 4

## Top of pages 2, 3 and 4

**Caption.** Enter Employer's Name and FEIN (if you can get it), Employee's name and Social Security Number, and your case number for both identifier entries.

## Top of page 2

**Remittance information.** On line 1, enter "California" in the blank field. On line 2, enter "10." On line 3, enter "service" in the first field and "5" in the second field. On line 4, enter "50." On line 6, enter "California".

## Page 4

**Bottom—Contact Information.** This is who the employer can contact for information about the withholding order—likely the agency that receives the employer's checks, but ask the court clerk to be sure there's not a local preference. Enter the name, phone, fax and email or website (if any), then the mailing address. Enter the name and address where the employer should send a termination notice, probably the same as above. Then repeat the contact information in the section below for who the Oblilgor (payer) can contact.

## More help

This is a complicated form. Form FL-196, the official instructions for FL-195, might help, or visit your local Department of Child Support Services or Family Law Facilitator and ask them to help you with it. For locations, see **www.nolodivorce.com/links**.

## Figure 19.1
## ORDER/NOTICE TO WITHHOLD INCOME FOR CHILD SUPPORT
### Form FL-195 (page 1)

Note: "Employer" in the instructions also refers to any other withholder upon whom the order might be served.

Check this box

Check this box.

Enter "California"

Enter your county

Employer's name and address.

Employer's Federal EIN number, if you can get it.

Name and birthdate of each child supported.

Enter amounts for:
child support
past-due ch. support
spousal support
Total

Enter total to be withheld, figured for each of these four pay periods.

Your case number.

Your case number

Employee's name (last name first) and Soc. Security number.

Custodial parent's name

If past due amounts ordered, check "yes" if over 12 weeks overdue, otherwise check "no."

Enter "month" for each item you use.

INCOME WITHHOLDING FOR SUPPORT

☐ ORIGINAL INCOME WITHHOLDING ORDER/NOTICE FOR SUPPORT (IWO)
☐ AMENDED IWO
☐ ONE-TIME ORDER/NOTICE FOR LUMP SUM PAYMENT     Date: _____
☐ TERMINATION OF IWO

☐ Child Support Enforcement (CSE) Agency  ☐ Court  ☐ Attorney  ☐ Private Individual/Entity  (Check One)

NOTE: This IWO must be regular on its face. Under certain circumstances you must reject this IWO and return it to the sender (see IWO instructions www.acf.hhs.gov/programs/css/resource/income-withholding-...). you receive this document from someone other than a state or tribal CSE agency or a court, a co... must be attached.

State/Tribe/Territory     California          Remittance ID (include w/payment) _____
City/County/Dist./Tribe _____                Order ID _____
Private Individual/Entity _____              CSE Agency Case ID _____

Employer/Income Withholder's Name _____     RE: _____
                                                Employee/Obligor's Name _____
Employer/Income Withholder's Address _____  Employee/Obligor's Social S... _____
                                                Custodial Party/Obligee's Name (Last, First, Middle) _____

Employer/Income Withholder's FEIN _____

Child(ren)'s Name(s) (Last, First, Middle)     Child(ren)'s Birth Date(s)
_____                                        _____
_____                                        _____
_____
_____
_____

ORDER INFORMATION: This document is based on the support or withholding order from _____
(State/Tribe). You are required by law to deduct these amounts from the employee/obligor's income until further notice.
$ _____ Per _____  current child support
$ _____ Per _____  past-due child support - Arrears greater than 12 weeks? ☑ Yes ☐ No
$ _____ Per _____  current cash medical support
$ _____ Per _____  past-due cash medical support
$ _____ Per _____  current spousal support
$ _____ Per _____  past-due spousal support
$ _____ Per _____  other (must specify) _____
for a Total Amount to Withhold of $ _____ per _____ .

AMOUNTS TO WITHHOLD: You do not have to vary your pay cycle to be in compliance with the Order Information. If your pay cycle does not match the ordered payment cycle, withhold one of the following amounts: this order
$ _____ per weekly pay period           $ _____ per semimonthly pay period (twice a month)
$ _____ per biweekly pay period (every two weeks) $ _____ per monthly pay period
$ _____ Lump Sum Payment: Do not stop any existing IWO unless you receive a termination order.

1

Document Tracking ID _____

⬅ Pages 2, 3 and 4

# Figure 19.2
## EARNINGS ASSIGNMENT ORDER FOR SPOUSAL SUPPORT
### Form FL-435

Note: Use this form only when there is no child support in your case, just spousal support.

**Type captions as shown in figure 7.1.**

**Check box 1a and enter amount of current spousal support order.**

**If you have order for past-due spousal support, check box 1b and enter amount.**

**Type in name and address of person or agency to receive amount at 1a.**

**Check box 3 and enter the name and address of person or agency to receive payment.**

**Your case number.**

**Type in name of paying spouse and his/her date of birth.**

**Type in total for items 1a and 1b.**

**If this modifies an existing withholding order, check here.**

**If spousal support arrearages being collected, enter total due and date amount was established.**

FL-435

ATTORNEY OR PARTY WITHOUT ATTORNEY (Name, State Bar number, and address):

FOR COURT USE ONLY

TELEPHONE NO.:    FAX NO. (Optional):
E-MAIL ADDRESS (Optional):
ATTORNEY FOR (Name):

SUPERIOR COURT OF CALIFORNIA, COUNTY OF
STREET ADDRESS:
MAILING ADDRESS:
CITY AND ZIP CODE:
BRANCH NAME:

PETITIONER/PLAINTIFF:

RESPONDENT/DEFENDANT:

OTHER PARENT:

EARNINGS ASSIGNMENT ORDER FOR SPOUSAL OR PARTNER SUPPORT
☐ Modification

CASE NUMBER:

TO THE PAYOR: This is a court order. You must withhold a portion of the earnings of (specify obligor's name and birth date)
and pay as directed below. (An explanation of this order is printed on page 2 of this form.)

THE COURT ORDERS
1. You must pay part of the earnings of the employee or other person who has been ordered to pay support, as
   a. ☐ $_____ per month current spousal or partner support
   b. ☐ $_____ per month spousal or partner support arrearages
   c. Total deductions per month: $_____

2. ☐ The payments ordered under item 1a must be paid to (name, address):

3. ☐ The payments ordered under item 1b must be paid to (name, address):

4. The payments ordered under item 1 must continue until further written notice from the payee or the court.

5. ☐ This order modifies an existing order. The amount you must withhold may have changed. The exis
   effect until this modification is effective.

6. This order affects all earnings that are payable beginning as soon as possible but not later than 10 days after you receive it.

7. You must give the obligor a copy of this order and the blank Request for Hearing Regarding Earnings Assignm
   within 10 days.

8. ☐ Other (specify):

9. For the purposes of this order, spousal or partner support arrearages are set at: $_____ as of (da

Date: _____

_____
JUDICIAL OFFICER

Form Adopted for Mandatory Use
Judicial Council of California
FL-435 [Rev. January 1, 2005]

EARNINGS ASSIGNMENT ORDER FOR SPOUSAL
OR PARTNER SUPPORT
(Family Law)

Family Code, §§ 298.6, 4200;
Code of Civil Procedure, § 706.031;
15 U.S.C. §§ 1672-1673
www.courtinfo.ca.gov

# HOW TO GET YOUR JUDGMENT

The goal of all your paperwork is to get a Judgment that will settle the legal issues of your case and order the marriage dissolved. There are two ways you can go about getting your Judgment: (A) by filing the Declaration form (below) with your final papers, or (B) by going to a hearing. Read the discussion below on both methods before choosing which to try first.

## Method A: Filing the Declaration form

This is the preferred method for getting your Judgment. All you have to do is prepare FL-170, the Declaration for Default or Uncontested Dissolution (below), and file it with your final set of papers (chapter 8, Step 4). A clerk, judge or commissioner will examine your documents and inform you of any defects if they find any. They like to avoid hearings, but if there are unusual features in your case—such as support that is too low or a division of community property with a net worth of more than $5,000 that is not about equal—and those features are not explained in an agreement, then it is possible that a judge will set a hearing where you can explain things in person.

### Preliminary Declarations of Disclosure (PD)
### and Final Declaration of Disclosure (FD):

- **Cases with no settlement agreement.** If you have no settlement agreement and no Response was filed, then—assuming you served your spouse with a PD and filed a proof of service and the Declaration in figure 14.3—you can waive the FD by checking box 5(b) on FL-170 Declaration for Default Dissolution (figure 20.1).

- **Cases with an agreement.** If you *do* have a settlement agreement, the judge must be able to look in your file and find proofs of service and the Declaration re Service (figure 14.3) showing that both parties served each other with the PD. Same for the FD unless it was waived by having *both* parties sign FL-144. If you have an agreement and the FD was neither completed by both parties nor mutually waived in your agreement or with form FL-144, you'd better call an attorney.

**Rejected Declarations.** In the unlikely event that your Declaration for Default or Uncontested Dissolution is rejected, all that happens is that you have to either correct your paperwork or, if the courts asks it, go to a hearing (see Method B below). The Declaration is more likely to work in cases that are routine—that is, if your requests appear normal, property division appears equal, and support is reasonable—otherwise the judge might want you to come in and be examined in person, so he can ask questions and be satisfied that everything is fair and correct.

**Los Angeles and Solano counties.** To proceed by Declaration, Respondent must approve your Judgment as to form and content as shown on page 187. There should be no response fee charged for filing the document (Government Code § 70671).

**Welfare.** If the recipient of support is receiving welfare, the District Attorney must also sign the Judgment.

**Patience.** Many courts are backed up to the point that it can take a very long time, several months to a year, to get default papers processed, so you have to be patient. Call and ask the clerk how long it might take. Here's something to try: ask the court clerk how soon you can schedule a hearing; papers are usually signed and filed right after a hearing, so going to a hearing might be faster. Read "How long does it take?" in **chapter 2.12** about getting a private judge to move your papers through faster. Get our free report on how to get a faster divorce at **www.nolodivorce.com/PJ**.

## Method B:  Going to a hearing

Most counties do not want hearings in uncontested divorce cases. However, if you are asked to go, don't worry; the hearing is easier than you might think. Since this is not a contested case, your spouse will not appear in court. The hearing will be very brief, almost a mere formality, and most of your time will be spent just waiting for it to start. The judge sees a lot of cases and will take no special notice of yours unless it is unusual. You won't be grilled mercilessly—the judge just wants to ask about the facts.

First, you have to arrange a date for your hearing, as described in section 20.2. When you appear, your name is called, you take the stand and make statements about the facts in your case. Your job is to present evidence to the court that will allow the judge to make decisions. Your testimony is evidence, but be sure to take with you any documents you have about the title and value of property (or debts) to be divided and, if there is to be support, take recent pay stubs, accounting statements and tax returns to show the income of you and your spouse.

Further instructions, including what to say at a hearing, are set out below in section 20.2.

## 20.1 Method A – Filing the Declaration form

You can almost always avoid going to a hearing by filing a sworn statement—form FL-170 Declaration for Default or Uncontested Dissolution—to take the place of your testimony in court. A "**default**" dissolution is when Respondent has made no appearance in the case and you file FL-165 Request to Enter Default to terminate Respondent's ability to enter the case. An "**uncontested**" dissolution is when one of you files an Appearance, Stipulation and Waivers (chapter 12.7) agreeing to let the other party complete the case as uncontested.

Proceeding by Declaration is the preferred method in most counties for cases where there is a settlement agreement or cases without property, debts, children, or spousal support. If you have property, debts, or kids but no settlement agreement, it can still work if your paperwork is clear, complete, and shows that you made full disclosure, property is divided equally, and the amount of support is backed up with a computer calculation such as CalSupport's Bench Report.

### How to do it

You can file the Declaration for Default Dissolution at the same time as the Request for Entry of Default (see checklist, chapter 8) or any time thereafter. If filed after, include a copy of the stamped Request for Default form. One source in LA tells us it's safer to file it *shortly after* the Default papers rather than with them; less confusing to the bureaucratic mind.

Fill out the Declaration as shown in figures 20.1, 20.2 and 20.3. Prepare the original and make three copies. You *must* also file the Judgment (chapter 18), wage assignment forms (chapter 19) if support was ordered in your case, and the Notice of Entry of Judgment (chapter 21). Don't forget to include stamped envelopes addressed to yourself and the Respondent with the Superior Court Clerk's return address. File these papers in person or by mail. If all goes well, you will get the signed Judgment back in the mail. If not, the court will tell you the reason why and ask you to fix your documents and refile. If the court sets a hearing, go on to the next section.

**Note 1.** If you have no settlement agreement and you have property or debts to divide, you must attach FL-160 Property Declaration (chapter 15) showing estimated values and your proposed division.

**Note 2.** If you have no settlement agreement and there are children, you must attach FL-150 Income and Expense Declaration (chapter 16).

**Note 3.** If spousal support is requested, or terminated, or the marriage is over 10 years in duration, you must attach FL-157 Spousal Support Attachment (on CD).

**Santa Clara.** If you have no settlement agreement but there are minor children, you must attach a sworn declaration stating basic financial facts: gross and net incomes of each party, the date support is to begin, amount of support requested for the spouse, amount requested for each child and in total, whether the recipient gets welfare, the name and birth date of each child, when the parties separated and who has been the primary caretaker since, that the parties are fit parents, and, for joint physical custody, what contact the Respondent will have with the child. Ask the clerk if they have local rules that spell out this requirement. For spousal support, you must include information relevant to the spousal support factors under Family Code §4320, stated in chapter 5.2. A computer printout of guideline calculation, including the findings page, can be used in place of the support portion information on the required declaration.

## Judgment Checklist

Look on the CD for form FL-182 Judgment Checklist. This is a detailed checklist that you should use as a guide to make sure you completed all documents needed for your Judgment. It can only help if you file this form with your Judgment to show the court what documents you have completed, but so far only San Francisco and Santa Clara counties require you to do this.

(continued on page 216)

# Figure 20.1  DECLARATION FOR
# DEFAULT OR UNCONTESTED DISSOLUTION
## Form FL-170   (Page 1)

Type caption as shown in figure 7.1.

Check this box.

Check this box.

If you filed a Request for Default (ch. 17), check box 4a.

If no settlement agreement, check 4a(3) either A or B.

If you had a settlement agreement, check 4b.

If a Response or Appearance and Waiver was filed, check box 4c.

Type in your case number.

If both parties filed FL-141 re: service of both Preliminary and Final Disclosures (FD), check box 5a.

If no Response, no agreement, and no proof of Final Disclosure from Respondent, check 5b.

If both parties waived the FD with FL-144 or in a written agreement, check box 5c.

---

**FL-170**

ATTORNEY OR PARTY WITHOUT ATTORNEY *(Name, State Bar number, and address):*

FOR COURT USE ONLY

TELEPHONE NO.:             FAX NO. *(Optional)*:
E-MAIL ADDRESS *(Optional)*:
ATTORNEY FOR *(Name)*:

SUPERIOR COURT OF CALIFORNIA, COUNTY OF
STREET ADDRESS:
MAILING ADDRESS:
CITY AND ZIP CODE:
BRANCH NAME:

PETITIONER:

RESPONDENT:

DECLARATION FOR DEFAULT OR UNCONTESTED
☐ DISSOLUTION   ☐ LEGAL SEPARATION

CASE NUMBER:

(NOTE: Items 1 through 12 apply to both dissolution and legal separation proceedings.)
1. I declare that if I appeared in court and were sworn, I would testify to the truth of the facts in this declaration.
2. I agree that my case will be proven by this declaration and that I will not appear before the court unless I am ordered by the court to do so.
3. All the information in the ☐ amended ☐ *Petition* ☐ *Response* is true and correct.
4. Type of case *(check a, b, or c)*:
   a. ☐ **Default without agreement**
      (1) No response has been filed and there is no written agreement or stipulated judgment between th
      (2) The default of the respondent was entered or is being requested, and I am not seeking any relie petition; and
      (3) The following statement is true *(check one)*:
         (A) ☐ There are no assets or debts to be disposed of by the court.
         (B) ☐ The community and quasi-community assets and debts are listed on the **completed** *Declaration* (form FL-160), which includes an estimate of the value of the assets and to be distributed to each party. The division in the proposed *Judgment* (form FL-180) division of the property and debts, or if there is a negative estate, the debts are assig
   b. ☐ **Default with agreement**
      (1) No response has been filed and the parties have agreed that the matter may proceed as a defau notice; and
      (2) The parties have entered into a written agreement regarding their property and their marriage or rights, including support, the original of which is being or has been submitted to the court. I requ approve the agreement.
   c. ☐ **Uncontested**
      (1) Both parties have appeared in the case; and
      (2) The parties have entered into a written agreement regarding their property and their marriage or rights, including support, the original of which is being or has been submitted to the court. I reque approve the agreement.
5. Declaration of disclosure *(check a, b, or c)*:
   a. ☐ Both the petitioner and respondent have filed, or are filing concurrently, a *Declaration Regarding S of Disclosure* (form FL-141) and an *Income and Expense Declaration* (form FL-150).
   b. ☐ This matter is proceeding by default. I am the petitioner in this action and have filed a proof of servi *Declaration of Disclosure* (form FL-140) with the court. I hereby waive receipt of the final *Declaratio* FL-140) from the respondent.
   c. ☐ This matter is proceeding as an uncontested action. Service of the final *Declaration of Disclosure* (f waived by both parties. A waiver provision executed by both parties under penalty of perjury is cont and *Waiver of Final Declaration of Disclosure* (form FL-144), in the settlement agreement or propos another, separate stipulation.

Form Adopted for Mandatory Use
Judicial Council of California
FL-170 [Rev. July 1, 2012]

**DECLARATION FOR DEFAULT OR UNCONTESTED
DISSOLUTION OR LEGAL SEPARATION**
(Family Law)

Family Code, § 2336
www.courts.ca.gov

---

**Item 4a(3)(B):** If you have property or bills to divide but no settlement agreement, you *must* attach a copy of the completed FL-160 Property Declaration (**chapter 15**) to this form unless a current FL-160 was already filed with the Request for Default (**chapter 17**).

## Figure 20.2   DECLARATION FOR DEFAULT OR UNCONTESTED DISSOLUTION
### Form FL-170   (Page 2)

**Type in names of parties as shown in figure 7.2.**

**Enter your case number.**

**If there is a child in your case, check box 6 and 6a and one box under 6a. Check boxes 6b or 6c if they apply to you.**

**Also check box 7 and 7a(1) IF it applies to you. Check either 7a(2) and attach a computer printout or check 7a(3) and state facts about the other parent's earning ability.**

**Check boxes at 7b(1) to show if you are receiving or applying for welfare for a child, and show in 7b(2) if the other party is receiving assistance.**

**If the child support recipient is receiving public assistance, check one box at 7c.**

**Check boxes at item 8 to show how you want spousal support to be treated in your Judgment.**

**If you check 8d for a spousal support order, check the first box under it and attach FL-157.**

FL-170

PETITIONER:

RESPONDENT:

CASE NUMBER:

6. ☑ Child custody and visitation (parenting time) should be ordered as set forth in the proposed *Judgment* (form FL-180).
  a. ☐ The information in *Declaration Under Uniform Child Custody Jurisdiction and Enforcement Act* (UCCJEA) (form FL-105)
    ☐ has ☐ has not changed since it was last filed with the court. (*If changed, attach updated form.*)
  b. ☐ There is an existing court order for custody/parenting time in another case in (*county*):
    The case number is (*specify*):
  c. ☐ The current custody and visitation (parenting time) previously ordered in this case, or current schedule is (*specify*):
    ☐ Contained on Attachment 6c.

  d. ☐ Facts in support of requested judgment (*In a default case, state your reasons below*):
    ☐ Contained on Attachment 6d.

7. ☐ Child support should be ordered as set forth in the proposed *Judgment* (form FL-180).
  a. If there are minor children, check and complete item (1) if applicable and item (2) or (3):
    (1) ☐ Child support is being enforced in another case in (*county*):
      The case number is (*specify*):
    (2) ☐ The information in the child support calculation attached to the proposed judgment is correct based on my
      personal knowledge.
    (3) ☐ I request that this order be based on the ☐ petitioner's ☐ respondent's earning ability. The facts in support
      of my estimate of earning ability are (*specify*):
      ☐ Continued on Attachment 7a(3).

  b. Complete items (1) and (2) regarding public assistance.
    (1) I ☐ am receiving ☐ am not receiving ☐ intend to apply for public assistance
    listed in the proposed order.
    (2) To the best of my knowledge, the other party ☐ is ☐ is not receiving public assistance.
  c. ☐ The ☐ petitioner ☐ respondent is presently receiving public assistance, and all support
    payable to the local child support agency at the address set forth in the proposed judgment. A re...
    child support agency has signed the proposed judgment.

8. **Spousal, Partner, and Family Support** (*If a support order or attorney fees are requested, submit a c...*
  Expense Declaration *(form FL-150)* unless a current form is on file. Include your best estimate of the ...
  *Check at least one of the following.*)
  a. ☐ I knowingly give up forever any right to receive spousal or partner support.
  b. ☐ I ask the court to reserve jurisdiction to award spousal or partner support in the future to (*na...*
  c. ☐ I ask the court to terminate forever spousal or partner support for: ☐ petitioner ☐ ...
  d. ☐ Spousal support or domestic partner support should be ordered as set forth in the propose...
    based on the factors described in:
    ☐ *Spousal or Partner Support Declaration Attachment* (form FL-157)
    ☐ written agreement
    ☐ attached declaration (*Attachment 8d.*)
  e. ☐ Family support should be ordered as set forth in the proposed *Judgment* (form FL-180).
  f. ☐ Other (*specify*):

FL-170 [Rev. July 1, 2012]

**DECLARATION FOR DEFAULT OR UNCONTESTED
DISSOLUTION OR LEGAL SEPARATION**
(Family Law)

## Figure 20.3   DECLARATION FOR
## DEFAULT OR UNCONTESTED DISSOLUTION
### Form FL-170   (Page 3)

> **Type in names of parties as shown in figure 7.2.**

> **Type in case number.**

> **Check box 9 if Petition listed a child born before marriage and check another box to show how parentage is being established.**

> **Check one of these boxes if wife's former name is being restored.**

> **Date and sign as indicated on form.**

---

FL-170

PETITIONER:

RESPONDENT:

CASE NUMBER:

9. ☑ **Parentage** of the children of the petitioner and respondent born prior to their marriage or domestic partnership should be ordered as set forth in the proposed *Judgment* (form FL-180).

    a. ☐ A Voluntary Declaration of Paternity is attached.

    b. ☐ Parentage was previously established by the court in *(county)*:

        The case number is *(specify)*:

       ☐ Written agreement of the parties attached here or to the *Judgment* (form FL-180).

10. ☐ **Attorney fees** should be ordered as set forth in the proposed *Judgment* (form FL-180)

    ☐ facts in support in form FL-319

    ☐ other *(specify facts below)*:

11. ☐ The judgment should be entered nunc pro tunc for the following reasons *(specify)*:

12. ☑ The petitioner ☑ respondent requests restoration of his or her former name as set forth in the proposed *Judgment* (form FL-180).

13. There are irreconcilable differences that have led to the irremediable breakdown of the marriage or domestic partnership, and there is no possibility of saving the marriage or domestic partnership through counseling or other means.

14. This declaration may be reviewed by a commissioner sitting as a temporary judge, who may determine whether to grant this request or require my appearance under Family Code section 2336.

**STATEMENTS IN THIS BOX APPLY ONLY TO DISSOLUTIONS**

15. If this is a dissolution of marriage or of a domestic partnership created in another state, the petitioner and/or the respondent have been residents of this county for at least three months and of the state of California for at least six months continuously and immediately preceding the date of the filing of the petition for dissolution of marriage or domestic partnership.

16. I ask that the court grant the request for a judgment for dissolution of marriage or domestic partnership based on irreconcilable differences and that the court make the orders set forth in the proposed *Judgment* (form FL-180) submitted with this declaration.

17. ☐ This declaration is for the termination of **marital or domestic partner status only.** I ask the court to reserve jurisdiction over all issues whose determination is not requested in this declaration.

**THIS STATEMENT APPLIES ONLY TO LEGAL SEPARATIONS**

18. I ask that the court grant the request for a judgment for legal separation based on irreconcilable differences and that the court make the orders set forth in the proposed *Judgment* (form FL-180) submitted with this declaration.

**I understand that a judgment of legal separation does not terminate a marriage or domestic partnership and that I am still married or a partner in a domestic partnership.**

19. ☐ Other *(specify)*:

I declare under penalty of perjury under the laws of the State of California that the foregoing is true and correct.

Date:

_____
(TYPE OR PRINT NAME)

▶ _____
(SIGNATURE OF DECLARANT)

FL-170 [Rev. July 1, 2012]

**DECLARATION FOR DEFAULT OR UNCONTESTED
DISSOLUTION OR LEGAL SEPARATION**
(Family Law)

Page 3 of 3

## 20.2 Method B – Going to a hearing

Going to a hearing is easier than you might think. Thousands of people before you have done it by themselves with little trouble and great success, so just follow the instructions below and you'll be okay.

**Judgment Checklist.** Print out form FL-182 Judgment Checklist (on the CD). This is a detailed list that you should use as a guide to make sure you completed all documents needed for your Judgment.

**Setting the hearing date.** To get a date for your hearing, you have to ask the Clerk's office to "set" your case on their trial calendar. You can request a hearing date when you file the Request for Default (see checklist, chapter 8) or any time thereafter. In some counties, you merely call the Clerk's office on the phone any time after they receive your Request for Default and ask for a hearing date, but others require a local form to be filed to request a hearing. The clerk will tell you this when you call. The L.A. local form is at the end of this chapter for purposes of illustration, but if you run into one that you can't figure out, just send two blank copies to Nolo Press Occidental, 2604 El Camino Real, Suite 353B • Carlsbad, CA 92008, with a stamped, self-addressed envelope and we will send instructions.

**Paperwork.** In general, you bring all papers to hand over for the judge to examine and sign, but some counties want them filed sooner. When you call to set your hearing, ask when they want the Judgment, Notice of Entry of Judgment, and, if you use them, the Wage Assignment papers.

**Disclosure.** If you have not already filed FL-141 declaring that you served Respondent with the required disclosure documents (chapter 14), bring the completed form with you to the hearing.

**Preview.** If you can take the time, it could be very helpful to watch some uncontested divorces before your own hearing day. This will give you a good idea of what to expect when your case comes up, what sort your judge is (if you know ahead who it will be), how the courtroom is run, and so on. Ask a clerk when and where uncontested dissolutions are usually heard.

### The day of the hearing—how to go and what to say

The way you look might matter, so dress cleanly and neatly. If you own any, wear business-type clothing. Get to the courthouse a little before your case is scheduled, to give yourself time to find the right place.

Most counties have more than one Superior Court judge. Each judge has his/her own courtroom, called a "department," which is identified by a number or letter. In some counties, you go straight to the assigned department for your hearing. In larger counties, you may go first to a "presiding" or "master calendar" department. In such a case, go there and listen for the name of your case to be called, stand up and answer, "Ready!" and your case will then be sent to some other department for the hearing. Sometimes they will want you to pick up your file and carry it to the hearing—find out by asking the clerk or bailiff when you appear for the hearing, or call and ask the clerk ahead of time.

Don't give the bailiff or the court clerk any grief, no matter how they act toward you. They're the judge's staff and in too important a position for you to take any chances. Be extra nice.

When you get to the proper courtroom for your hearing, tell the clerk or bailiff that you are present. If you haven't already filed them, hand the clerk the original and three copies of your proposed Judgment, the Notice of Entry of Judgment, wage attachment forms if you use them, and stamped envelopes addressed to yourself and Respondent. If you have a settlement agreement that has not been previously filed, hand it over.

When your case is called, answer "Ready!" Go right on up, get sworn, and take the stand. Take time to arrange your papers. Relax. Some judges will ask you questions to get the information they want, but most will just tell you to begin. Tell the judge facts and information about your case and the orders you want made. Always call the judge "Your Honor."

**Testimony Guide.** The outline starting on the next page is your guide; use the portions that apply to you. Do not take this book to the stand. Instead, either make complete notes, or print the Testimony Guide found on the CD in the Forms folder (Nolo-2 Testimony Guide) and take it to the stand with you.

Cross out parts that do not apply to your case and use the rest. Check off each item as you go along to make sure you don't forget to say any part of it. Take your time. If the judge asks questions, it is only in order to become better informed and be satisfied that justice, as he or she understands it, is being done. Don't worry, just answer *briefly and exactly* what is asked. Do not volunteer information that is not asked for.

## I. IN EVERY CASE GIVE THE FOLLOWING INFORMATION:

A. "Your Honor, my name is _____ , and I am the Petitioner in this case."

B. "All of the facts stated in my Petition are true and correct."

C. "(I/ Respondent) resided in California for more than six months, and in *(county your court is in)* County for more than three months, immediately prior to the filing of the Petition."

D. *Using exactly these words, tell the judge:* "During the course of our marriage, there arose irreconcilable differences which led to the irremediable breakdown of our marriage. There is no chance for a reconciliation. Your honor, I ask that the marriage be dissolved."

## II. USE THE PORTIONS THAT APPLY TO YOUR CASE:

### If you have a settlement agreement, you say:

"Your Honor, the original copy of our settlement agreement has been submitted with the Judgment. My signature is on it, and I recognize the other signature as that of Respondent. I ask that it be admitted into evidence. I request that the court make the orders set out in the Judgment which I have submitted for your signature, which correspond to the terms of our settlement agreement."

*Ask the judge if he or she would like more detail on the orders you have set out in the proposed Judgment and, if so, go on as described below.*

### If you have no settlement agreement, you say:

A. CHILDREN:

   1. None: "Your Honor, the Respondent and I have no minor children, and none are expected."

   2. If you have children:

      a. "Your Honor, the Respondent and I have ___ child(ren)." *Give the full name, age, and birth date of each child.*

b. "I know that (I am/ Respondent is/Respondent and I are both) fit and proper to have custody of the child(ren), and it would be in the best interest of the child(ren) to have the court award

i. Legal custody to both parents jointly with primary physical custody to (me/Respondent)."

ii. Primary legal and physical custody to (me/Respondent)."

iii. Both legal and physical custody to both parents jointly."

*For joint physical and legal custody, the judge may ask for reasons why this is suitable in your case and may want details about how it will work in actual practice.*

c. Visitation: *Say,* "I request that the court order the parenting arrangements described in the parenting plan in the proposed Judgment." *(Be prepared to describe and discuss your plan if the judge wants you to.)*

## B. CHILD SUPPORT AND SPOUSAL SUPPORT:

1. No children and no request for spousal support:

a. Where Petitioner is the wife: "Your Honor, I do not want spousal support, and I understand that if I waive my claim to it now, I lose all claim to it forever."

b. Where Petitioner is the husband: *If you have a written waiver of spousal support, hand the original to the judge and say,* "I recognize the signature on this waiver of spousal support to be that of Respondent, and I request that it be admitted into evidence." *If the waiver is part of a settlement agreement, say nothing. If you don't have a written waiver or a settlement agreement with Respondent, the court may retain jurisdiction or make a nominal support award.*

2. If you want spousal support and/or child support:

a. "The information in the Income & Expense Declaration is true and accurate to the best of my knowledge and belief. Before separation, our gross combined family income was $_____ per month, with average expenses of $_____ per month. My current monthly income is $_____ per month and current monthly expenses is $_____ per month, all as reported on the most current Income and Expense Declaration."

b. If there are children: "Under the proposed parenting plan, the custodial parent will have physical custody of the child ___% of the time. After the divorce, my actual federal tax filing status will be _____ and my spouse's will be ____. The total number of exemptions claimed by each party will be ____for myself and ____ for my spouse." *This should be enough, but be prepared to give more details if the judge asks. Don't worry, just tell it the best you can. If you get stuck, ask for a continuance. Ideally, you will hand the judge a copy of the Bench Report produced by CalSupport software, as that will save the judge a lot of trouble.*

c. "I request that (Petitioner/ Respondent) be ordered to pay (Respondent/ Petitioner) $___ per month for spousal support, to continue until _____."

d. "For child support, I request that (Petitioner/Respondent) be ordered to pay to (Respondent/Petitioner) $___ per month for one child and $____ per month for the next child and . . . *state the amount for each additional child*, a total of $___ per month." *If support is to continue beyond the age of 18, that must be stated here. If the child is being supported with welfare funds, say* "(I am/Respondent is) receiving welfare to help support the child(ren), so support payments should be made through *(title of officer for your county)*."

e. "Your Honor, I request that the parties be ordered to share uninsured health care costs for the child(ren) as follows: Mother to pay __% and Father to pay __%.

f. "(Respondent/Petitioner) (has/does not have) health insurance available at a reasonable cost, so I now request that health (life, other) insurance be ordered at this (a future) time as set forth in the proposed Judgment." *Be prepared to give details about what is or is not available through employment, and costs.*

g. "Finally, I ask that the Order for Wage Assignment be issued."

## C. PROPERTY AND BILLS:

1. None: *If you checked box 5a on the Petition, then tell the judge,* "There is no property subject to disposition by the court."

2. Divided by agreement: *If you checked box 5b on the Petition and have an agreement, then say,* "Our property is divided in the agreement previously received in evidence."

3. Divided by the Court: *If you listed property at item 5b on the Petition, tell the judge,* "The information in the Property Declaration is true, accurate, and complete, to the best of my knowledge and belief. I request that the property be divided as set forth in the Judgment submitted for Your Honor's signature." *Be prepared to answer questions about the property or your requested division if the judge wants to go into it in more detail.*

Notes on pension plans: *If there is a community interest in a retirement plan, take care of it by one of the following methods (see chapter 3.6(b)). If you have it, bring an expert's report or other papers to show the value of the community share.*

a) Trade-off: *The pension is listed and valued with the other property in the Property Declaration. Say nothing unless the judge asks questions.*

b) Waiver by Petitioner: *Tell the judge,* "Your Honor, I know I may have some right to part of Respondent's pension plan which is listed in the Property Declaration, but I have thought it over and I don't want or need any part of it. I waive any and all rights I may have in that pension plan."

c) Written waiver by Respondent: *Hand the judge the original and one copy of the waiver and say,* "Your Honor, this is Respondent's waiver of rights to my pension plan. I recognize the signature as the Respondent's. Would you please admit this into evidence?"

Note on family home: *If the home is awarded to one spouse, say nothing unless asked. If, however, you want an order for a deferred sale, say,* "In order to benefit the minor child(ren), I request that the sale of the family home be deferred as set forth in the proposed Judgment."

4. Separate property: *If you checked box 4 in the Petition, then say,* "The property listed under item 4 of the Petition is separate property, and I ask

that it be confirmed as such." *The judge may want to ask questions about how some item was acquired or debt incurred, so be prepared, and bring any related documents you may have.*

## D. DECLARATIONS OF DISCLOSURE:

1. Both parties have complied: "Your honor, the case file will show that both parties have complied and served each other with the Preliminary and Final Declarations of Disclosure."

2. Respondent has not complied: "Your honor, the case file will show that I have served Respondent with the Preliminary and Final Declarations of Disclosure, but Respondent has not complied. I waive the Final Disclosure requirement and ask that you enter the Judgment in this case without it."

## E. RESTORATION OF WIFE'S MAIDEN NAME:

"Your Honor, (I want my/Respondent wants her) former name restored as set forth in the Judgment."

## F. CONCLUSION: "Your Honor, that concludes my testimony."

When your testimony is finished, the judge will recite the orders being made in your case; take notes. You do not need any witnesses. The clerk may hand you your signed copy of the Judgment. If not, it will be mailed to you, as will your copy of the Notice of Entry.

The Judgment you prepared *must* correspond to the judge's spoken orders. If the judge orders something different from what is in your prepared form, take careful notes on what the judge says; ask him/her to repeat if necessary. Then get your forms back from the clerk, make the necessary changes, and return them as soon as possible for the judge's signature. The orders in your Judgment do *not* become effective until the Judgment is signed by the judge *and* entered in the clerk's record book.

## Troubleshooting guide

We said it before and say it again: 99 times out of 100 there will be no trouble with a hearing. However, it will make you feel better if you know what to do in case you are that unfortunate one out of the 100.

### 1. Before the hearing begins.

It sometimes happens that the people who work in the court forget that they are there to serve the public. It usually does no good to remind them. Rather, if the clerk or bailiff (or even the judge) is less than helpful or polite, just keep calm, be nice, and quietly but firmly pursue your goal. You have a right to be there and a right to represent yourself. Whatever you do, don't get short with the judge's clerk or bailiff, even if you don't like the way they are treating you—these people work with the judge every day and you have enough problems without getting on their bad side. Walk softly. Be polite no matter what. Consider it a mark of your new maturity.

If someone is making things difficult for you, it is very possible that there is a reason. If so, you must find it out and correct the problem. Ask what is the matter, and at least try to get some hint about the general area of the problem. If necessary, ask to speak to another clerk or to a supervisor. Don't get upset. What is important is to correct the problem. Go over this book and double check everything. You can always return to the Clerk's office or to court another day.

### 2. After your hearing begins

This is a scary time for something to go wrong, but don't worry, you have an excellent escape hatch (or panic button) that you can use if all else fails. Lawyers use it all the time. It is called the continuance.

If the judge is very difficult, or refuses to grant your dissolution, this means he or she thinks you have left out something essential. Ask the judge, politely, to explain, as it is likely that you can give additional testimony that will solve the problem. If things go very wrong and you can't figure out what your problem is, or if you get into any kind of situation you can't handle, just tell the judge, *"Your Honor, I request that this matter be taken off calendar, to be reset for hearing at another time, so that I may have time to seek advice and further prepare this case for presentation."* During the next recess, see if the clerk or bailiff can help you, or ask to see the judge in chambers. Go over this book and double-check everything.

Assuming you figure out what went wrong, have your case set for hearing again, just like you did the first time, and do the hearing over again. If you think the problem was personal to that judge, ask the clerk if there is an informal way to avoid a judge who doesn't seem to like you or people who represent themselves.

### 3. After the hearing

If the judge grants your dissolution but refuses to sign your Judgment, this means the judge thinks there is something wrong with it. Probably it is different from the orders announced in court. Ask the clerk what is wrong (or look at the clerk's docket sheet or minute order, a public record) and make up a new Judgment form. Do it as soon as possible, and bring it in for the judge's signature.

# Figure 20.4  REQUEST FOR DEFAULT SETTING
## Local form for Los Angeles County

**Type caption as shown in figure 7.1.**

**Check a box to show the kind of case you have.**

**Read carefully and check each box that applies to your case.**

**Check box(es) to show if your case involves any of these requests.***

**Enter "one half"**

**Date and sign.**

---

NAME, ADDRESS, AND TELEPHONE NUMBER OF ATTORNEY OR PARTY WITHOUT ATTORNEY.

STATE BAR NUMBER

Reserved for Clerk's File Stamp

ATTORNEY FOR (Name)

**SUPERIOR COURT OF CALIFORNIA, COUNTY OF LOS ANGELES**
COURTHOUSE ADDRESS:

PLAINTIFF:

DEFENDANT:

**REQUEST FOR DEFAULT SETTING**

CASE NUMBER:

DEPT.

The Petition filed in this case is for:
- [ ] **Dissolution**
- [ ] **Legal Separation**
- [ ] **Paternity**
- [ ] **Nullity**
- [ ] **Other**_____

More than 30 days have passed since service of the Summons and Petition and the:
- [ ] Request for Entry of Default has been filed and entered
- [ ] Request for Entry of Default is included in the Judgment packet
- [ ] Response was not filed prior to the entry of the Request for Entry of Default

Petitioner seeks to obtain a judgment and requests to set this case for an uncontested trial based on a:
- [ ] Request to terminate spousal support in a marriage of over 10 years
- [ ] Request for no visitation or supervised visitation
- [ ] Request for a specific amount of spousal support
- [ ] Request for child support other than guideline
- [ ] Other_____

Trial time estimate is _____ hours.

I declare under penalty of perjury under the laws of the State of California that the foregoing is true and correct.

**Date:**

_____      [ ]Petitioner's [ ]Attorney's Signature
Print or Type Name

**NOTICE:  The [proposed] judgment must be submitted with this form.**
If the Court finds that a hearing is not required and the Judgment meets the criteria [set by statute], your judgment will be entered.  If the Court finds that a hearing, declaration, or further evidence is required, a request or a notice of the date, time and location will be sent to you.

FAM 031
Revised 08/05/2011

**REQUEST FOR DEFAULT SETTING**

Family Code § 2336

---

***Note.** If you check any of the boxes in the third (last) group of check boxes, come to court with a marital settlement agreement or documents and evidence to prove your right to the requests made.

You can download this form at **www.lacourt.org/forms/familylaw**.

# NOTICE OF ENTRY OF JUDGMENT

## What it is

To become effective, the written order of the court *must* be entered in the Clerk's Judgment Book. To let you know that the entry has been made, and when it was made, a clerk mails a notice to both parties. You prepare this form for the Clerk's office, but leaving blanks which they fill in.

After the Judgment is entered and returned to you, make sure to mail Respondent a court-stamped copy of the Judgment and Notice of Entry to show when the Judgment was correctly completed.

## How to fill it out

Fill it out as shown in figure 21.1 on the next page. Prepare the original and make three copies.

**Note:** When you file this form, you *must* also include two stamped envelopes with the court clerk's return address: one addressed to you, and one addressed to your spouse's last known address. Weigh your packet of papers and include enough postage.

**Note:** If divorce will end your group health coverage under your ex-spouse's plan, you have 60 days to give written notice of your divorce to the Plan Administrator and your desire to continue at your own expense under the plan.

## Figure 21.1  NOTICE OF ENTRY OF JUDGMENT
### Form FL-190

FL-190

ATTORNEY OR PARTY WITHOUT ATTORNEY (Name, State Bar number, and address):

FOR COURT USE ONLY

TELEPHONE NO.:                    FAX NO. (Optional):
E-MAIL ADDRESS (Optional):
ATTORNEY FOR (Name):

**SUPERIOR COURT OF CALIFORNIA, COUNTY OF**
STREET ADDRESS:
MAILING ADDRESS:
CITY AND ZIP CODE:
BRANCH NAME:

PETITIONER:

RESPONDENT:

**NOTICE OF ENTRY OF JUDGMENT**

CASE NUMBER:

You are notified that the following judgment was entered on (date):

1. Dissolution
2. Dissolution—status only
3. Dissolution—reserving jurisdiction over termination of marital status or domestic partnership
4. Legal separation
5. Nullity
6. Parent-child relationship
7. Judgment on reserved issues
8. Other (specify):

Date:

Clerk, by _____ , Deputy

—NOTICE TO ATTORNEY OF RECORD OR PARTY WITHOUT ATTORNEY—

Under the provisions of Code of Civil Procedure section 1952, if no appeal is filed the court may order the exhibits destroyed or otherwise disposed of after 60 days from the expiration of the appeal time.

STATEMENT IN THIS BOX APPLIES ONLY TO JUDGMENT OF DISSOLUTION
Effective date of termination of marital or domestic partnership status (specify):
**WARNING: Neither party may remarry or enter into a new domestic partnership until the effective date of the termination of marital or domestic partnership status, as shown in this box.**

**CLERK'S CERTIFICATE OF MAILING**

I certify that I am not a party to this cause and that a true copy of the Notice of Entry of Judgment was mailed first fully prepaid, in a sealed envelope addressed as shown below, and that the notice was mailed
at (place): _____ , California,  on (date):

Date:

Clerk, by _____ , Deputy

Name and address of petitioner or petitioner's attorney        Name and address of respondent or respondent's attorney

Page 1 of 1

Form Adopted for Mandatory Use
Judicial Council of California
FL-190 [Rev. January 1, 2005]

**NOTICE OF ENTRY OF JUDGMENT**
(Family Law—Uniform Parentage—Custody and Support)

Family Code, §§ 2338, 7636, 7637
www.courtinfo.ca.gov

*Callout annotations:*
- Type caption as shown in figure 7.1.
- Type in your case number.
- Check this box.
- Enter date marital status ends (see chapter 18 text note).
- Petitioner's name and address.
- Respondent's name and last known address.

# Part Three:
# Summary Procedures

# THE SUMMARY DISSOLUTION

If you haven't already done so, read chapter 2.2 about the advantages and disadvantages of the Summary Dissolution. You should also read through all of Part One, no matter which procedure you choose.

After many years of experience, it seems striking how *little* the Summary Dissolution is used. This could be because of the disadvantages pointed out in chapter 2.2. Now that we have the burden of the disclosure requirements (chapter 14) added to the Summary Dissolution, it loses a lot of its advantage of ease of use. Please remember our main advice: don't do it if you think your spouse might file a revocation during the long waiting period, and don't rush into it just to make the deadline. The Regular Dissolution is not much harder to do and it has some advantages over this shorter method.

If you are qualified to use the Summary Dissolution, and if you choose to use it instead of doing a Regular Dissolution, then you will need the official *Summary Dissolution Booklet*, form FL-810. You will also need forms FL-800, FL-825, FL-830, and FL-150. Get these forms from your Clerk's office, from the companion CD that comes with this book in the forms folder in their own separate folder, or download them from **www.courtinfo.ca.gov/selfhelp/family/divorce/summary.htm.**

**The Summary Dissolution Booklet (FL-810).** The law *requires* both spouses to read this booklet before you can file, so you might as well do it now. The Booklet is clear and easy to follow, so just do as it says. It urges you several times to see a lawyer, but our advice is that you do not retain a lawyer to handle your case, but rather see a lawyer just for a consultation if you have specific questions you want answered or a problem you can't solve yourself.

Below are a few things you'll need to know or have clarified.

## Captions

The captions (the information at the top of each form) are filled out as shown in chapter 7 at figures 7.1 and 7.2.

## Judgment (FL-825)

You file your Judgment (FL-825) along with your Petition. The Judgment should be signed by the judge and entered by the clerk at least by the time six months have passed after your Petition was filed. This should be automatic, but if you don't get it after the six-month waiting period, either party can file FL-820, the Request for Judgment. Your divorce becomes effective on the date that appears on the Judgment, but you are not divorced until the Judgment has been signed and entered by the clerk and returned to you.

## Request for Judgment (FL-820)

Do the caption as described above.

**Item 3.** Check box (a). Box (b) is for cases where the final Judgment was not properly requested and/or entered when you first had a right to it, and for some good reason you need to have it made effective as of the earlier date. For example: If you were told and believed that your spouse entered the final Judgment, then you got married again and later found out your divorce was not entered, you might get the Judgment made effective as of the end of the waiting period, *if* the proceeding has not since been revoked or dismissed.

**Item 4.** If a party's former name was not requested on the Petition, it can be requested here, but *only* if the party is the one filing this form. Check this box and type in the full name you wish to have restored.

Put in the date and place where the form is signed, type your name on the dotted line, and put your signature on the solid line.

On the back of the form, fill in only the boxes with the husband's and wife's names and last known addresses.

## The Notice of Revocation (FL-830)

This form is used to stop the dissolution if it is filed before the six-month waiting period has passed. Either spouse can file it. *Do not* file it unless you want the divorce proceeding to be permanently stopped.

The caption is filled out as shown in Fig. 7.1. Don't forget the case number. In the first paragraph, put in the date the Petition was filed (the date stamped at the clerk's office). Then put in the date and place signed, type your name on the dotted line and add your signature on the solid line.

Fill in the party's names and last known addresses in the boxes provided.

# TERMINATION OF DOMESTIC PARTNERSHIP

If you haven't already done so, read chapter 2.2, which discusses who is qualified to use the summary procedure and, for those who are qualified, the advantages and disadvantages of doing it that way. You should also read through all of Part One, no matter which procedure you choose.

Please remember our main advice: even if you are qualified to use it, don't proceed by Notice of Termination of Domestic Partnership if you think your partner might file a revocation during the long waiting period, and don't rush into it just to make the deadline. The Regular Dissolution is not terribly difficult and it has some advantages over this shorter method.

If you are qualified to use the Notice of Termination procedure, and if you choose to use it instead of doing a Regular Dissolution, then you will need to obtain and carefully read the Termination brochure prepared by the Secretary of State and the Termination forms. These can be found on our CD in the Forms folder in their own separate folder, or you can download the latest brochure and forms from the Secretary of State's web site at **www.ss.ca.gov/dpregistry**.

For your convenience, the full text of the statute that defines the summary procedure to terminate a domestic partnership is reproduced below.

## Family Code §299: Termination of Domestic Partnership

(a) A domestic partnership may be terminated without filing a proceeding for dissolution of domestic partnership by the filing of a Notice of Termination of Domestic Partnership with the Secretary of State pursuant to this section, provided that all of the following conditions exist at the time of the filing:

(1) The Notice of Termination of Domestic Partnership is signed by both domestic partners.

(2) There are no children of the relationship of the parties born before or after registration of the domestic partnership or adopted by the parties after

registration of the domestic partnership, and neither of the domestic partners, to their knowledge, is pregnant.

(3) The domestic partnership is not more than five years in duration.

(4) Neither party has any interest in real property wherever situated, with the exception of the lease of a residence occupied by either party which satisfies the following requirements:

(A) The lease does not include an option to purchase.

(B) The lease terminates within one year from the date of filing of the Notice of Termination of Domestic Partnership.

(5) There are no unpaid obligations in excess of the amount described in paragraph (6) of subdivision (a) of Section 2400, as adjusted by subdivision (b) of Section 2400, incurred by either or both of the parties after registration of the domestic partnership, excluding the amount of any unpaid obligation with respect to an automobile.

(6) The total fair market value of community property assets, excluding all encumbrances and automobiles, including any deferred compensation or retirement plan, is less than the amount described in paragraph (7) of subdivision (a) of Section 2400, as adjusted by subdivision (b) of Section 2400, and neither party has separate property assets, excluding all encumbrances and automobiles, in excess of that amount.

(7) The parties have executed an agreement setting forth the division of assets and the assumption of liabilities of the community property, and have executed any documents, title certificates, bills of sale, or other evidence of transfer necessary to effectuate the agreement.

(8) The parties waive any rights to support by the other domestic partner.

(9) The parties have read and understand a brochure prepared by the Secretary of State describing the requirements, nature, and effect of terminating a domestic partnership.

(10) Both parties desire that the domestic partnership be terminated.

(b) The domestic partnership shall be terminated effective six months after the date of filing of the Notice of Termination of Domestic Partnership with the Secretary of State pursuant to this section, provided that neither party has, before that date, filed with the Secretary of State a notice of revocation of the termination of domestic partnership, in the form and content as shall be prescribed by the Secretary of State, and sent to the other party a copy of the notice of revocation by first-class mail, postage prepaid, at the other party's last known address. The effect of termination of a domestic partnership pursuant to this section shall be the same as, and shall be treated for all purposes as, the entry of a Judgment of dissolution of a domestic partnership.

(c) The termination of a domestic partnership pursuant to subdivision (b) does not prejudice nor bar the rights of either of the parties to institute an action in the superior court to set aside the termination for fraud, duress, mistake, or any other ground recognized at law or in equity. A court may set aside the termination of domestic partnership and declare the termination of the domestic partnership null and void upon proof that the parties did not meet the requirements of subdivision (a) at the time of the filing of the Notice of Termination of Domestic Partnership with the Secretary of State.

(d) The superior courts shall have jurisdiction over all proceedings relating to the dissolution of domestic partnerships, nullity of domestic partnerships, and legal separation of partners in a domestic partnership. The dissolution of a domestic partnership, nullity of a domestic partnership, and legal separation of partners in a domestic partnership shall follow the same procedures, and the partners shall possess the same rights, protections, and benefits, and be subject to the same responsibilities, obligations, and duties, as apply to the dissolution of marriage, nullity of marriage, and legal separation of spouses in a marriage, respectively, except as provided in subdivision (a), and except that, in accordance with the consent acknowledged by domestic partners in the Declaration of Domestic Partnership form, proceedings for dissolution, nullity, or legal separation of a domestic partnership registered in this state may be filed in the superior courts of this state even if neither domestic partner is a resident of, or maintains a domicile in, the state at the time the proceedings are filed.

**INDEX?**

A combined index covering Book 1 and Book 2 is available online at **www.nolodivorce.com/index**. Using your browser, you can print it or download it and use it on your computer. You will need Adobe Acrobat Reader which, if you don't already have it, comes with this book's companion CD.

**Why isn't the index printed in the books?** Good question.

**First:** Although new laws and forms typically take effect January 1 and July 1, we often get forms at the last minute, then have to process them for book and CD, then rush to press, which has a three- to four-week turnaround, then there are delays for shipping and distribution. So, in order to get the latest information on the street as quickly as possible, we can't wait for a time-consuming index revision.

**Second:** These two books are not necessarily revised at the same time, so if we printed the index in each book, an index printed in one book could become out-of-sync with the index in the other book. An online index is more reliable once it is updated.

# Order of Forms

All Judicial Council forms mentioned in this book are on the companion CD in the Forms folder and can be filled out and printed on any computer. These forms have been "enabled," so you can save the data you enter with the "File > Save As" function if you use Adobe Reader 8 or later. Forms are listed below in the order mentioned in this book.

| Chapter | Form Number | | |
|---|---|---|---|
| 9 | FL-110 | • | Summons |
| 10 | FL-100 | • | Petition |
| 10 | FL-105 | | Declaration Under UCCJEA |
| 7.1 | MC-020 | | Additional Page |
| 11 | FL-120 | • | Response |
| 12.7 | FL-130 | | Appearance, Stipulations, and Waivers |
| 13 | FL-115 | • | Proof of Service of Summons |
| 13 | FL-117 | | Notice and Acknowledgment of Receipt |
| 13 | FL-335 | | Proof of Service by Mail |
| 13 | FL-330 | | Proof of Personal Service |
| 14 | FL-140 | • | Declaration of Disclosure |
| 14 | FL-142 | • | Schedule of Assets and Debts (4 pages) |
| 14 | FL-141 | • | Declaration Re Service of Declaration of Disclosure |
| 14 | FL-144 | | Stipulation and Waiver of Final Declaration of Disclosure |
| 15 | FL-160 | | Property Declaration (used if there's no written agreement) |
| 15 | FL-161 | | Continuation of Property Declaration " |
| 16 | FL-150/1 | • | Income and Expense Declaration |
| 16 | FL-150/2 | • | Income Information |
| 16 | FL-150/3 | • | Expense Information |
| 16 | FL-150/4 | * | Child Support Information |
| 16 | FL-155 | | Financial Statement (Simplified) |
| 17 | FL-165 | • | Request to Enter Default |
| 18 | FL-180 | • | Judgment |
| 18 | FL-182 | • | Judgment Checklist |
| 18.4 | FL-350 | | Stipulation to Establish Child Support (in a few counties) |
| 18.4 | FL-191 | * | Child Support Case Registry Form |
| 18.4 | FL-192 | * | Notice of Rights and Responsibilities, Health Care Costs |
| 18.4 | FL-192/2 | * | Information Sheet on Changing a Child Support Order |
| 19 | FL-195 | † | Order/Notice to Withhold Income for Child Support |
| 19 | FL-435 | † | Earnings Assignment Order for Spousal or Partner Support |
| 19 | FL-450 | † | Request for Hearing Re Earnings Assignment (blank sent to Respondent) |
| 20.1 | FL-170 | • | Declaration for Default or Uncontested Dissolution (not used if you go to court) |
| 21 | FL-190 | • | Notice of Entry of Judgment |

- • Used in every case. Forms not marked are used only in special circumstances.
- † Used in every case with either child or spousal support.
- * Used in every case with child support.